BK 331
POWER AN
19
30
St. Lou

D0984212

FV
WITHDRAWN

331.88 R464p
REYNOLDS
POWER AND PRIVILEGE : LABOR
UNIONS IN AMERICA
                              14.95

 St. Louis Community College

Library

5801 Wilson Avenue
St. Louis, Missouri 63110

POWER
AND
PRIVILEGE

POWER AND PRIVILEGE

Labor Unions in America

Morgan O. Reynolds

A Manhattan Institute for Policy Research Book

UNIVERSE BOOKS
New York

Published in the United States of America in 1984
by Universe Books
381 Park Avenue South, New York, N.Y. 10016

© 1984 by Morgan O. Reynolds

All rights reserved. No part of this publication
may be reproduced, stored in a retrieval system, or
transmitted, in any form or by any means, electronic,
mechanical, photocopying, recording, or otherwise,
without prior permission of the publishers.

84 85 86 87 88 / 10 9 8 7 6 5 4 3 2 1

Printed in the United States

Library of Congress Cataloging in Publication Data

Reynolds, Morgan O., 1942–
    Power and privilege.

    "A Manhattan Institute for Policy Research book."
    Bibliography: p.
    Includes index.
    1. Trade-unions—United States.   I. Title.
HD6508.R44   1984   331.88'0973   83-18194
ISBN 0-87663-438-2

To my Dad,
a good union man,
and my Mom,
who sometimes disagrees

Contents

Tables and Figures

Foreword

One of the healthier developments in the American intellectual climate is the recent appearance of articles that reconsider the economic role of labor unions. Some authors examine union work rules that prevent qualified employees from working outside narrow categories. Others note that our sickest industries tend to have the most powerful unions and pay the highest wages. That such articles appear in publications like *The Atlantic Monthly* and *Harper's* is refreshing.

But these articles are also disappointing. While their authors cut through many myths about labor unions, they accept others.

We have been told that Local 802 of the American Federation of Musicians, by insisting that the producers of *The Best Little Whorehouse in Texas* hire twenty-five musicians rather than the nine they wanted, forced the musical to end its Broadway run. We have been told that NuCor, the large nonunion steel company, has a labor cost of $65 per ton, while U.S. Steel's is $160 per ton. NuCor's president attributes half of this cost advantage to the absence of work rules.

We have also been given ample evidence that the idea that unions represent society's underdogs is a myth: many union airline pilots make over $100,000 a year, while auto and steel workers earn $30,000 to $40,000 in wages and fringe benefits, far higher than the average income for all American workers.

But while the authors of such articles uncover many of the problems with unions, they fail to mention their exclusion of minorities and women from high-paying jobs, their role in reducing wages of nonunion workers, and their leaders' frequent disregard for even their own members' interests. And while these authors may understand that real wages are tightly linked to productivity, they often credit unions for the increase in labor's share of national income over the last 50 years. Also, they rarely challenge the assumption that unions are needed to offset the power of employers.

What we have needed is a *book* that reconsiders the economic role of labor unions, and does so by challenging fundamental assumptions. Here it is, in *Power and Privilege*. Anyone who seeks a comprehensive treatment of the effects of labor unions, as well as the legal and economic reasons for those effects, would do well to read this book. Morgan Reynolds shows that unions prevent women and minorities from working in highly skilled jobs (Chapter 10) and cause reductions in the wages of nonunion workers (Chapter 7). While agnostic on whether unions increase labor's share of national income, Reynolds presents conclusive evidence that labor's share of income in industries is not correlated with unionization (Chapter 7). Reynolds also explains why union corruption is widespread and why government regulation has done little to restrain it (Chapter 10).

Reynolds's book is full of startling facts. He tells of pressmen at the *Washington Post* in 1975 destroying over one million dollars of computerized presses. He quotes W. E. B. DuBois, the famous 19th-century American black leader, who said that trade unions are "the greatest enemy of the black working man." Reynolds gives evidence that workers, not employers, often insisted on so-called yellow-dog contracts. He also suggests a new view of the labor injunctions used by employers during employee strikes in the late 19th and early 20th centuries. He points out that almost every reported injunction was to halt union violence.

No other book I know of comes close to *Power and Privilege* in bringing together such a wealth of information about unions. And Professor Reynolds goes even further. He asks what the source of union power is and proposes reforms to reduce it.

Most union power, says Professor Reynolds, depends on unions' ability to withhold competing labor from employers. Rarely can union members achieve wage gains or other benefits simply by striking. If that were all they did, then employers would replace them with other workers. To be successful, union workers must use threats and sometimes violence to keep other workers from taking their places.

This insight is not new, but many writers miss its significance. Obviously picket lines during strikes are meant to prevent other workers from entering a plant. That's why one of the dirtiest words in the union lexicon is "scab." But what happens to "scabs" and potential "scabs" if the union succeeds? Professor Reynolds notes that workers who don't get jobs in an industry because of a union have to settle for less satisfactory jobs elsewhere. Which means that the conflict in strikes is not just between workers and management; it is also between striking workers and their potential replacements.

Keeping this conflict in mind, Reynolds looks at the effect of labor unions on the distribution of income. It is commonly believed that unions' main impact is to redistribute income from employers (that is, owners of capital) to labor. But because unions restrict the supply of labor in unionized industries, the workers kept out go to nonunion companies. This influx of labor drives down nonunion wages. Thus, nonunion labor helps pay for union labors' gains. Unions simply don't benefit all workers.

Still, many people who can accept Professor Reynolds's analysis might reject his proposal to remove the special privileges government grants labor unions. They may believe that without government support, unions would be disadvantaged in their bargaining with employers.

Professor Reynolds addresses this belief. He agrees that isolated incidences of labor exploitation occurred during the 19th and early 20th centuries, when moving costs were high relative to wages. But exploitation is much less likely now that laborers are so mobile. Today's employers have very little monopoly power in hiring workers because they must compete with other employers located not just in their own regions, but in other areas of the country as well. For employers to control wages, they have to collude. But there are so many potential employers for each worker that collusive agreements are impossible. And there is little evidence that employers do collude.

The only instances of employer collusion that Reynolds finds, other than when they deal with monopoly unions, are in college and professional sports. And economists who have studied the athletic market agree that collusion succeeds only when the members of the colluding league face little or no competition from other leagues and when the colluding employers are exempt from antitrust laws. Collusion therefore is unlikely in the typical labor market, where there are so many more potential employers and collusion is illegal.

Professor Reynolds also shows the great harm done by labor legislation, two of his best examples being the minimum wage law and the Davis-Bacon Act. The minimum wage keeps low-productivity people out of work by making it not worthwhile for employers to hire them. Many of the people hurt by the law are young black men. The Davis-Bacon Act dictates artificially high wages for workers on federal construction projects, preventing lower-wage labor from competing for this work. Many of the displaced laborers are members of minorities.

Both laws, which labor unions strongly support, prevent people from getting skills they need to climb the economic ladder.

Some readers may think *Power and Privilege* and its author anti-worker. If so, these readers miss the point. Unions, rather than benefiting all labor, pit workers against their fellow workers and, as Reynolds documents, many unions mistreat even their own members. Nor is Professor Reynolds antiunion. Rather, he is against giving unions special privileges. And keep in mind those who are among the victims of compulsory unionism; by opposing legal privileges for unions, Professor Reynolds takes the side of these victims. If *Power and Privilege* must be labeled, it is far more accurate to call it pro-poor, pro-woman, and pro-black.

David R. Henderson

David R. Henderson is a Senior Staff Economist with the Council of Economic Advisers.

Acknowledgments

This book began in 1979 when Harold Hochman, then employed by ICEPS, the predecessor to today's Manhattan Institute for Policy Research, sought someone to do a book on labor unions. At the Public Choice meetings he asked James T. Bennett for a suggestion, and it was me. I was delighted with the idea at the time, but it has been a wild up-and-down experience since then. People changed, the scope of the book changed through many rewrites, publishers changed, but finally the task has been accomplished. What a relief. All's well that ends well.

Some people who deserve my thanks include George Gilder, Dan Heldman, Howard Dickman, and some anonymous referees for their incisive comments on the manuscript. I also want to thank seminar participants at the University of Chicago, the University of California–Davis, Texas A&M University, W. H. Hutt, Peter Lindert, Gary Libecap, and Murray Rothbard for comments that shaped my thinking on various points. My apologies to them all for being too bullheaded to adopt every suggestion. For intellectual inspiration, I want to single out W. H. Hutt and Sylvester Petro, both of whom continue courageously to pursue the truth about labor unions without a trace of bias or concession to academic popularity. Thanks to Bill Hammett and Joan Kennedy Taylor for sticking with this project and to Lou Barron, who pleasantly proved the expression "The only good editor is a dead one" to be incorrect.

My gratitude also goes to the editors of the *Journal of Labor Research,* the *Journal of Social, Political, and Economic Studies,* the *Government Union Review*, and the *Journal of Libertarian Studies* for their permission to use all or parts of articles that I have previously published in their journals.

For financial support along the way, I want to thank the Manhattan Institute for Policy Research. They made this book possible. For help on related union-research projects that improved this book I want to mention the University of California–Davis, the Center for Libertarian Studies, the Liberty Fund, the National Right to Work Legal Defense Foundation, and Texas A&M University. For typing help, I have to thank everyone on the secretarial staff of the departments of economics at Texas A&M and at UC–Davis. They did stellar work over the years.

And to my wife, Suzie, what can I say? I don't know what I'd do without you.

Preface

This book is about labor unions. Its purpose is to explain and interpret the behavior of unions and unionists—what they do, why they do it, and what effects their actions have. I try to discuss most of the important and basic questions about unions in light of contemporary economic analysis.

Unions and unionists are often involved in controversies—controversies charged with emotion and polemics. Interested parties and their apologists fan the fire and smoke, so we must be especially on guard against sentimentality, romantic notions, and confusion about the nature of unionism. The broad warning issued by Edmund Burke applies here: "It is a general error to suppose the loudest complainers for the public to be the most anxious for its welfare."

The only way to arrive at correct conclusions about how unions actually work is to use economic reasoning. It helps us to think as clearly as possible. We simply cannot rely on our humanitarian impulses to reason correctly for us. We must go beyond the natural impulse to picture things in terms of good guys and bad guys.

The sober task of economics is to understand how markets work, including markets for labor services. How are wages, hours, and working conditions determined? How do interventions by unionists or government work? Do union actions have the effects that their advocates claim? What does the evidence show? The answers cannot be described as "liberal" or "conservative"; they can only be right or wrong. My purpose is not to praise or blame unions, but to pursue the truth about them as openly and dispassionately as I can. This book will not please everyone, but I believe that it reflects careful reasoning and an honest sifting of the evidence. I might add that disagreement is not entirely undesirable, because knowledge often advances as a result of disagreement rather than agreement. And in an area as charged with polemics and controversy as unionism, controversy is inevitable.

The effort to understand unions, in a reasonably detached way, is not new. Shelves in almost every university library in the country groan under the weight of all the material written about unions, collective bargaining, and industrial relations. The subject has been approached through almost every discipline imaginable: economics, sociology, political science, psychology, history, business administration, industrial relations, and law. Perhaps no topic of comparable scope has received so much attention.

So why another book about unions—aside, that is, from the possible gains to the author and publisher? I believe that the efforts to understand unions, by and large, have not been very successful. Partly this reflects the general problem that there is unlimited room for the improvement of knowledge in almost every field. The analysis of unions, however, is underdeveloped in view of the vast amount of intellectual effort expended. Why?

The general answer is that many writers are unwilling to *think hard* about unionism, just as they are unwilling to think hard about other collective movements that promise to improve the lot of the common man. Many writers have a weakness for worker protest, a fondness for (apparent) underdogs, and an unspoken opinion that individuals really don't matter very much—that only the "workers" or the "masses" do. Less extreme writers are not so romantic about unionism but support it, rather murkily as an essential ingredient of the "middle way." By this view, unions partially offset the "excesses of capitalism"; they serve as a balance wheel, a bulwark against communism, a corrective in a society that would otherwise be more unjust than it is.

Behind both views is a wrongheaded and tenacious myth of economic life: that individual workers are weak, exploited, and impoverished by market capitalism. According to this doctrine, concentrations of capital—say, in the corporate form of enterprise—inevitably imply that unorganized employees must suffer reduced shares of the receipts from production. We are repeatedly told that wages, hours, and working conditions for the mass of the laboring classes can be improved only by the force of combinations of workingmen (unions) or by governmental decree, in the face of the so-called strength of employers. Natural sympathy for the underdog and a belief that the distribution of income is extremely unequal—workers laboring for low pay while investors enjoy an ever-richer diet of "unearned" income—has led many writers to take an uncritical attitude toward trade unions. As C. Wright Mills says, "In many liberal minds, there seems to be an undercurrent that whispers: 'I will not criticize the unions and their leaders. There I draw the line.' " This attitude continues to hinder systematic investigation and understanding of the conditions, processes, and effects of unionism. This book goes some distance toward overcoming these obstacles.

The Plan of the Book

Chapter 1 discusses the evolution of the prevailing ideas about wages, working conditions, and the role of unions. Chapter 2 lays out the economic logic of unions. The emphasis is on the key insights of economic analysis, which strip away the confusion surrounding unions and collective bargaining. The difficulties of maintaining an economically effective "workingmen's combination" imply dependence on governmental intervention to support unionism, despite talk about the free trade union movement and free collective bargaining. Chapter 3 discusses some common economic errors propagated by unionists, and Chapter 4 explores the new Harvard-NBER work on unions as the "collective voice" of the working class.

Chapter 5 diagnoses the origins of the primary legislation of the 1930s, which supports unionism in the private sector in this country, and Chapter 6 examines additional regulation on behalf of unionism from the 1930s, including the Davis-Bacon Act and the minimum-wage law. Chapter 7 analyzes the array of effects unions have on the economy, including the relative pay of union members, labor's share of income, and unemployment.

Chapter 8 examines the explosion of unions in the public sector from 1 million in 1960 to 6 million in 1982. Approximately 45% of public employees are now unionized as opposed to less than 20% of employees in the private sector. The same logic applies to public employee unions that applies to unions in the private sector, but there are differences, especially since the marketplace cannot protect the general public from union actions quite so well as the private sector can. Chapter 9 discusses the role of unions in the inflationary spiral, and Chapter 10 looks at a series of contradictions in unionism, from their proclaimed support of free enterprise to compulsory union dues.

Chapter 11 closes with a look at the role of unions in modern economic systems. Amid the muddled thought that approves of unionism and the aspirations of workingmen is the stark fact that unions fit into neither a capitalist nor a socialist system. Whether the brand of unionism shaped in America by legislation can survive in the same form into the 21st century remains to be seen. The need to reconsider the labor policies of a free society was made very clear by Henry Simons in 1944 when he wrote, "a community which fails to preserve the discipline of competition exposes itself to the discipline of absolute authority." The growth of unionism in governmental employment makes these words as relevant today as they were forty years ago.

1

The Enduring Controversy
over Labor Unions

It is ideas, not vested interests, which
are dangerous, for good or evil...indeed
the world is ruled by little else.
—J. M. Keynes

It is merely a question of time until the
views now held by intellectuals become the
governing force of politics.
—F. A. Hayek

Labor unions are a prominent feature of life in every Western economy. According to government statistics, labor unions and employee associations in the United States have 23 million members, hold nearly 200,000 contracts, and collect more than $5 billion annually in dues, fees, and assessments. Nearly one in every four American families includes a dues-paying member of a union. Every day of our lives we depend on things that are produced, delivered, or sold by union employees. The largest union—the International Brotherhood of Teamsters, Chauffeurs, Warehousemen, and Helpers of America—has 1.8 million members in 740 local unions, employs 7,000 officers and business agents, and negotiates 80 new contracts each business day. Unions can shut down an uncounted number of enterprises, including General Motors, U.S. Steel, the National Football League, small businesses, schools, and police departments across the country. The power, prosperity, and security of U.S. unions appear undeniable.

It was not always so. At the end of the nineteenth century, union membership in the United States was only 500,000, which was less than 2% of the labor force. Only a dozen unions claimed more than 10,000 members. The largest union was the Locomotive Engineers with 30,000 members; the Cigarmakers were second with 28,300. Samuel Gompers, probably the most famous president of the American Federation of Labor, came from the Cigarmakers. With the development of automatic machinery, the Cigarmakers' membership declined to 2,500 by 1974, and the union disappeared in a merger with the Retail, Whole-sale, and Department Store Union. Unions existed in many trades in the nineteenth century, but they organized a substantial share of employment in very few instances, mainly construction, printing, railroads, and the postal service.

In the early 1900s union membership rose to 6% of the labor force, where it remained until 1917. Under pressure of World War I and the government's War Labor Board, membership expanded rapidly, hitting 12% of the labor force. But it did not last. By 1924 only 8% of the labor force was organized, and by 1933 the proportion has eroded to the same 6% as in 1903. The number of union members had fallen from a peak of 5 million in 1920 to fewer than 3 million in 1933, a 40% decline.

Before 1934 unionization was substantial only in coal mining, contract construction, printing, men's and women's outerwear manufacturing, railroads, local transit and trucking, the stage and theater, and the postal service. Even in these industries, only one-third of the persons employed were unionized.[1] Unions were concentrated in a narrow range of industries and occupations, mainly in big cities. The bulk of economic activity—services, wholesale and retail trade, manufacturing, agriculture, and government—was nonunion.

Then came the New Deal. In the decade from 1935 to 1945 the fraction of the labor force organized into unions jumped fourfold to 25%. No one who looks at the history of labor unions in this country can fail to recognize the impact the Great Depression had on unionism and the changes the 1930s produced in public opinion and labor legislation. Governmental policy swung sharply toward active promotion of unionism and collective bargaining. Legal constraints on union tactics were removed. Whether one views this shift of governmental policy as a product of desperation, wisdom, pursuit of the general good, or submission to special interest groups, one cannot disregard the sudden spurt in union growth. It would not be much of an exaggeration to say that American experience with large-scale, national unions is less than fifty years old.

The fraction of the labor force organized by unions continued to rise slightly between 1945 and 1953, to nearly 30%, but has declined ever since. It now stands barely above 20% of the labor force, although it is sometimes reported as 25% of nonagricultural employment.[2] Either way, the gradual decline of unionization has drawn comment from nearly every observer of the labor market. Union membership has risen in absolute terms since the early 1950s; in fact, substantial growth of unionism has occurred among teachers and government employees, but these increases have not been large enough to prevent steady erosion in the unions' share of a rapidly expanding work force.

The recent direction of change for unions has not been especially favorable in other respects either. Opinion polls consistently show that unions have the lowest public rating of any major institution in our society. Unions lost 3 out of 4 of the 902 elections to decertify the union as collective bargaining agent in 1980, and the number of elections has tripled over the last decade. Corruption in union finances, especially pension money, is daily newspaper fare. Periodic violence and convictions of union leaders have not brightened the image of unions. Union lobbying to change federal labor laws to permit easier organization of workers and to impose common situs picketing in construction was unsuccessful in the late 1970s. The political prospects for pro-union change in labor laws are slim. Unions can still muster their political clout—witness, for instance the defeat of a 1980 referendum on a right-to-work law for Missouri and continued blocking of attempts to repeal the Davis-Bacon Act—but fighting against adverse political proposals is not a mark of political ascendancy.

Unions and the Intellectuals

Ideas have played an important role in the evolution of public policy toward unions and union tactics. Ideas are important in sustaining general approval of any institution and its actions, and their importance cannot be overemphasized in the matter of unions because, to the public, so much of union behavior appears antisocial. The power of unions to win financial concessions through disruption, threats of disruption, and other forms of economic pressure ultimately rests on some kind of vague acceptance in, or at least tolerance by, the general community. Unions of government employees intensify the issue because some familiar union arguments are not very persuasive when used in public-sector disputes. For instance, it is hard to claim that union gains in the public sector help *all labor* because nobody believes that taxes to pay higher compensation come exclusively from a handful of rich capitalists.

Intellectuals and academics, by design and otherwise, have supplied arguments to make the actions of unions appear reasonable. Perceptions of labor unions are colored by the belief that employers are likely to exploit employees unless a union protects them. This doctrine, almost unthinkingly accepted on a wide scale, underlies almost all news reporting of labor disputes, as well as the labor legislation of the twentieth century. For example, if a truck driver is injured or killed in a brawl with strikers at a plant gate, journalists report it as a "labor-management conflict."

Emotion always has caused many intellectuals and social activists to sympathize with unions. The excitement of the "struggle" and the persistent belief that the distribution of income is unjust—workers earning too little and investors earning too much—make support for unionists and their tactics predictable enough among intellectuals. In fact, it is accurate to say that many intellectuals are bored with social stability and a gradual advance in economic conditions. They tend to prefer fireworks and social conflict. Yet economic progress is impossible without a relatively stable framework of laws, rules, and a measure of security for persons and their property. This proposition has been demonstrated over and over again.

If we put aside sentimental appeals centering on poverty and exploitation of workers, the intellectual argument for unions historically has rested on two propositions: (1) individual employees are helpless in dealing with employers, and (2) a union is essential to give employees the ability to deal on an equal basis with an employer. In the terminology of economics, buyers (employers) commonly enjoy monopoly power in deciding what terms to offer the sellers of labor services, and monopolization by the sellers (workers) is the appropriate remedy to offset the buyers' power. Even if the first statement were true on theoretical and empirical grounds, the acceptability of the proposed remedy is not implied, because its effects must be compared with those of other policies, say, promoting more independent, competitive behavior among buyers in their competition for labor services. Regardless of the factual validity of the prevailing view, however, its popular and judicial success is undeniable.

Skeptics in universities have not been numerous or very effective. To question the virtue of organized workers, their leaders, or the doctrine of unionism seems to align doubters with the unholy (read: "businessmen") and against dedicated, selfless unionists whose public task is to represent "labor's interests." Even scholars who normally boast of their unfettered, objective analyses of any and all social issues somehow never generate bold ideas about unions and unionists. Ralph Harris (Lord Harris of High Cross), a founder of the Institute for Economic Analysis in London, has remarked that the belief in trade unionism is close to theology, an unchallengeable religious belief. He is correct. Nor is such uncritical sympathy toward unionism confined to people whose livelihood directly depends on a steady flow of union dues.

The helpless individual is the central feature of most social analysis, although this is rarely stated explicitly. It is the all-purpose rationalization for expansion of the power of government from consumer protection to safety legislation, from minimum-wage laws to maximum-interest-rate ceilings. Without active direction by the state—so the reasoning goes—people would pay too much, work for too little, buy bad products, accept the wrong jobs, entrust their investment money to the wrong people, and generally exploit one another in the marketplace. At no time was this notion more assiduously promoted than in the second half of the nineteenth century by Marxist-syndicalists of every hue and color. By the turn of the century, the helpless workman, obviously incompetent to manage his own affairs in an increasingly complicated modern industrial society, had become a cliché that many people, including politicians and judges, accepted unthinkingly. Trade unionists and their supporters in journalism and the universities labored with enormous success to gain the advantage of being thought of as underdogs. The clichés soon found their way into the laws of the land.

Even the writing of otherwise impartial economists show a garbled sentimentality toward unions. No one is more prominent in this regard than the father of free-market economics, Adam Smith. "Masters," he wrote, "upon all ordinary occasions, have the advantage in the dispute, and force [workmen] into a compliance with their terms." The reasons Adam Smith offered for this advantage were that "The masters, being few in number, can combine much more easily....In all such disputes the master can hold out much longer....Masters are always and every where in a sort of tacit, but constant and uniform combination, not to raise the wages of labour above their actual rate." Adam Smith said that the subsistence wage rate was *not* determined by the wage necessary to maintain just a workman but by requirements for raising a family; otherwise "it would be impossible for him to bring up a family, and the race of such workmen could not last beyond the first generation."[3]

This muddled theory was challenged by Edwin Cannan. If masters have this power, he asked, why would they concern themselves about the labor supply of the next generation? "Trade rings," he said, "usually adopt the motto, 'After us the deluge.' "[4] Even more telling, Adam Smith himself unconsciously abandoned his own theory of subsistence wages because he said that in "certain circumstances...wages [rise] considerably above this rate;...masters...bid against one another, in order to get workmen, and thus voluntarily break through the natural combination of masters not to raise wages."[5] The truth is that Adam Smith had silently given up his subsistence theory of wages for a supply-and-demand theory of wage determination.

W. H. Hutt traces the tenacity of the notion of the employer's advantage among serious economists such as Thornton, Jevons, Hawtrey, Longfield, and Edgeworth.[6] The eminent Alfred Marshall continued to explain in 1920 that labor was at a disadvantage in bargaining because it was "perishable" and because labor was vexed with a "want of reserve funds and of the power of long withholding."[7] His prestige may have been decisive in sustaining the erroneous doctrine. R. G. Hawtrey had an especially colorful expression for the argument: "labour is more perishable than cut flowers."[8] The persistence of this view tied into the classical belief in the subsistence theory of wages. Hutt patiently points out that advocates never were pressed to explain why so many observed events were contrary to the theory of labor's disadvantage. Why were real wages nearly always rising under nonunion capitalism? Why was there so much job-switching if workers were immobile and under the thumb of their employer? Why did workers with great savings receive no higher wage than those with zero savings, even though they could "hold out longer"? Why did large firms pay higher wages than small firms, despite greater bargaining power by large enterprises "against" their labor force? Why was there virtually no factual evidence of conspiracies among masters to depress wages or hold them down? Employers' bargaining associations seemed to spring up only in cases where unionists successfully monopolized the labor supply of an entire industry. Maybe it was considered impolite to challenge prevailing doctrine, especially a doctrine of such obvious compassion. Compassionate rhetoric, however, is not identical with correct analysis, nor is it the same as compassionate policy.

There is no doubt of the long history of intellectual support for unionism, but most of it emanated from noneconomists. The exciting idea of clashes between capital and labor prevailed over quieter notions like the incentive of investors, managers, and employees to cooperate to their mutual advantage in the production process. Labor economists like Sidney and Beatrice Webb, Selig Perlman, John R. Commons, in addition to Marxists, emphasized solidarity and collective action as the primary vehicle for economic improvement among workers. The Webbs, for example, refer to

> the uncontrolled power wielded by the owners of the means of production, able to withhold from the manual worker all chance of subsistence unless he accepted their terms. . . . Individual bargaining. . . must be, once and for all, abandoned. In its place, if there is to be any genuine "freedom of contract," we shall see the conditions of employment adjusted between equally expert negotiators, acting for corporations reasonably comparable in strategic strength.[9]

Unionists have adopted slogans and catchwords from these and other writings to powerful effect.

Nor has this view of unionism yet died of natural causes. Here is a sample of contemporary remarks from the scholarly literature:

> To gain a voice in establishing the terms of their employment, therefore, workers were required to act in concert through a bargaining agency with sufficient power to deal with the large employers. . . Majority rule of course, entails a loss of some minority rights.
> —Irving Bernstein, *The New Deal Collective Bargaining Policy* (Berkeley: University of California Press, 1950)

> Lifting the suffocating burden of absolute managerial control from the working lives of Americans. . . was one of the greatest chapters in the historic struggle for human liberties in this country.
> —Jerry Cooper, *Labor History* (Spring 1977)

> the centerpiece of the game: the awesome power which a company wields over its employees. This suzerainty. . .
> —David Montgomery, *Workers' Control in America* (New York: Cambridge University Press, 1979)

> In America the state was more interventionist, because it saw the need to redress a serious imbalance of power between employers and workers.
> —Gaston Rimlinger, *Journal of Economic History* (March 1977)

For the most part, intellectuals find it difficult to imagine how individuals can control their own lives except through collective political mechanisms, a classification that includes unions.

The New Agnosticism

Times, however, have changed since the days of the Webbs. After fifty years of real experience with large-scale national unions, intellectuals no longer can arouse any real passion for unions, union tactics, or union leaders. The dissipation of belief has led to some recent soul-searching in the intellectual community about the nature of unionism and the state of industrial relations.

The most interesting aspect of the recent articles on unionism is the more or less open admission that their authors have not quite figured unions out. "Attitudes toward unions, pro and con, are emphatic enough," says Irving Kristol. "But of serious thinking about unions—what kinds of institutions they are, and why, and to what purpose—there is precious little."[10] Other writers are not quite so open about the prevailing confusion, but it is transparent enough. Nicholas von Hoffman, for example, attributes the decline of unions to "image problems," citing the unions' failure to support civil rights, antiwar, and women's movements, plus continued hostility on the part of business and the mass media. He concludes that a bad union is better than no union at all because "for most of those people [working for somebody else], without union power there is no power."[11]

Intellectual floundering is especially obvious in recent academic papers about the issue of unions. Clark Kerr's overall review of industrial relations is representative. He describes the field of industrial relations as

> a contribution of theory and practice...an interdisciplinary view ...a rejection of ideology...an attitude of neutrality...an effort to see reality in its several dimensions...countervailing forces...mixtures of good and bad...workable policies... among the "bumps and grinds" of the real world.

The continuing failure to consider the fundamentals of unions is obvious in his conclusion:

> Labor economics will make a greater contribution if it is on the borderline between theory and practice than if it is only on the borderline of theory; or only uses a single methodology; or only refers to a single ideology; or abandons a relationship to theory entirely. It can contribute most where the world of theory and the world of practice meet.[12]

Another review of the research in industrial relations is more explicit about the lack of an "integrating theory" on unions. George Strauss and Peter Feuille refer to

> the difficulty of defining precisely what industrial relations includes...some authors feeling that industrial relations should have a theoretical base of its own and others concluding that the only appropriate theories were those of the more basic disciplines, such as economics...a growing perception that industrial relations was becoming a practitioners' rather than a researchers' field....American industrial relations research may have stressed policy too much, seeking immediate application rather than basic understanding. We see little likelihood of a specifically industrial relations theory being developed in the U.S.

Strauss and Feuille come close to stating one of the major reasons for much of the dissembling by academics in the field when they say that "industrial relations scholars increasingly sought to facilitate union-management cooperation, and in the process they became technicians and defenders of the status quo."[13] An accurate translation is that industrial relations specialists and labor economists in major universities are labor consultants, arbitrators, conciliators, fact finders, and mediators. They have a financial interest in a labor conflict system and in maintaining their own aura of impartiality. The failure to come to grips with the fundamentals of unions is no surprise: it sometimes pays to be confused.

Economists gave little attention to unions until a few years ago. Professor George Johnson calculated that 9% of the space in leading economic journals during the 1940s was devoted to articles on unions, 5% in the 1950s, 2% in the 1960s, and less than 1% up to 1975. Major reasons offered to explain the decline were that unions had ceased to grow; their existence and security were no longer as much of an issue, and thus they received no research money; and welfare programs (research money) attracted the attention of labor economists. Another factor was that the investigation of labor unions had been a traditional preserve of old-style labor economists rather than a research issue among mainstream economists.

Recently, however, there has been a major resurgence of research on labor unions. Increasing space in academic journals is devoted to labor unions, and new journals (e.g., *The Journal of Labor Research* and *The Journal of Labor Economics)* have been established. Richard B. Freeman and James L. Medoff and others connected with the Harvard-NBER group have been especially prolific. Their claim that economists traditionally treat unions as monopolies is seriously misleading because it is necessary to examine the "collective voice/institutional response" role of unionism to understand fully what unions do in modern industrial economies. They argue that, on balance, unions positively affect the economic and social system by providing workers with a voice at the work place and in the political arena, that unions generally increase productivity, reduce turnover, promote economic equality, and operate as democratic, noncorrupt organizations. Freeman and Medoff marshal data and opinion for their view and conclude that their findings "present a reasonably valid picture of modern unionism in our country—one which stands in sharp contrast to the monopoly model and many popular beliefs about trade unions."[14]

To be sure, there is some truth in the claim that unions are like service agencies which are responsive to the collective wishes of their members. But that is far from the whole truth about national labor unions. The complex effects of union actions must not be allowed to overwhelm a basic, rigorous analysis of what unions are and what their tactics are. The foundation to analyze what unions are, what they do, and why, already exists, particularly in the work of W. H. Hutt, Henry Simons, H. G. Lewis, Fritz Machlup, Ludwig von Mises, and Milton Friedman.[15] Unfortunately, this fundamental work on unions has received so little attention from the current generation that few people are aware of it. The field has been left to the ambiguities of specialists in industrial relations for so long that even many economists believe that unions do not fit into contemporary theory. There are few issues where we are in a better position to clear up confusion.

2
The Economic Nature of Unionism

Workers can only prosper when they are
free to fight.
—George Meany, 1979

After God had finished the rattlesnake,
the toad, the vampire, He had some awful
substance left with which he made a scab.
—Jack London

As the nineteenth century drew to a close, labor unions had experienced very little success in the United States. The century was scattered with occasional union triumphs, and unions had a slight grip in a few industries, but the power, control, and security that unionists sought for themselves and their organizations had clearly eluded them. Unionists cast about for ideas and tactics that might bring them a measure of success. Nearly everything was tried in some form or another: socialism, syndicalism, anarchism, cooperatives, political unionism, and perhaps the most seductive idea of all, welding everybody into one giant union. Unions and unionists were a diverse brew. Many unions were here one day and gone the next because union efforts collapsed on a wide scale during hard economic times. Other unions were secret societies that adopted names like the Knights of St. Crispin or the Knights of Labor and had secret membership rolls, held secret rites, and concealed their organizational campaigns.

An aura of collective protest, high-pitched emotion, and even tinges of revolution accompanied unionism nearly everywhere. And with it came the specter of union violence. Bombings and killings in the anthracite fields during the 1870s (sometimes attributed to the Molly

Maguires), the anarcho-syndicalist flavor of the Haymarket riot in 1886, the violence of railroad and steel industry disputes, and many other incidents raised an image of unionists and organized workers as a threat to general peace, prosperity, private property rights, and, indeed, to individual liberty. Unionism commanded little allegiance or respect in the nineteenth century because individualism, not collectivism, was the ethic of the day. American capitalism was in its heyday, and the concepts of free enterprise and individual freedom in general had a grip on popular opinion that is hard to imagine in our contemporary environment.

The United States was infertile soil for unionism, and the explanation for this runs much deeper than the flat assertion that employers were especially defiant or greedy compared with those of the rest of the world. The immigrants building North America were not a random draw from their native lands but mainly those who sought adventure, new opportunities, and fewer restrictions, and who believed that they could make it on their own in a land where some said the streets were paved with gold. Immigrants were chiefly self-confident individuals who sought no help through collective action against established order.

Sentiment was not necessarily antiunion; it just was not pro-union. We might say it was nonunion, because people generally wanted to go about their individual business peaceably in a fluid, rapidly growing land of opportunity. If they encountered a labor dispute in the course of their daily activities, they generally preferred to be left alone. They didn't want to choose sides, as unionists demanded. Public sentiment may have fluctuated with the times, especially if labor violence was on the front pages, but a Marxist-style sympathy for the "plight of the working class" was never a dominant mood. More often, people were horrified by periodic outbreaks of labor violence and union disruption of production and trade, especially if the outbursts had revolutionary overtones. Although America had a history of mob violence committed by lynch mobs, vigilantes, and the Ku Klux Klan, those groups were not quite so menacing as unionists because they did not threaten to overthrow the existing order or the incumbent government. They were guilty of temporary outbursts of mob action, without the semicoherent ideology of unionism.

The rough and untrained character of many union leaders only reinforced public skepticism about them and their motives. And unionists in America could not rely on a common workingman's ideology of social class stemming from the medieval era. The common heritage of

Europe, and the main cement for unions there, did not exist in the United States. There were no long-smoldering class resentments based on accidents of birth, bondage, and legal privileges to fuel the fires of unionism in America, and as a result, unionists often resorted to force.

At the beginning of the twentieth century a dominant strain of unionism emerged as a survivor in this unfavorable environment. Experiments with political radicalism largely gave way to *business unionism* —the notion that unions must pursue immediate, tangible gains for their memberships within a private-enterprise economy. The idea was to accept capitalism, the wage system, and the political system and thereby achieve marginal gains for members. This model of unionism succeeded so well that it now forms the basis of the common definition of "labor union" in American dictionaries: "an organization of workers formed for the purpose of advancing its members' interests in respect to wages, benefits, and working conditions." Some definitions add the phrase "through collective bargaining with employers," presumably to distinguish labor unions from associations that are not quite unions—say, employee associations or professional bodies like the American Medical Association or the American Bar Association, and other kinds of trade associations that are unionlike blocs in many respects.

The goals of unionists had been lowered by the practical exigencies of trying to unionize in a capitalist nation. The ambitions of social visionaries and reformers who saw unions as a vehicle for comprehensive change in a capitalist society gradually fell by the wayside. Unions, under the emergent philosophy of business unionism, had to accept the capitalist system, avoid conscious pursuit of its overthrow, and act primarily as bargaining agents for their members, winning greater remuneration for them in a piecemeal, ad hoc fashion. And so the successful formula for American unionism was forged. The message appealed to union members and many potential members, and met less hostility among the general public than did cries of revolution. It elicited reasonably general approval as a feasible and laudatory task for unions, and seemed to fit the spirit of capitalism, encompassing, as it did, the pursuit of financial gain, an appeal to the workingman's pocketbook. Trade unionism is the capitalism of the proletariat, as George Bernard Shaw put it.

The creator of this dominant tradition for twentieth-century unionism was the American Federation of Labor and especially its leader, Samuel Gompers. The AFL was founded in 1886 as a federation of national trade unions, each composed of a particular kind of craftsman. This kind of organization enabled unions of workers in a single trade to survive in a private-property, market economy by banding similar workers together and bargaining for their services as one unit. No more divide-and-conquer strategy by capitalists. This economic philosophy was never practiced in its pure form, with unions confining their activities to the economic marketplace and totally abstaining from political lobbying. Nonetheless, unions did devote most of their resources to actions in the market, such as organizing, picketing, striking, bargaining, and boycotting.

The appeal of U.S. unionism was *economic*: a union could gain something of material value for its members, whether higher wages, shorter hours, or better working conditions. "We are practical men," Adolph Strasser told a committee of the U.S. Senate in 1885. "We have no ultimate ends. We are going on from day to day. We are fighting only for immediate objects—objects that can be realized in a few years."[1] Strasser, president of the Cigarmakers and one of Gompers's close associates, spoke for the AFL. Samuel Gompers was even more pointed when he was asked what he wanted and what unionists really wanted. "More," was his tart reply.

The human desire for more goods, better pay, and a more comfortable existence is universal and well understood. Many people immediately sympathize with the wish for high wages and good working conditions; they then endorse unionism without further ado because unions are so vocal in claiming to pursue these objectives. A high-wage society is a high-income society, after all, because the bulk of income derives from compensation for labor services. And nearly everybody favors a high-income society. Few people openly argue for the opposite of material prosperity—poverty. There are, it is true, opponents of economic growth, like religious preachers and environmentalists (secular preachers), who denounce materialism and the ubiquitous thirst for market goods. The casual observer might accept these people as what they claim they are: opponents of material abundance. But it is hard to treat them seriously because they always ask their audiences to donate more money. They denounce command over market goods and services and yet plead for more of it for themselves, to spread the good word (naturally).

Since the basic appeal of unionism is economic, the methods of economic analysis, to the extent that they are valid, certainly are appropriate in any inquiry into the objectives, methods, and effects of unions.

It simply will not do to accept Strasser's assertion that unionists are practical men of limited vision and inquire no further. It is not enough to believe that unionists have good intentions and worthy objectives and then conclude that their actions and their effects on union members, investors, managers, nonunion workers, and consumers must be benign. The world is not so simple.

Consider the union objective of higher wages. How could anyone but a heartless employer be opposed to such a demand? As Finis Welch has said, "The notion that everyone should earn a decent wage is as appealing as the idea that everything good should be cheap."[2] If only it were so easy. The problem is that high wages are not the *cause* of successful economic activity; they are the *result* of successful economic activity. By the same token, low prices are not the *cause* of an abundant supply of goods, low prices are an *effect* of productive economic activity. Directly forcing wage rates or other prices to be something they otherwise would not be in a free market cannot produce greater wealth in the community. On the contrary. It impoverishes the community.

Other economic questions immediately follow about the objectives and techniques of unionism. If Gompers or another unionist demands more, we are entitled to ask, Yes, but in exchange for what? Surely he would not offer shorter working hours in return. If unionists insist that they be paid more, who is going to pay for it? Where does the money come from? From higher production? From the returns of investors? Aren't profits a shallow purse? What if other workers, unemployed or not so well paid, are willing to do the job for less than union workers demand? If people seeking to hire labor services wish to deal with people who want to remain nonunion, what techniques can unionists use to change their minds? How far can unions go in the pursuit of their purposes? What can other people, who may not agree with unions, do to resist them? Once we go beyond the naive view of just nodding our agreement that high wages are good, we must face a series of controversial questions surrounding unionism.

Union Activities—A Positive View

The basic legitimacy of labor unions—in other words, the right of people to form and join labor unions—remains a live issue of government policy around the world and even continues to surface in mild form in the United States. So-called conservative political candidates, for example, sometimes are asked by unionists to endorse the basic legitimacy of unions. From a purely scientific perspective, we could avoid the whole question by making the factual assertion that multi-person organizations called unions exist and, if we are to understand them, we must develop some theories about their behavior and check against experience to see if the observed behavior of unionists and their apparent effects are consistent with theory. This strategy avoids the normative, value-loaded question of "legitimacy," an undefined word if ever there was one. A declaration of legitimacy might be construed as a sweeping endorsement of all union objectives and any means they choose to use in pursuit of their ends.

There is, however, a qualified way to endorse the basic legitimacy of unions, based on widely accepted Western values. The argument is that government should not forcibly restrict the right of men and women to associate freely with one another, provided that such private associations seek no unlawful objectives and use no unlawful means. People ought to be free to form, join, and quit private, voluntary associations provided they do not use force, fraud, or threat of force to deny others their equal and concurrent right to form, join, and quit associations of their own choosing. Of course, this rationale implies that people are free to exercise their right to refuse to join, or to quit, voluntary associations, including labor organizations, assuming that severance does not break legally enforceable contractual obligations. In the language of market economics, consenting adults should be free to trade with one another as they choose, free from the coercive interference of others.

In principle, then, associations of workingmen are as consistent with a free and prosperous society as are any other voluntary associations. There is nothing inherently objectionable about "combinations of labor," any more than about combinations of investors who might pool their financial assets, say, in the corporate form of enterprise in hope of increasing their wealth. Unions would be just another form of "joining" to which Americans are supposed to be so addicted. Organizations are the common way to get things done around the world: families, households, partnerships, social clubs, cooperatives, churches, and corporations. The mutual advantages of cooperating within voluntary organizations make them attractive to individuals because, by definition, personal benefits exceed personal costs of association for each person. Otherwise, they would withdraw, quit. The right of workers voluntarily to form and join private labor organizations has been secure for a long time in the United States and, in fact, this right was never a serious issue of public policy, despite frequent claims to the contrary. (This issue receives more attention in Chapter 5.)

Labor organizations *can* perform services that benefit their members *and* benefit enterprises and their customers, or at least avoid harming them. That is, unions in principle can be socially productive organizations whose net effect on national income is positive rather than purely redistributive; they need not be adversarial organisms whose gains for members and leaders come at the expense of larger losses by others in the economy. Labor representatives can smooth over misunderstandings and resolve conflicts between managers and employees by means of a formal grievance process. For example, a union could control the actions of an abusive foreman whose behavior benefits neither employees nor the owners of the business. In general, unions can provide employees with another way to voice their concern and discontent to management, in addition to the person-to-person conference with the supervisor who is available in nonunion situations, or to that other sign of discontent, quitting. These improvements can reduce absenteeism and turnover, thereby enhancing productivity and encouraging management to invest in more specific training of its employees. Seniority systems for transfer, promotion, and layoff can improve worker security and perhaps encourage experienced workers to give more informal training to inexperienced workers, because unionism reduces competition between workers. Unions can help workers to increase their productivity directly through union-sponsored training programs. To the extent that unions improve the intangible aspects of work situations—employee morale, pride, and dignity—they can raise production and improve quality control, on-time shipments, and the on-the-job safety record. Unions also provide a means for members and officers to suggest work-rule changes or different techniques of production that can benefit employees, managers, owners, and, ultimately, customers.

A labor organization can supply information about job opportunities and act as a clearinghouse for employers and workers. This is the traditional economic function of the infamous middleman, who increases the efficiency of a market by matching offers to buy with offers to sell more cheaply and effectively than traders can without his services. The union hiring hall performs a similar function, although it ordinarily is mixed with a high degree of monopoly power, too. Unions can benefit their members through joint-purchase programs that reduce the cost or raise the quality per dollar of dental care, prescription glasses, life insurance, and other goods. Finally, labor representatives can act as specialists for their members in monitoring employer payment of complex fringe benefits like insurance and retirement programs. These services, especially grievance procedures and the establishment of communication channels within companies, are valuable, but unions, particularly adversarial unions, are not needed to perform them. And many nonunion enterprises today are demonstrating this.

If unions pursued these objectives in peaceable, legal ways, many employers would welcome unions into their enterprises. In fact, some employers did welcome labor unions in the past, including such magnates as Andrew Carnegie. Many businessmen were (and are) self-made men from working-class families. They harbored no grudges against workingmen, no desire to exploit and abuse them, even if they could. They wanted only to trade, produce, and sell by doing business fairly. The picture, commonly portrayed by unionists, of working places as seething pools of worker resentment simply was not true then and is not true today. Work places, of necessity, generally are characterized by cooperation and mutual respect in a market economy, not by bosses lashing and driving frightened, faceless crews of quasi-slaves. From the point of view of maximum profits, businessmen seek the most economical methods of production, which is not the same thing as pursuing low-priced labor services per se.

Entrepreneurs want the lowest possible labor costs per unit of output, all else being equal. If union actions improved the productivity of their members, say, by 20%, their wage rates could rise by 20% *without* raising labor costs per unit. Union actions could raise the compensation of their members, and it would be financed out of more production, without deliberate harm to anyone else. Labor costs in union firms then would be no greater than in nonunion firms, and therefore unionized firms would be competitive without special regulations or privilege. Under these circumstances it is hard to imagine why unions would be more controversial than country clubs or business partnerships.

Associations, voluntary or coercive, continue only as long as they benefit some individuals. Unions must deliver benefits to *somebody,* even if, on balance, they harm other participants in the economy like investors, nonunion workers, rival union members, foreign workers, consumers, or taxpayers. Perhaps the most obvious beneficiaries of unions are the people on the union payroll. Clearly unions are vehicles of power, prestige, and income for union leaders. For full-time staff employees of unions, the union also is the source of their economic livelihood, although not necessarily the source of power and prestige that it might be for "labor leaders," as they are too broadly called.

Many union officials—perhaps all, in the long run—could not survive in office if they did not serve the interests of a substantial share of the membership. In other words, it is reasonable to argue that all unions cannot be dismissed as self-perpetuating oligarchies or bureaucracies that quietly suck money from the pockets of unwilling workers and entrepreneurs in return for no visible service, except perhaps the promise of "labor peace." Some unions, however, would fit any reasonable definition of labor racketeering; they could hardly be described as benefiting anyone except their leadership—for instance, some locals of the longshoremen.

Local union officials are probably the best examples of leaders who are responsive to member sentiment. Local officials, especially in industrial unions, commonly are elected by direct vote of the membership, remain at their blue-collar jobs, do union work as unpaid volunteers, except for reimbursement of expenses for union business, and face contested elections and high turnover in office, unlike national union officials. These leaders are in close daily contact with members, and their pay is not greatly in excess of that of members.[3] Further, they generally do not have *the power to decide which members work and which do not,* the key feature that makes most craft unions entirely different in terms of the power of union officials over union members.

Unions can give members a feeling of participation, of community with their fellow employees. Call it solidarity. To some extent, this fraternal feeling is generated by working with others and by membership in associations like the Rotary Club, the Elks, the Veterans of Foreign Wars, and countless other social and professional organizations. Unions differ from most groups, however, in their reliance on the notion of a common enemy, the employer. It is difficult to read much union literature without being impressed by the stream of invective directed at corporations, bankers, and "outlaw" employers. Officials at union headquarters constantly preach the litany of the collective interest of the members: us against them. In union there is strength. So goes the union slogan, and collectivism definitely is the ideology. Some union members may be impressed with these union views of the world, but I seriously doubt that everyone is.

The dominant reason that employees support unionism is the belief that they enjoy higher wages and benefits than they would otherwise. "Unions," says Ernest van den Haag, "capitalize on the feelings of members that they ought to get more power and money and promise to get both for them."[4] Sometimes the facts indeed support the claim of union leaders that they raise the wages of their members, although not nearly as often as union leaders would like to take credit for. Many union leaders talk as if only their Herculean efforts prevent a collapse of all American wage rates to zero.

The value of formal work rules and grievance procedures to members is difficult to gauge. In the end, unions have never been able to forestall new technology and more productive machinery indefinitely, nor have they been able to prevent eventual shifts in the allocation of resources through relocation of people and plants. Unions, however, undeniably can provide temporary respite from change. For some members, the existence of unionism gives an overall feeling that they can tell the boss off without fearing for their jobs. It is not clear, however, that unionism has reduced the overall amount of incivility and rancor on the job. It would be easier to argue the reverse.

Many intellectuals have placed great emphasis on unions acting to moderate managerial abuses of workers on the job. The quotations in Chapter 1 about "the suffocating burden of absolute managerial control" and the "awesome power which a company wields over its employees" convey the fervor of conviction felt by many writers. Yet there is surprisingly little evidence about the value that workers place on these union effects. One of the few efforts to quantify the value of the nonpecuniary conditions of employment is that of L. F. Dunn, who interviewed nonunion textile workers in a rural southern mill in 1971.[5] Dunn systematically asked how much each employee would be willing to sacrifice in wages for various improvements and then how much in additional working time. The workers were not willing to sacrifice money or to work longer hours for a well-enforced seniority system to govern job choice, shift, and layoff. In fact, some said they would pay *not* to have such an arrangement. Only 20% of the workers were willing to pay something for a "well-defined and fair" set of work rules and a grievance system, but the average supporter was willing to give up only 89 cents per week, or 19 cents per week over all those sampled. Average weekly earnings were $87. To put it in perspective, the average worker valued the lifting of "absolute managerial control" at one first-class postage stamp per week.

Another study, by George J. Borjas, analyzed the relationship between unions and satisfaction on the job in a national sample of white workingmen between fifty and sixty-four years of age.[6] The major empirical finding was that union members reported significantly *lower* levels of job satisfaction than nonunion employees, a result that held within occupational classes and in both craft and industrial unions. Although the correlation might be explained on the grounds that unions tend to organize individuals who work in unpleasant jobs, Borjas found that even after statistical control for the two-way dependence between unions and job satisfaction, unions had the strong independent effect of reducing expressed satisfaction. Surprisingly, workers with the longest tenure in unionized jobs expressed the most dissatisfaction. Borjas explained this result on the grounds that unions effectively politicize the work force within an enterprise, leading to more expressions of dissatisfaction. Also, senior employees were especially dissatisfied because unions compress the wage structure (the standard rate) so that senior workers achieve little wage advantage through their union. Borjas concluded that these results were not conclusive and that further studies by technical economists would improve our understanding of the on-the-job effects of unions.

A study by Richard B. Freeman, on the other hand, found that trade unionism is associated with significant increases in employee attachment to firms—that is, longer job tenure.[7] He analyzed three bodies of data on individual work experience and concluded that the increase in attachment could *not* be attributed to union wage increases, reductions in employer-initiated separations like layoffs, or a tendency of unions to organize workers who would be more stable anyway, but rather to changes in the work setting brought about by union actions. Freeman conceded that it was difficult to pin down exactly what aspect of unionism was responsible for increasing tenure, all else being equal, but he argued that it was due to grievance systems and specific work rules like seniority, based on regression results, which included variables for grievance and seniority clauses in collective contracts across manufacturing industries. The results were consistent with his view that unions increase tenure because of their "voice" function and the development of an industrial jurisprudence system under collective bargaining, which he considers socially beneficial, at least partly, because it reduces employee turnover, which is costly, and thus raises productivity. Obviously his results and interpretations are not entirely consistent with those of Dunn or Borjas.

Perhaps more direct evidence of the benefits of unionism can be found in public opinion surveys, in which about 75% of union members say they are satisfied with their union, while about 30% of nonunion workers would vote union in an election.[8] These results are subject to the usual deficiencies of public polling; in particular, responses depend on the exact wording of the questions and opinions must be rendered in public to a well-educated stranger. As a result, public opinion is not the same thing as popular opinion and is very much a product of educated media representatives, to whom people express opinions that are respectable, that sound responsible, while popular opinion is a far more earthy, even shocking thing, usually undiscussed, even unknown, in more refined company.

If we accept the results of opinion polls at face value, however, they support a less favorable interpretation of unions—namely, that they do not benefit all their members all the time, only about 75% of the time. This is not surprising. There are conflicts of interest within any group. A primary reason why some members feel they receive few benefits is that some unions are ineffective at raising compensation for members. In other unions that do raise wages, some members cannot secure work at the union wage, suffer more frequent unemployment, or work only part-time. Union work rules also can limit the earnings in union jobs of high productivity workers, who must slow down their own production to avoid becoming "rate busters." Some workers don't like unions, or anything about them, for political, ideological, cultural, or religious reasons. Some do not want to cooperate with the union because they abhor strike actions or violent confrontations, or because they don't want to displease the boss or jeopardize their promotion possibilities.

A possible response to a 25% disapproval rating among union members is that democratic unionism need please only a majority of the membership. Disgruntled members can campaign for new policies or new leaders and can even try to bring in new unions or turn the shop into a nonunion establishment. True, although this claim does not falsify the observation that a union always has unhappy members. Aside from political campaigning to change union policies, the major option for those who work in unionized establishments but do not feel that they benefit from union representation is to quit and seek employment in less unionized trades, industries, or locations. Based on the proportion of the labor force that is nonunion, we can say that the majority of economic activity (80%) in the U.S. economy is nonunion and constitutes the crucial safety valve for individuals who want nothing to do with unions. Nevertheless, the concentration of unions in certain sectors and regions restricts the labor market options available to nonconformists. Greater conformity is a familiar consequence of *all* political mechanisms, including unionism, but the most disturbing cases occur when union control over a trade is so extensive that expulsion from the union is tantamount to economic death—the victim cannot work in his craft again—a more frequent occurrence in England or Australia, where half of the labor force is unionized and virtually 100% is unionized in some trades and industries.

Union Purposes and Activities—A Dissenting View

Labor unions remain the most controversial private organizations in our society despite more than 150 years of experience with them. As Douglass Brown and Charles Meyers put it, "Basically, we are impressed by what seems to have been before 1930, and what seems to exist today, a feeling of 'unease' in the presence of unions on the part of large segments of the population."[9] Why? It cannot be general contempt for self-interest or greed per se that creates unease over labor unions. Americans have no general objection to groups of people who seek to enhance their own prosperity. In fact, almost all economic activity would fit under such a broad rubric. Nor are Americans opposed to the announced objective of labor unionists, namely, raising the standard of living for all wage earners.

I think the answer ultimately lies not in the goals toward which unions work, but in the *means,* the *tactics* that they use to pursue their economic gains. The use of intimidation, coercion, and violence by unionists is a continuing issue for public policy. Strikes, picketing, and boycotts create potentially violent confrontations and help to explain the multitude of laws, regulations, and rulings directed at union tactics. There are other issues, too. There is ample room for concern over some of the objectives that unionists pursue, from pushing up wages and benefits and enforcing closed shops, to demanding the dismissal of nonunion employees. The economic side effects of union actions are important too. How, for example, do union wage rates, fringe benefits, work rules, and strikes affect employment, unemployment, output, inflation, income inequality, investment, and the amount of competition in our economy? What are the *political effects* of union pressures for more government spending, protective tariffs, building codes, welfare programs, and so on? And, finally, are union leaders corrupt, self-serving seekers of personal power and wealth or are they responsive, democratic representatives of their members' wishes? The issues can be summarized as (1) tactics, (2) objectives, (3) economic effects, (4) political effects, and (5) corruption.

Many writers emphasize that unions are complex creatures with political, social, and economic aspects. Unfortunately, though, pointing out that the world is complicated is not really helpful from a scientific point of view. In approaching unionism and other observable phenomena, it is useful to have a simple, coherent idea about what is going on. Truly useful theories are compact, yet they explain or predict a wide variety of observed and yet-to-be-noticed behavior.

The monopoly theory of unionism is just such a vehicle. Although, like all theories, it has limitations, none is fatal, and we can get a tremendous amount of mileage from a handful of correct statements about unions.[10] A labor union can be defined as a group of labor suppliers who individually have little or no market control over wages and working conditions but who want to control (raise) compensation as a group. Expressed this way, there is nothing different in principle between combinations of workers and combinations of sellers in other markets (businessmen, farmers, oil producers, physicians) who attempt to restrict supply and push up the prices of their services. As Edward H. Chamberlin wrote, "It is fundamental to distinguish between the labor market and the product market, but it is also common to place far too much emphasis on the distinction."[11] Unions are fundamentally cartels—groups of producers with sectional interests diametrically opposed to those of consumers. Unions are labor OPECs.

This states the main economic purpose of unions, albeit in unflattering terms. Trade unionists never really spend much effort concealing their main objective anyway, because a classic union slogan has been to "take competition out of wages" and to "take labor out of competition," results that could hardly redound to the benefit of consumers. Imagine if other sellers vowed to "take competition out of prices" or take their services out of competition. Arthur J. Goldberg, former general counsel of the AFL-CIO, wrote a grudging acknowledgment of the anticompetitive nature of unions in an article defending union exemptions from antitrust laws:

> Technically speaking, of course, any labor union is a monopoly in the limited sense that it eliminates competition between employees for the available jobs in a particular plant or industry. By concerted economic action, these workers attempt to increase the wage at which the employer will be able to purchase their labor.[12]

Although Goldberg attempted to denigrate the importance of this bit of truth by saying that he was speaking only "technically," he was stating the precise truth: *a union is a monopoly.* Unions are the primary anticompetitive ingredient in labor markets.

Suppose that unions somehow succeeded in entirely eliminating wage rates determined by competitive supply-and-demand conditions throughout our economy. What would be the result? It would spell the death of any market system, despite the frequent protestations among unionists that they want no such thing. The reason is that labor costs are by far the largest component of the cost of production, and if these costs were not connected to some kind of market price determination, only a socialist command mechanism could reconcile the conflicts of interest among participants in the economic process.

Employee compensation is 76% of national income in a typical year and all labor earnings total about 80% of national income, since approximately two-thirds of the 6% of national income received by proprietors is also a return to labor services. The remaining 20% of national income is received by suppliers of nonlabor factors of production who earn returns in the form of corporate income, rent, and interest payments. To get a grip on general magnitudes, consider that employee compensation was $1,856 billion in 1982, and corporate profits after corporate tax and with capital consumption and inventory valuation adjustments were $113 billion, according to the U.S. Department of Commerce.[13] These figures dramatize that profits are a shallow purse as a source of union wage gains, because employee compensation typically exceeds profits by nine- or tenfold in enterprises. These wage and prfoit figures are correct to compare in terms of tax liability because employees must pay personal income taxes on wages, while corporate owners (shareholders) must pay personal income taxes on dividends and capital-gains taxes (eventually) on any higher value of shares from investment of retained earnings. Thus, if the income paid to labor and investors were pictured as a pot of money to be divided between them, labor got 90% and investors 10% of the income from corporate activity during the 1960s and 1970s.[14]

Unionists continually decry profits as "too high" or "excessive," and maybe they should do so, but unfortunately their lament reflects little understanding of the economic process. Profits are a *residual,* anything left over from revenues after contractual expenses have been met. Wages, on the other hand, are *prices* for labor input. They are not residuals. Wage rates simply are not comparable to profits as economic phenomena. More than one-third of corporations report negative net income (losses) in any reporting period. In 1977, figures available from the U.S. Treasury's *Statistics of Income* showed that 36.5% of corporations reported losses amounting to $26 billion, while positive earnings amounted to $149 billion. Even union leaders probably would admit that losses do not constitute excessive profits. An unknown fraction of the remaining firms earn a lower rate of return on their invested capital than they could on the interest from low-risk treasury notes. But consider the two out of three enterprises with positive net income and imagine that somehow unionists confiscated all these profits. If investors then expected permanently to receive no return, investment would cease, the productive stock of capital would decay, production would plummet, and the basis for our prosperity would be destroyed in the process. Such a union "success" in seizing investor returns would gain a 10% or 12% wage boost at the expense of capital owners, but it would be terribly costly. Only ill-informed or ill-intentioned analysts would claim that events would unfold any other way if private-investor returns were confiscated through union wage pressure.

Many unionists, however, recognize the useful function of profits and losses in regulating efficient production, a prominent example being the statement of Samuel Gompers: "The worst crime against working people is a company that fails to operate at a profit."[15] Union wage pressure, work rules, and harassment nonetheless are constant problems because even mild encroachment on investment returns discourages investing and distorts its pattern away from that preferred by consumer spending. In the process we become collectively poorer, although partial confiscation of returns by union action surely yields less damage than total confiscation.

If we suspend the question of who pays for union gains, we can ask *how* unions might deliver on their promises to raise compensation above the market prices that otherwise would prevail. The key is that unionists must restrict the available supply of labor services *or* directly impose higher wage rates on enterprises. Analytically, this same proposition is at work in the theory of cartels and monopolies, where either price or quantity can be viewed as the decision variable. A monopoly must restrict production to enhance profits *or* directly fix a higher price and then reduce production in accord with the lower rate of sales. In the case of trade unions, as Henry Simons wrote in 1944, "control of wages *is* control over entry."[16]

For a trade union, the closed-shop arrangement corresponds rather closely to a business monopoly that restricts production. Both are instances of an "artificial scarcity" that produces artificial abundance elsewhere in the economy. Under an effective closed shop, buyers of labor services are compelled to hire only union members, and, of course, union membership is rationed among favored individuals in order to limit the supply of labor. Obviously this arrangement depends on the use of force or threat of force to prevent enterprises from dealing with nonunion workers or members of other unions, because employers might be unhappy about the cost, quality, or availability of the labor services allowed by the union. Employment and outputs are smaller, wage rates higher in the closed-shop sector, and employment and outputs are larger and wage rates lower in the nonunion sector as a result of these union restrictions.

Strikes and wage negotiations are nearly superfluous if a union can enforce a closed-shop arrangement since competition among independent, noncolluding employers would bid up the price of artificially scarce labor to the desired level. The closed shop is generally associated with a union hiring hall and still can be found in the building trades, longshoring, and the hotel-restaurant industries. However, the literal closed shop is *not* the common means that unionists use to raise labor costs because it is relatively difficult to impose on enterprises (which want control over the exact individuals hired), and the tactic has been illegal since the 1947 Taft-Hartley amendments to the National Labor Relations Act.

The most popular union device is to try to fix wages above market rates via wage negotiations, popularly called collective bargaining. Although the term "collective bargaining" is widely accepted and used, it is basically a misleading phrase. It conveys the notion that labor representatives are simply expert negotiators and bargainers for their members' services, much like attorneys who represent clients in legal disputes. If it were as simple as that, few could object to the arrangement, because if unionists only bargained for members' services *and* abstained from the threat of using organized force against those who disagreed with their demands, wage rates and working conditions would be no higher than the market for their members' skills would allow. But there is more to union bargaining than simply informing employers of their employees' wishes and discussing the nature of current and prospective labor market conditions.

Strikes

The strike or threat of strike is the principal tactic that unionists use to impose higher wage rates and superior working conditions on buyers of labor services. A great deal of confusion deliberately has been spawned about the right to strike. Most writers leave the impression that strikes are nothing more than a peaceable withholding of labor services by unhappy employees. If so, relatively few would object to a strike, provided that strikers did not breach legal contracts with owners of the enterprise. Strikers, in other words, would be exercising their basic right to refuse to deal on unsatisfactory terms. Two conditions would be necessary for a *noncoercive work interruption* to achieve economic gains for strikers: (1) an employer would have to offer substandard wages and working conditions—in other words, wages and conditions that are below prevailing market rates and (2) employees would have to be dissatisfied enough to regard an organized walkout as the best means of voicing their displeasure.[17] Under these conditions, an employer would quickly discover that his offer is substandard because he could not attract enough replacements of comparable quality without raising the ante.

Most strikes, however, are not simple denials of striking employees' labor services to the enterprise. If they were, picket lines would not be used at all, because striking employees could stay home or work elsewhere until the enterprise realized the wisdom of their demands and some mutually agreeable pact was consummated between the enterprise and its experienced work force. Ordinarily when a strike is called by union officials, some employees prefer to continue working, including members of the union who are unsympathetic with the particulars of the specific strike. Other people, currently unemployed or employed elsewhere at less attractive terms, seek the work abandoned by the strikers. Also, during the course of a strike, some strikers become discouraged or find that their employer offers a better package than they can hope for elsewhere, and they gradually return to work. A union's problem is painfully obvious: organized strikers must shut down the enterprise, close the market to everyone else—uncooperative workers, union members, disenchanted former strikers, and employers—in order to force wages and working conditions above free-market rates. If too many individuals defy the strikers, if they go their own way, if they are happy to accept the work the strikers abandoned, then unionists often resort to force. Unionists ultimately cannot impose noncompetitive wage rates (monopoly wage rates) unless they can prevent employers from hiring consenting adults on terms that are mutually satisfactory. Unions must actively interfere with freedom of trade in labor markets in order to deliver on their promises.

An ironic aspect of this insight is that union-organized strikes typically do not reflect worker solidarity at all. Nor are strikes the much ballyhooed conflict between management and labor (a form of buyer-seller conflict), because labor, capital, and management services basically are cooperating factors in the production process. Instead, strikes expose the basic conflict among competing sellers in the market for labor services, namely, the conflict between organized labor and unorganized labor. Stated in the earthy (and divisive) idiom of unionism, the central problem for unions is the existence of "scabs," "rats," and "strikebreakers," not the presence of capitalists, investors vexed by excessive greed, or large corporations. A successful strike depends on the union's ability to persuade *everyone* to strike.

Unfortunately, most academic discussions of labor relations and unions ignore the coercive aspect of unionism or else treat it as unimportant. Yet, understanding unionism requires a positive analysis of what unions *actually do*. People who cross a picket line might hear only pleas to honor the line, at first. But union tactics are rarely confined to verbal pleasantries and appeals to each person's sense of social justice. Tactics are well known, especially to those who have used them or felt their sting: mass picketing, insults, threats, throwing rocks and bottles, car chasing, abusive phone calls, physical assaults, property destruction, and sometimes even murder. Vivid examples are easy to cite, and a few are cited in later chapters, but here it is enough to emphasize the basic cause: the violent history of unionism is an inevitable effect of a political-legal system in which organized groups, within flexible limits, are allowed to use force in labor disputes.

Unionists generally claim that their struggle is with abusive employers, but most union intimidation is directed at uncooperative workers who do not feel that unions serve their interest. If managers and owners were the main antagonists of unions, we should expect unionists to assault them when they tried to enter their struck places of business instead of assaulting and intimidating other workers trying to enter places of business. Labor disputes are basically *conflicts between organized and unorganized workers,* and also within the group of organized workers; they are not conflicts between capital and labor. The prevailing confusion over the nature of labor disputes is rather like the widely accepted claim that the urban racial disturbances during the 1960s were directed at "whitey." But when we look at what actually happened we find that blacks burned and looted businesses and residences in their very own neighborhoods, regardless of the color of the managers, employees, or owners. Attacks and looting were not directed at white people and white-owned property any more than they were during the 1977 power failure in New York City. Ideology can blind people to the most self-evident truths.

Union leaders are often quoted as deploring violence. The expression of such admirable sentiments places them among a very safe majority, which includes leaders of the Soviet Union, who publicly condemn violence as a way to resolve conflicts. On the other hand, unionists commonly consider it their right to blockade businesses that fail to meet union demands. It is hard to imagine anything less consistent with free enterprise, a concept sometimes lauded by unionists, or more contrary to the interest of consumers, whose satisfaction is the ultimate purpose of economic activity. Workers who do not cooperate with union officials are considered subhumans who run the risk of getting what they "deserve" in a strike because, according to unionists, a willingness to work incites the spontaneous outrage of strikers. After a few bombings, rifle shots, and assaults, union leaders are quick to point out that they certainly do not condone violence but they can't be responsible for everyone's behavior.

Police protection to enable nonstrikers and the general community to go peaceably about their business, including crossing picket lines, is called strike-breaking and union-busting. If it were union-busting, of course, it would amount to an open admission by unionists that their success depends on the use of coercive methods. Many governmental officials, however, within fairly broad limits do little to protect law-abiding citizens from union coercion. The police and courts, reinforced by a substantial amount of public opinion, accommodate union threats and use of violence because they believe that it furthers the public purpose of helping labor. The view that the ends advocated by unionists justify their means has been promoted by a century of effort in the intellectual community. Hitting a person over the head with a baseball bat to take $20 from his wallet is a crime on the street, but it is much less likely to be treated as criminal if the person wielding the bat is an organized worker in a labor dispute, despite the fact that access to work is worth considerably more than $20.

Many believe that government officials act in favor of employers if the police intervene to protect nonstrikers from attack. In a sense, this impression is correct: government officials attempt, perhaps halfheartedly, to secure the human right of an employer to operate his business under such circumstances. But a more complete description recognizes that government is acting to secure everyone's rights in the situation: the right of strikers to withdraw their labor services and disrupt production in concerted, peaceable protest; the right of managers and owners to operate their enterprise in a peaceable, noncoercive manner;

and the right of individual employees and potential employees peaceably to seek the work abandoned by strikers. In the bad old days, companies frequently used additional security guards, weapons, and ammunition to protect company property and assert their right to continue production during a strike. Pro-unionists commonly regard outbursts of violence under these circumstances as unprovoked attacks on workers by capitalists and their hired goons. Although company agents may have fired the first shot in some instances, the fact is that citizens are likely to attack one another if the government fails to guard its right to use violence. When government fails to secure the common property rights of people to do business, people resort to private substitutes to secure their right to earn a livelihood.

These observations about some methods of unionism may seem distasteful, ugly, even shocking to some readers, but the task at hand is to pursue the truth about how unions actually behave. The relevant question is whether these assertions about behavior are true or false, not whether they are tasteful or distasteful. Although coercion and threats are not all there is to unionism, they are a part of union behavior in the United States—probably the most important part. We must go beyond the observation that union representatives help to resolve (and inspire) worker grievances in work places under existing collective agreements.

To put the use of union coercion in perspective, we can draw on the nearly exact parallel between business enterprises and households. Businesses are formed to advance the interests of their owners, while families advance the interests of their members; otherwise they would dissolve. Both groups try to purchase things they want as cheaply as possible—businesses to maximize the value of the company for owners, and families to get as much satisfaction as possible from their limited budgets. Labor unions, at their most powerful, forcibly deny enterprises access to vital labor services, except on terms demanded by unionists. It is as if a group of suppliers had banded together and attempted to cut off a household's supply of a vital product until the targeted family submitted to the group's demands. Suppose, for instance, a group of grocers got together, insisted on higher food prices, and then "struck" families who refused to buy or deal with them. The grocers' union could throw up pickets around selected homes and try to cut off families' access to food from scab grocers and fast food outlets. Painters, plumbers, and appliance repairmen could do the same thing. Such direct assaults on families would not be condoned by the courts or legislatures over a sustained period, but they are permitted against businesses. The ideological justification for the privilege is that unions are "underdogs" that do not harm consumers, only corporations and rich investors. If the rule of law prevailed, however, organized labor would not be permitted to coerce anyone, regardless of the victim's social position or means of livelihood.

Union picketing of private residences is not wholly unknown, although it usually involves homes of nonstriking workers in a labor dispute. For example, twenty pickets marched in front of the residence in Salinas, California, of a woman who worked at the Bruce Church, Inc., farm during a lettuce strike in 1979.[18] Pickets carried the red and black flags of the United Farm Workers (UFW) and called the woman a "witch, rat, whore, adulteress, dog and old lady in heat." The woman agreed to quit working after one of the pickets told her, "Come on out. Otherwise I'm going to take your [16-year-old] daughter and make her a Chavista [follower of UFW President Cesar Chavez]...and...when we have children, they will be Chavistas." The same day at least twenty-two demonstrators also picketed at the home of an irrigator who worked at Bruce Church farm, calling him, his wife, and their seven children "traitors, cheap scabs and animals" and threatening to damage family cars parked in front of the house. In King City, pickets marched around mobile homes occupied by workers who had crossed picket lines at California Coastal Farms. Strikers threatened to break down the door if an occupant of one home did not talk to them, warned another occupant that he would have to "face up to the consequences" for himself and his family if he did not quit working, and told another that "things would go bad for sure" for himself and his family. The Agricultural Labor Relations Board (ALRB) in California responded ten months later by ordering the UFW to apologize to residents in Salinas and King City and stop "restraining and coercing" farm workers at their homes. The ALRB refused recommendations by two administrative law judges to ban picketing of private residences in agricultural labor disputes or to establish rules for home picketing.

Some economists point to the strike statistics to support the claim that union violence and disruption are an inconsequential part of unionism. Strikes represent a small proportion of total work hours in the economy (less than 0.5%) primarily because they can be considered "mistakes," much like wars. If unions and managers had perfect foresight, it generally would pay them to agree to the post-strike settlement and avoid incurring the costs of a strike. But since the world is filled with uncertainties, different perceptions of the environment, and resolve among contestants, perfect foresight exists only in theory.

A competing explanation for strikes is that they are a device to restrict production and raise prices in an industry. The argument is that strikes serve industry as a supplemental source of profit, assuming that entry of new firms or nonunion firms does not completely erase the price effects of strike-restricted output. Unions can play this role in principle because they are exempt from antitrust law while enterprises are not, so that labor organizations can effectively be used to propel an industry toward a cartel. An example comes from the coal mining industry whose leader, John L. Lewis, used to call strikes or work stoppages whenever the supply of coal above ground threatened to force prices down. A similar example comes from trucking, where a story is told about Dave Beck, head of the Teamsters' Union, who was negotiating higher wages for drivers of brewery trucks in the state of Washington when he was told that eastern beer would undercut local beer if the breweries were forced to pay such wages. Beck asked what price for eastern beer would allow the higher wages he demanded, and when a figure was named he supposedly replied, "From now on, eastern beer will cost that much."[19] The generality of this model of strikes and union behavior appears highly limited, however, because business firms in a nonunion industry ordinarily do not seek industry-wide unionization as another source of profit. Costs of unionization simply outweigh benefits to the industry. Even after unionization, enterprises have problems in deciding and coordinating which company will suffer strikes; each company still has incentives to turn nonunion; and new nonunion enterprises are attracted into the industry.

During the 1970s an average of 5,300 reported work stoppages occurred each year, or twenty new strikes each business day. Between 60,000 and 70,000 contracts were negotiated each year, so about 8% of negotiations ended in a strike. Most of the remaining settlements, however, occurred under the pressure of a strike deadline and avoided strikes at the last minute. Grants of concessions can eliminate strikes, appeasement can work, but this strategy suffers the long-run problem of feeding a union's subsequent appetite, perhaps beyond all ability to satisfy it.

A complete absence of strikes, violence, and disruption would not change the coercive nature of monopoly unionism, though. In blunt terms, wages and working conditions above free-market results can be preserved only by force or threat of force. Islands of monopoly returns in a competitive sea can be sustained only by sea walls that keep people out. If everyone knows that a union has overwhelming power to exclude and disrupt, the power need not be used and can give the mistaken impression that union power does not rest on force. As Henry Simons wrote,

> Where the power [of coercion and intimidation] is small or insecurely possessed, it must be exercised overtly and extensively; large and unchallenged, it becomes like the power of strong government, confidently held, respectfully regarded, and rarely displayed conspicuously.[20]

To understand how strikes work is not to be antilabor or antiunion. People of all persuasions correctly refer to the strike as a weapon. The word "weapon" may be disconcerting, but a truthful analysis explicitly shows that wages and working conditions above free-market results depend on credible threats of violence. Regrettably, I cannot find a more pleasant way to state the truth.

Weighing the Pros and Cons

Which aspects of unions, positive or negative, dominate and represent "real" unionism? As with most important questions about economic life, there is room for reasonable people to disagree. Few social propositions command universal belief. Both positive, productive features and negative, destructive aspects of unions exist, most observers would agree, but the relative weight to assign to each is open to disagreement. To some extent, the area of disagreement can be diminished by the advance of positive knowledge about unionism and its effects, although not all disagreement will disappear, because there is room to differ over the values that public policy ought to promote. Moreover, empirical evidence never constitutes "proof"; it can only confirm (fail to reject) an idea or hypothesis. So, as always, we must rely on informed judgments about the nature of things.

It will come as no surprise to learn that I believe that monopolistic, coercive aspects of unionism have been the primary features of U.S. unionism in the past. The evidence in support of this opinion is quite powerful, and I hope to establish it beyond reasonable doubt in the remainder of this book. A preeminent product of liberal Western thought is the conclusion that means must be evaluated on their own, that they tend to determine ends, indeed that they are the ultimate ends. To me, the most important passage of Milton Friedman's *Capitalism and Freedom* is the following:

> A common objection to totalitarian societies is that they regard the end as justifying the means....If the end does not justify the means, what does?...To deny that the end justifies the means is indirectly to assert that the end in question is not the ultimate end,

that the ultimate end is itself the use of proper means. . . . To the liberal, the appropriate means are free discussion and voluntary cooperation. . . .[21]

The behavior of American trade unions provides more evidence than we might want in support of this conclusion. Founded largely on coercive techniques, unions tend to use coercion or the threat of coercion on a more or less regular basis. Even if the economic and political effects of aggressive unionism were thought to be good, public policy could hardly approve of it as an unmixed blessing. In fact, the dependence of unionism on its own coercive methods and the legislated coercion of government amount to an indictment. If unions are so good for workingmen, why must so many be forced into joining? The question nearly answer itself and forms the core of the problem for public policy.

It is fruitless and naive to blame unions for their use of force to pursue monopoly gains or to urge them to reform themselves. They are responding to incentives that allow them basically to operate outside of the rule of law, despite the huge and expanding web of labor rules and regulations. The long-run answer to the power of unions is to eliminate their special legislation, their legal immunities, and their special governmental agencies and to treat unionists in a manner consistent with everyone else under contract and tort law.

If other private associations had similar immunities to unions, they would act the same way. Sylvester Petro seems undeniably correct in saying,

If, for example, businessmen were allowed to compel the purchases of their customers, to assault them when they showed any intention of removing their patronage, and to block access to competitors—there is very little reason to believe that such conduct would not become common business practice.[22]

The way to promote the best features of unions is to treat them as responsible, representative organizations under the same legal framework that rules for everyone else in this society.

3
The Mythology of Unionism

*Before we had strong unions, Congressman, the
employer by arbitrary decisions decided the level
of wages, and he just said, "This is it," and the
worker either took it or went hungry.*
—*Walter Reuther*

*They know how to break the eggs, all right.
But where's the bloody omelette?*
—*Roy Campbell*

Many who sympathize with unionists acknowledge the use of coercion and threats but argue that they are the price we all must pay to further unionists' good ends. Felix Frankfurter and Nathan Greene, in their influential book *The Labor Injunction,* provide a legal version of this popular strain of thought: "The damage inflicted by combative measures of a union—the strike, the boycott, the picket—must win immunity by its purpose. But neither this nor any formula will save courts the painful necessity of deciding whether, in a given conflict, privilege has been overstepped."[1] The authors also refer to union "instruments for damage" and the resulting "area of judicial discretion."

A more recent example comes from Archibald Cox and Derek C. Bok, who sympathize with unionism in their prominent text on labor law, yet are surprisingly frank in their recognition that unionists use force to pursue their objectives:

> Counter-attack lay in concerted activities designed to injure the employer's business until he came to terms. If the employer refused to recognize the union, the union had to choose between acquiescence and resort to economic compulsion. Moreover, the employees of some establishments could be organized only by pressure from the outside and in such instances the strike, boycott and picket line were indispensable weapons.[2]

This passage is remarkable, yet typical of many quotations in the academic and judicial literature, apparently because so many observers view economic activity as an arena for conflict. They make no distinction between the side effects of cooperative, noncoercive activities of ordinary production and outright vandalism, assault, and intimidation. They make no distinction between mutual agreement to trade among consenting adults and refusal to trade until mutually satisfactory terms of trade are arrived at. For example, a threatened lockout by an employer supposedly is the counterpart to a strike. It is not. First, lockouts are so rare as an employer tactic that the government has not bothered to gather data on their frequency. Second, and more important, an employer does not threaten the economic livelihood of employees in a lockout because he does not pretend to cut off the strikers' alternative economic opportunities, whereas strikers try to shut down the entire operation of a plant, cutting off the employer from labor services and other supplies until he submits.

Cox and Bok speak of the attempt to "injure the employer's business." This idea may be the most amazing thing of all about unionism—the notion that injuring the employer will profit the employees. The employer, though, is a middleman, an intermediary between consumers (the real employers) and the owners of productive inputs (i.e., the dispersed owners of capital, land, and labor services). Entrepreneurs organize production, and if they are efficient at keeping costs low and anticipating buyers' most pressing demands, they will prosper, expand, invest, and everyone will ultimately profit, including investors, consumers, and employees. Harming creative and successful entrepreneurs is the road to poverty, not prosperity.

If an employer refuses to deal with a union, Cox and Bok claim that a union must choose between acquiescence and compulsion. This shows, if nothing else, what can pass as erudite analysis in the academic community. What if a potential buyer refuses to deal with an anxious seller of some other kind of service? Ordinarily in business affairs, the seller must respect another person's refusal to accept an offer *or* offer him a better deal. Presumably Cox and Bok would agree with this proposition if a peddler offers jukebox services, beer, or janitorial supplies to tavern owners, but they make an exception for bartenders or waitresses, to whom they would allow use of "friendly persuasion" on tavern owners, provided, of course, that the bartenders were organized into a recognized union.

The view that the good effects of unionism warrant special privileges in our legal framework is common in the industrial relations community. Labor unions clearly required special dispensations from the law in order to succeed. They were difficult to organize and sustain in the United States because so many obstacles to forming private combinations intruded. Union leaders, business managers, and all others were expected to behave in a noncoercive way under the evolving common law prior to the 1930s, because courts enforced law in a relatively even-handed way, although perfection never was achieved. This legal framework restricted unionists from freely using their tactics and led unionists to wage intensive political campaigns for legal privileges and immunities that could allow unionism to flourish in a sustained way. Their efforts finally paid enormous returns during the confusion of the Great Depression.

The evidence for this view is quite strong, despite many textbook treatments to the contrary. The wording of assorted legislation and legal rulings is always tortured enough to reveal the special privileges in a straightforward way. Consider, for example, Section 602a of the Landrum-Griffin Act of 1959:

> It shall be unlawful to carry on picketing on or about the premises of any employer for the purpose of, or as part of any conspiracy or in furtherance of any plan or purpose for, the personal profit or enrichment of any individual (except a bona fide increase in wages or other employee benefits) by taking or obtaining any money or other thing of value from such employer against his will or without his consent.

The parenthetical exclusion speaks volumes about the nature of the special union-management legislation and legal structure that have been erected since 1930. Congressmen, legislators, regulators, and the courts decided to permit labor unions as cartels fixing terms of employment and then tried to regulate the succeeding behavior of union leaders and organized workers. This amounted to promoting monopoly in labor markets and then requiring cartel leaders to use their power "reasonably."

Unions are beneficiaries of regulatory favors by government, but still, the net economic effect of unions could be beneficial. Unionism could be part of the middle way, a happy medium between laissez-faire capitalism and socialism. Defenses of our present brand of unionism, however, rest on a simple and often naive misunderstanding of the economic process and of unionism. This chapter discusses the common justifications for unions and their actions; Chapter 4 will introduce more sophisticated arguments for unionism and will argue that they cannot stand critical examination either.

"Unions protect workers from employers' superior bargaining power"

This is the most important argument for unionism. Its adherents range from devout believers to lukewarm adherents who talk about the "obsolete concept of individual bargaining" in an economy of a "few corporate giants." In the jargon of economics, they believe that buyers (employers) of labor services have an immense amount of power to dictate the terms of trade in labor markets *and* that the appropriate policy to offset this monopoly power on the demand side is to monopolize the supply side. Even if we accept the assertion about the degree of market power among buyers, the policy recommendation does not necessarily follow because it must be weighed against competing remedies—for example, promoting more competitive, independent behavior among buyers of labor services, say, through antitrust policy.

Unionists, intellectuals, and a substantial share of the general public believe that employers have superior bargaining power that they can employ to abuse the wages, hours, and working conditions of employees who lack union protection. Unionists especially point to the real and imagined evils of the nineteenth century and claim that unions partially offset the excesses of capitalism, thus acting as correctives in an unjust society by promoting an equitable sharing in the decision-making power and the fruits of production. In sum, actual labor markets depart so much from the competitive model of economics that unions are an inevitable and desirable by-product of a real-world market economy.

The belief in employer power over wages and working conditions is almost entirely without basis. It is largely a result of union propaganda, the distortions emanating from the intellectual community, and public gullibility and lack of interest. Professional economists never offered much support for the doctrine, although they are far from blameless in the matter.

Generally, enterprises are forced by competition among businesses to pay competitive prices for *all* scarce, productive commodities, including labor services. Individual enterprises are not free to fix wages wherever they want because, if they choose to offer very low wages, they cannot attract the quality of labor services in the quantity they want; if they choose to pay very high wages, employment must be rationed among an excess supply of eager, qualified applicants. Also, if wages are too high, a firm necessarily overpays its labor suppliers, and the equity value of a private enterprise plummets. Inefficient managers would be displaced because the firm would go under or be taken over by more efficient managers via proxy battles, tender offers, or other capital-market techniques.

Wage rates are determined by the interaction of supply and demand among large numbers of potential buyers and sellers for each type of labor. Individual employers, no matter how large, cannot depress wages and working conditions for any significant period of time, because they must compete for productive labor by paying wages at least at the level paid by the next highest bidders.

It is easy to mistake the caution of employers in bidding up the price of labor as "superior bargaining power," but, in truth, it is the real groping process by which actual markets converge on prices that "clear markets," a vivid phrase to describe pricing that maximizes trade volume and avoids both shortages and surpluses. The facts clearly do not support the idea of immobile employees exploited by employers. More than 4.5 million enterprises hire labor; more than 500,000 new ones appear each year (a smaller number expire each year); and more than 2 million people quit their jobs each month. Dynamic competition and mobility are the rule in the labor market. Moreover, if conspiracies among employers to depress wages below competitive rates ever were an important phenomenon, it is hard to explain why there were no prosecutions or civil suits under our antitrust laws, especially prior to 1914, the year Congress tried to redefine labor services as no longer commodities.

Individual employers, no matter how large, have negligible ability to exploit labor by depressing a worker's wage below the market rate for his skills. The only prominent exceptions are buyer combinations in some professional sports and among NCAA colleges to depress wages for athletes. Monopoly on the buyer's side is called *monopsony.* Although it has occurred, there is an exaggerated belief in its power and ubiquity. Union leaders naturally are interested in promoting an exaggerated view of the scope of industrial monopoly and monopsony because such a view encourages the public to accept unions as a desirable countervailing power.

True, there is immobility among employees because it is costly to change jobs. Older employees who invested in skills specific to a particular firm might be cited—a senior administrative secretary, for example, who knows the ropes. In theory, an employer can lower wages of such employees, to some extent, without fear of losing them if—and I emphasize the word "if"—their firm-specific skills are significantly less valuable to other employers. By the same reasoning, however, such an employee can withhold his individual services in order to exploit his monopoly skills. The employer's alternative to accepting the employee's offer is costly firm-specific training of another employee. Each party can try to exploit this temporary immobility in the bargaining process, but we can make no general statement about the outcome, because it is a bilateral monopoly situation. There is no reason to expect that employees consistently suffer the worse end of deals that offer some scope for bargaining, especially since large employers have an incentive to maintain a reputation for fair dealing in the labor market.

Unskilled and semi-skilled manual workers, however, have a wide range of alternative employment because they are not specialists nor do they have skills that are highly specific to a single employer. It is true that low-skilled people are more likely to limit their geographic mobility for family and other personal reasons than are highly skilled people, but that is an option the less skilled are free to choose. Turnover rates in semiskilled jobs certainly support the contention that mobility and adaptability are the rule. In manufacturing, for example, annual turnover exceeds 50%. Semiskilled and skilled blue-collar workers are the traditional backbone of unionism, of course, yet such employees do not really fit into the theory of firm-specific training and immobility.

In most discussions of labor immobility, almost no one, except W. H. Hutt, points out that there is little parallel between the immobility of labor services and that of huge capital facilities.[3] Most talk of exploitation is about labor, but a good deal of it should be redirected to investors who supply the complementary capital that multiplies the output of human effort. Once installed, much of the capital equipment is relatively fixed and immobile by nature. Unionization has far more to do with exploiting the income earned by investors on their previous investments in transportation facilities, ports, manufacturing plants, mines, and public utilities than with the reverse, namely, the exploitation of workers by investors. The opportunities and legal privilege to exploit are more abundant among unionists than among investors. This process can be termed "opportunistic behavior,"[4] but in the long run neither investors nor hired employees can be truly exploited because they adjust their expectations and subsequent investing and work behavior. Investors protect themselves from exploitation by unionists, but unfortunately, we are poorer as a result, because otherwise profitable, productive investments are not exploited due to fear of union opportunism.

Businesses use a staggering variety of goods and services and only collude, according to union lore, to depress the prices of labor services, but never the prices of other commodities. This is a very odd theory. Presumably some businessmen could redirect their energies to depressing prices of nonlabor commodities, especially those that form bigger shares of total costs than labor expenditures. Yet we hear absolutely nothing about monopsony power over prices in markets other than labor. It is a threadbare idea, kept alive by constant reiteration by unionists. Nevertheless, it still forms the ideological basis for unionism and the labor policy of all Western governments.

"High living standards in the United States are due to a strong union movement"

Union leaders are eager to take credit for the long, historical advance in the standard of living in the United States. Not only is it immodest for union officials constantly to repeat this boast, it is also demonstrably wrong. As a historical matter, real wages rose about 2% per capita each year in America on average long before the advent of powerful unions, and wages rose at a comparable rate after the formation of big unions. The 1970s had zero growth in real wages and pulled the post-1930s big-union era down to the historic average.

If high wages could be achieved on an economy-wide scale by union wage pressure (or wage legislation), it would be easy for even the poorest nations of the world to get rich quick. The government of Sri Lanka or Sierra Leone or Egypt could simply encourage powerful labor unions and watch poverty disappear, or issue a decree simply declaring high wages for everyone (rather like presidential candidate George McGovern's "$1,000 for everybody" in 1972). The idea, of course, is preposterous. It reverses the essential line of causation: High productivity of labor causes high wages, not vice versa.

The United Kingdom provides another easy instance of the fallacy. If unions cause high wages for all, we should expect to find real wages higher in more highly unionized countries. Yet the U.K. is much more unionized than the United States—55% versus 20% of the labor force—yet real wages are at least 40% lower in England. And British unions are as militant as any. The same could be said of some other European countries and of Australia, but their situations are not quite so clear-cut as the British example because union membership figures are unreliable. European unions also tend to be political and religious associations besides being economic-interest groups. Also, more wage-setting and income policies occur at the level of the central government in these economies.

The sad fact is that unions, tough bargaining, and political pressure do not create real wealth. A highly productive economy, with its accompanying high real wages, depends on abundant physical capital, educated and skilled people, and an institutional framework that allows individuals to work to improve their lives. Governmental policies, in other words, must avoid destroying people's incentive to work, save, and invest.

Material output can be divided into two components: (1) the number of people working, and (2) the output produced per person, or "productivity." Union actions, rhetoric aside, do nothing to increase either, and they often do a great deal to harm both the employment situation and productivity. Union actions frequently destroy employment opportunities in the high-productivity sectors of the economy through strike actions, high wage rates, and so on. Unions also hobble measures to raise productivity by imposing restrictive work rules, opposing the installation of new equipment and techniques of production and fostering a depression mentality that encourages members to save some work for the next guy. It is much more correct to argue that wages—real wages, that is—are lower in our society because of labor unions rather than the reverse, because unions discourage investment in high-productivity, unionized sectors, they restrict employment there, restrict output on the job, prevent efficient deployments of labor at the work place, and thereby depress real demand for goods produced by noncompeting labor, increase the supply of labor in less productive employments, and raise the level of unemployment in the economy.

The true source of our prosperity is capital plus efficient management and efficient labor, not unions. If we were to arrange these factors in order of importance, we must rank capital first, because even the most ambitious managers and employees, without capital assets, are much less productive than are unenthusiastic people with machinery to work with. "We are better off than earlier generations," as Ludwig von Mises said, "because we are equipped with the capital goods they have accumulated for us."[5]

Unionists point to two things in support of their claim to be the main source of workers' prosperity: (1) Union workers are generally well paid, and (2) employers resist union wage demands in collective bargaining and, therefore, would not grant raises without union threats. Both of these claims are factually true, more or less, but the explanation (theory) of unionists is wrong. Union workers ordinarily would be well paid, with or without unions. People in plumbing, construction, long-haul trucking, mining, railroads, and printing were well paid before unionism and will continue to be well paid after unions disappear (which they will, I suspect). In addition, if unions do raise wages for their members, this does not imply higher wages for *all* workers, or even necessarily higher earnings for union members. Since more labor is forced into the nonunion sector by high union wage rates, the greater supply reduces wage rates there, with the net result that unionism does not raise wages for all workers.

With respect to resistance by employers to union wage demands, the answer is yes and no. In the nonunion sector, on the one hand, wages are quietly adjusted upward on a more or less continuous basis, in accord with market conditions and turnover. No headline-grabbing confrontations, strike deadlines, and mediating accompany the process. In unionized negotiations, on the other hand, companies often would grant wage increases without union pressure because to do so would be in accord with market realities, especially when a contract has not been reopened for three years in an inflationary era. If union leaders, however, are to protect their own prestige and powers, they must demand considerably more than management might grant as negotiations approach, so that whatever settlement might be reached, union leaders can point to the gains they obtained for their members from a stingy company.

Quite often in the ritualized and costly negotiation process, the problem is to save face for union leaders, and both management and union negotiators know it. It is a charade. The controversy over Boulwarism is a perfect example of this process. As personnel director of General Electric Corporation (GE) in the late 1950s, Lemuel Boulware proposed going into union negotiations with an offer that was well publicized before the general public, employees, and shareholders and that management considered fair in light of market conditions and past experience. The management of GE believed that union members would make the right decision if they had the facts. Union leaders objected vehemently and filed an unfair labor practice suit, which was ultimately upheld by the National Labor Relations Board.[6] GE management was prohibited from communicating directly with the firm's employees and could deal only with union representatives thereafter. Union bargaining must appear to be tough and arduous, especially if union members are to continue believing that union efforts are the source of their big paychecks. This is not to deny, however, that some unions impose higher wage rates and benefits than would otherwise occur; it is simply to point out that not all do. Some settlements are more or less open admissions of a union's inability to affect rates of pay. As W. H. Hutt points out, preserving the prestige of union officials is akin to conducting diplomatic dealings with leaders of newly independent states, whose sensitivities and prestige must be preserved, while the interests of the inarticulate masses are of no account.[7]

"The enemy is the company"

This is completely false. Unions do not compete against employers, despite superficial appearances to the contrary. Sellers compete with sellers and buyers with buyers. When people ask, "What's the competition got?" they mean, "What do other sellers have to offer?" Unions compete with those who sell substitutes for their members' services, which means other forms of labor—members of rival unions, foreign workers, strikebreakers, nonunion workers—as well as machinery and other nonlabor commodities that can substitute for direct labor, or, in effect, the labor of those who produce and service machinery that can substitute for the services of organized workers.

Union control of labor markets has always been incomplete, in spite of the substantial governmental machinery supporting unionization since the 1930s. As a result, organized workers must prevent competing workers, who want to improve themselves, from entering a unionized labor market and thereby restoring open-market conditions.

Bitter jurisdictional disputes among unions dramatically illustrate the fact that the main "enemy" is competing labor. Unions assert exclusive jurisdiction (properly speaking, monopoly jurisdiction) over particular kinds of work and workers, much as national governments claim suzerainty over people and territory. Interunion disputes break out at times, accompanied by strikes, picketing, boycotts, and violence. Two craft unions, for example, can claim the same work, especially if a new technique or material is introduced, and the employer often is caught in the middle of a union battlefield.

As Woodruff Randolph, who ruled the International Typographical

Union from 1944 to 1958, said, "The ITU is a craft union exercising jurisdiction over all composing room work. Our jobs are dependent on that work. The life of our trade is dependent upon that jurisdiction. Whatever weakens or destroys our jurisdiction destroys our union."[8] William L. Hutcheson's Carpenters' Union claimed to cover everything from the growing tree to the finished product: "Once wood, it is always the right of the carpenter to install it."[9] Unionists are not much interested in other unionists' welfare despite all the cant about "the labor movement," "solidarity," and "brotherhood."

One of the venerable clichés of the union movement is that "labor is not a commodity," a phrase that has served as an all-purpose response whenever anyone raises difficult questions about whether unionists are monopolists, whether they interfere with commerce or use strong-arm tactics. Supposedly, people who ask such graceless questions are callous propagandists in comparison with union leaders who have such deep concern for the less fortunate. This high-minded cry that labor is not a commodity is even enshrined in the Clayton Act of 1914 in order to justify union exemption from antitrust laws. Congress, by declaration, attempted to exempt pricing of labor services from the same economic laws that govern pricing of tires, kumquats, and Lionel trains. The hypocrisy is that unionists know that labor services are commodities and that people trade their labor services in markets every day. Unionists' livelihoods depend on bargaining for the sale of other individuals' labor services.

Unions battle one another over jurisdiction essentially because they treat people as commodities, as pawns in labor empires. An examination of any union constitution confirms the validity of the charge. The documents begin by solemnly identifying a group of people who "belong" to the union. The UAW, for example, declares that it takes in and holds jurisdiction over all employees in automobile, farm implement, and aircraft plants "and such other branches of industry as the International Executive Board shall decide."[10] In other words, workers are the property of the union organization. And woe to any other sectionalist labor group that fails to recognize this.

An important purpose of the AFL-CIO is to keep interunion conflict within bounds. The AFL-CIO constitution declares that "each affiliated national and international union is entitled to have its automony, integrity and jurisdiction protected and preserved" (article III, section 7), and it provides for the AFL-CIO Council to issue charters to new organizations if they do not conflict with present affiliates. A "no raiding" agreement requires unions to respect tne established collective bargaining and work relationships of all affiliates, and there is elaborate dispute-settlement machinery to encourage a "proper" degree of respect. Between 1962 and 1975 there were 1,616 jurisdictional-dispute cases filed with the AFL-CIO, most of which were settled by mediation or impartial umpire, although sanctions (suspension, publicity) were imposed in twenty cases.[11] The notion of territorial integrity often extends far beyond interunion disputes, in the opinion of union officials. In 1932 William Green, head of the AFL, felt so strongly about the "absolute sovereignty" of the international (that is, the national union) that he wrote to a union official after the courts unseated him for corruption: "The laws of your international should be respected, and should not be set aside by the courts."[12]

"The strike is the basis of union power"

The strike per se is not the basis of union power. More precisely, the ability to deny an employer access to labor at prices below those demanded by strikers is the basis of power. Strikes ordinarily are not simply withdrawals of labor by current employees, because successful unions must cut off (control) the wider labor supply to enforce wage demands on an enterprise.

"Unions protect workers against the abuse of managerial authority"

This notion is a variant of the first myth and cannot withstand scrutiny either. Workers are not captives. In a competitive labor market employers are forced by competition for productive labor to offer wages and working conditions that cater to the preferences of workers. This includes equitable treatment of workers' grievances by management, because failure to supply attractive working conditions implies that an employer must pay higher wages in order to attract and retain workers. It pays companies to develop reputations for dealing fairly with employees because this keeps labor costs lower than they would otherwise be. A competitive labor market is the ultimate protection for employees, not union grievance procedures.

Three additional points should be made about this issue. First, the value of grievance procedures, whether union or nonunion, depends on how easy it is to change jobs. Employees place no value on a complaint system if mobility among employers is without cost, but they value it highly if there is only one available employer (the socialist state?). Most real cases lie somewhere between these two extremes of costless mobility and prohibitive cost of mobility. Second, managerial abuse can occur in situations where union-imposed pay scales are higher than pay in the competitive sector because so many employees are eager to retain their high-paying jobs. Managers can demand more productivity from workers and still attract a plentiful labor supply. Naturally, unionists contest managerial authority over working conditions in such cases, although if a union succeeds in controlling most of the grievance process, it is unclear which employees will be helped and which harmed by the change. Third, empirical studies by L. F. Dunn and George J. Borjas suggest that the nonpecuniary effects of unionism are virtually zero or even negative in the minds of employees, although the question is far from resolved as a matter of empirical study.

The more general problem is that unionism eliminates free labor markets and substitutes controlled (unfree?) markets, controlled by union officials. Consider the testimony of Walter Reuther, president of the United Auto Workers, before the House Committee on Education and Labor in 1953:

REUTHER: We [UAW] do not control the workers at all, and I do not control a single worker in America....no one has control over anybody. I don't control a single General Motors worker. They have much more control over me than I have over them....He [the employer] surely is free, and he is free to say no and they often say no.

REP. GWINN: Well, he certainly is not free to go into the market and find other workers, is he?

REUTHER: Well, you see, labor is not a commodity which you go and shop for in the free marketplace....We are trying to develop collective bargaining, to advance.

GWINN: No, it seems to me it is quite offensive to have a monopoly of human flesh, and I think that they are different.

REUTHER: ...The whole concept of monopoly is where you get into a field where you are carrying out practices which are unethical and which are deliberately directed toward the restraint of free trade and free competition. We are not doing that.

GWINN: ...and where is the free competition in this whole business?

REUTHER: The competition is between General Motors Corporation and its workers at the collective bargaining table. That is where the competition is. You just treat labor as a commodity, and labor is not a commodity. Labor is people.

GWINN: I know. That is an old story, and I do not treat it as a commodity. I want to make it free, and I am talking about free men and not a commodity.[13]

4

The New Rationale for Unionism

I am a businessman. I sell labor.
—Dave Beck, former Teamsters' president

Solidarity forever
Solidarity forever
Solidarity forever
For the union makes us strong.
—verse from union song

Interest among economists in research on the behavior and effects of labor unions languished for many years. Although there was more than one reason for this, a major factor was that labor economists were divorced from mainstream economics in their approach, concentrating on description and subjective evaluation of labor institutions and shunning optimization theory, the competitive model, general equilibrium, econometrics, and the other modern paraphernalia of economics. Academic labor specialists today largely congregate in the separate field of industrial relations, rather than in economics, and the literature on unions still is dominated by institutionalists who are much more sympathetic toward unions than are the bulk of economists trained in market analysis. Kenneth Boulding said in the late 1940s that everywhere he turned he found labor economists and industrial relations specialists jumping up and down on what they thought was the corpse of supply and demand, proclaiming, "The labor market is dead, long live human relations."[1]

A new economic rationale for unionism now has appeared with a more formidable academic pedigree than the failing institutionalist story about unionism offsetting the oppressive managements committed to satisfying the rapacity of stockholders. Based on modern economic theory and econometric techniques, Richard B. Freeman, James L. Medoff, and others in the Harvard–National Bureau of Economic Research group treat unionism in an analytical yet sympathetic way.[2] They claim that the traditional treatment of unions as monopolies—as exemplified by this book, for example—is seriously misleading because it is necessary to examine the "collective voice/ institutional response" role of unionism to understand fully what unions do in modern industrial economies. The Freeman and Medoff argument appears sophisticated and far-reaching, but the main contentions can be easily summarized in four statements:

1. A trade union is a vehicle for collective voice—that is, for providing workers with a means of communicating at the work place and in the political arena.
2. Unions generally increase productivity.
3. Unions promote economic equality.
4. Unions are democratic, noncorrupt organizations.

Freeman and Medoff marshal data and opinion for their analysis and conclude that their findings "present a reasonably valid picture of modern unionism in our country. It stands in sharp contrast to the monopoly view of trade unions and to many popular beliefs about them."[3]

Their portrait, despite the authors' academic credentials, does not capture the essential features of unionism. Suspicions should be aroused whenever anyone advertises the "newness" of his views, whether it is John Maynard Keynes writing in 1936, the current crop of historians with "radical" reinterpretations of history, the new Chrysler Corporation, or Freeman and Medoff on unions. The trouble with the Freeman-Medoff version of unionism lies partly in what they say in their analysis and even more in what they fail to say. Their analysis, for example, is strangely silent about how union officials induce managers of businesses and governmental agencies to listen so attentively to the voice of the "collective." Yet the coercive tactics of unions certainly are a central problem for public policy. The Freeman-Medoff story commits a serious sin of omission, as do so many other academic discussions of unionism.

The newly proposed rationale for unionism is unsatisfactory on its own terms as well. In the first part of this chapter, I intend to reproduce the essential features of the Freeman-Medoff argument, as well as cite their evidence, in as neutral a fashion as I can muster, reserving my critical remarks for the remainder of the chapter. Their analysis, I believe, is fatally flawed in a number of ways, although the problems take three general forms: (1) some hypotheses are inconsistent with the main features of U.S. unionism; (2) most of the analysis cannot be falsified by empirical experience; and (3) the main issue for public policy—the use of threats, intimidation, and coercion—is ignored because their analysis evaluates only the economic *effects* of unionism, not the process or means used by unionists.

Unions as Collective Voice

Freeman and Medoff follow Albert Hirschman's book, *Exit, Voice, and Loyalty,* in identifying two mechanisms for dealing with divergences between "desired social conditions and actual conditions."[4] The first is the classic market mechanism of mobility: "The dissatisifed consumer switches products; the diner whose soup is too salty seeks another restaurant; the unhappy couple divorces. In the labor market, exit is synonymous with quitting, while entry consists of new hires by the firm."[5]

Individuals leave poor jobs for better jobs, and enterprises offering unattractive working conditions are penalized or punished by the market competition for qualified employees. Freeman and Medoff, however, warn that "as long as the exit-entry market mechanism is viewed as the only efficient adjustment mechanism, institutions such as unions must necessarily be viewed as impediments to the optimal operation of a capitalist economy" (pp. 70–71).

The second mode of adjustment is political mechanisms, termed "voice" by Hirschman. Voice is defined as direct communication or talking about problems, and "in the job market, voice consists of discussing with an employer conditions that ought to be changed, rather than quitting the job" (p. 71). Freeman and Medoff recognize that individuals communicate with one another; they assert, however, that collective bargaining, not individual bargaining, is necessary for effective voice at the work place—for two reasons. First, many aspects of an industrial setting have "public good" or "externality" characteristics that affect the well-being of every employee—for instance, safety conditions, lighting, heating, speed of a production line, policies on layoffs, work sharing, promotions, grievance procedures, and pensions. Freeman and Medoff say these conditions "all obviously affect the entire work force in the same way that defense, sanitation, and fire protection affect the entire citizenry" and therefore "require collective decision-making" (pp. 71–72). Reliance on individual initiative to change conditions does not work because incentives are weak: costs are concentrated on one person, but benefits are spread over all, so a "free rider" problem makes individual adjustments insufficient.

The second reason that individual action must be replaced by collective action is that workers who don't want to leave a firm are afraid of punishment. "Since the employer can fire a protester," say Freeman and Medoff, "individual protest is dangerous; so a prerequisite for workers having effective voice in the employment relationship is the protection of activists from being discharged" (p. 72). Freeman and Medoff point out that U.S. labor law supplies protection for such collective action.

In competitive markets the authors say that firms are responsive to mobile, "marginal" workers, those who depart or are attracted by changes in conditions, while firms ignore "within some bounds" preference of "inframarginal," older workers who "are effectively immobile" (pp. 72-73). Since unions are political institutions whose elected leaders are responsive to all the workers, unionists collect information about preferences, and this leads firms "to choose a 'better' mix of employee compensation and a 'better' set of personnel policies" (p. 75). If bargaining issues involve sizable fixed costs or public goods, a union contract can be "socially more desirable than one based on the marginal preference—that is, it may even be economically more 'efficient' " (p. 73).

Imperfect information, existence of public goods in industrial settings, conflicting interests in the work place and political arena are all a part of their rationale for unionism as an alternative to the market process. Freeman and Medoff add, however, that the effect of unionism also depends on management response:

> If management uses the collective-bargaining process to learn about and improve the operation of the workplace and the production process, unionism can be a significant plus that improves managerial efficiency. On the other hand, if management reacts negatively to collective bargaining or is prevented by unions from reorganizing the work process, unionism can have a negative effect on the performance of the firm...there are two forces determining the economic effects of collective bargaining, managements and unions. (p.74)

Their model of unionism, which they term collective-voice/institutional-response analysis, "stresses the role of unionism in increasing democracy at the workplace by providing workers with a channel for expressing their preferences to management and increasing workers' willingness to complain about undesirable conditions" (p. 90).

Productivity

The Freeman-Medoff rationale focuses attention on the ways that unionism can raise productivity, although it acknowledges some of the negative effects of unionism, too. Four effects are discussed. First, collective voice saves some of the costs of mobility because "as workers' voice increases in an establishment, less reliance need be placed on the exit and entry mechanism to obtain desired working conditions" (p. 76). This saves on hiring and training outlays in the enterprise, and reduces lost production from disrupted work groups. Second, the voice model proposes that: "promotions and other rewards tend to be less dependent in any precise way on individual performance and more dependent on seniority. As a result, in union plants feelings of rivalry among individuals are likely to be less pronounced than in nonunion plants and the amount of informal training and assistance that workers are willing to provide one another is greater" (p. 77).

Third, unions pressure managements into raising efficiency by introducing modern personnel practices, tightening job-production standards, and rationalizing production. Fourth, the apparatus of collective bargaining opens up a two-way communication channel to improve the flow of information between workers and management. This can "possibly improve the productivity" (p. 78) of an enterprise because managers can learn of improvements in production techniques from employees, while managers, in turn, find it easier to communicate with employees.

Freeman's empirical work finds that unionism reduces employee quits and turnover after controlling for other factors with multiple regression analysis.[6] A few statistical studies that relate output per worker to unionization, controlling statistically for capital per worker, the skill of workers (in some analyses), and other factors, find that unionism raises productivity. Brown and Medoff claim that unionism raises productivity in manufacturing 20% to 25%, Frantz found 15% in wooden household furniture, Clark 6% to 8% in cement, Allen 33% to 51% in construction, and Freeman, Medoff, and Connerton found a 25% to 30% productivity increase in underground bituminous coal in 1965, but a 20% to 25% reduction in the same industry in 1975.[7] Freeman and Medoff attribute the dramatic tumble of the United Mine Workers' statistical effect on productivity to the industry's rapid growth, which "yielded supervisors who are on average younger and less experienced in labor relations than was typical prior to the late 1960s" (p. 81).

Freeman and Medoff claim that the productivity effects of union-ism depend on specific industrial-relations settings and never make an overall statement about the net effect of unions on productivity:

> To repeat, unionism *may increase productivity* in some settings and decrease it in others. If the increase in productivity is greater than the increase in average unit costs due to the union wage effect then the profit rate will increase; if not, the rate of profit will fall. There is limited tentative evidence that, on average, net profits are reduced somewhat by unionism, particularly in oligopolistic in-dustries, though there are notable exceptions. At present, there is no definitive accounting of what proportion of the union wage ef-fect comes at the expense of capital, other labor, or consumers, and what portion is offset by *previously unexploited possibilities for productivity improvements.* (p. 81, emphasis added)

Economic Equality

Freeman and Medoff point out that the monopoly view of unionism implies that workers displaced from unionized firms by union wage rates increase the supply of labor to nonunion firms, therefore reduc-ing wages for comparable workers. Economists also traditionally em-phasized that organized workers tend to be more skilled and higher paid than other blue-collar workers, highlighting the potentially dis-equalizing effects of a "labor elite" who benefit at the expense of lower-skilled and lower-paid employees. Freeman and Medoff, how-ever, claim that the wage-equalizing tendencies of unionism dominate the disequalizing effects of monopoly. They argue that, since union decisions are based on a political process, they tend to reduce wage in-equality. Members with below-average earnings tend to favor equal-ization, and union ideology and organizational solidarity support it, too. Also, union rules reduce managerial discretion in wage-setting and reduce the possibility that "arbitrary supervisory judgment will deter-mine the career of a worker" (p. 86). The authors recognize that these reductions in inequality occur "possibly at the expense of efficiency, which may be lessened because the reward for individual effort is reduced" (p. 86). Freeman and Medoff also claim that trade unions raise the earnings of blacks relative to those of whites and thus, on the whole, help reduce differences based on race. Their basic reasons for equalization are the blacks are slightly more unionized than whites because blacks are overrepresented among blue-collar factory workers, while union standard-rate and promotion-by-seniority policies com-press earnings within unionized work places.

Freeman offers empirical support in a subsequent paper.[8] His analysis uses variances of logarithms of earnings as measures of wage dispersion ("inequality") and finds lower dispersion in the union sector after controlling for other characteristics of organized workers. He says in conclusion: "Overall, the within-sector effect of unionism on dispersion appears to more than offset the increase in dispersion of earnings across industries, so that on net unionism reduces inequality."[9] Standard-rate policies plus narrowing the blue-collar/white-collar earnings differential statistically dominate the more widely studied impact of unionism on widening dispersion of average wages across industries, according to Freeman.

A related paper finds that the higher the percentage of the work force that belongs to unions in a state, the closer to equality is the distribution of family income.[10] Thomas Hyclak uses a single equation regression with data for 1950, 1960, and 1970 among the forty-eight contiguous states. The Gini coefficients on family income or percentage of families with low income are measures of inequality and are regressed on right-hand-side variables like median age, percent nonwhite, unemployed, high school graduated employed in manufacturing, urban percentage, and percent unionized. Unionization has a significant negative association with degree of family income dispersion, all else being equal, and so is considered to be an equalizing factor. Curiously, no dummy variable for the South was introduced to see if the percentage unionized might not reflect the higher income inequality in southern states and lower income inequality in northern states rather than the degree of unionization being the crucial equalization factor. Freeman and Medoff sum up their two views of unions in Table 4-1.

Democracy and Corruption

Freeman and Medoff correctly point out that "under the monopoly view of unionism, the potential to use union monopoly power to raise wages and to extort funds from firms—particularly small, weak firms—fosters a significant amount of corruption and undemocratic behavior in the union movement" (p. 88). They argue, however, that "the vast majority of evidence appears to support the voice view that unions generally are democratic political organizations and are responsive to the will of their members" (p. 88).

As evidence, they cite union constitutions, which typically mandate

Table 4-1
Two Views of Trade Unionism

	Union Effects on Economic Efficiency	Union Effects on Distribution of Income	Social Nature of Union Organization
Monopoly View	Unions raise wages above competitive levels, which leads to too little labor relative to capital in unionized firms. Union work rules decrease productivity. Unions lower society's output through frequent strikes.	Unions increase income inequality by raising the wages of highly skilled workers. Unions create horizontal inequities by creating differentials among comparable workers.	Unions discriminate in rationing positions. Unions (individually or collectively) fight for their own interests in the political arena. Union monopoly power breeds corrupt and nondemocratic elements.
Collective-Voice/ Institutional-Response View	Unions have *some positive effects on productivity* (1) by reducing quit rates, by inducing management to alter methods of production and to *adopt more efficient* policies, and (2) by improving morale and cooperation among workers. Unions collect information about the preferences of all workers, which leads the firm to choose a "better" mix of employee compensation and a "better" set of personnel policies. Unions improve the communication between workers and management, leading to better decision-making.	Unions' standard-rate policies reduce inequity among organized workers in a given company or a given industry. Union rules limit the scope for arbitrary actions concerning the promotion, layoff, recall, etc., of individuals. Unionism fundamentally alters the distribution of power between marginal (typically junior) and inframarginal (generally senior) employees, causing union firms to select different compensation packages and personnel practices than nonunion firms.	Unions are political institutions that represent the will of their members. Unions represent the political interests of lower-income and disadvantaged persons.

Sources: Richard B. Freeman and James L. Medoff, "The Two Faces of Unionism," *The Public Interest,* 57 (Fall 1979), p. 75.

democratic procedures; U.S. labor laws against undemocratic practices within unions; "strong federal sanctions"; few charges of im-
proper elections filed by dissidents with the U.S. Department of Labor
(1965–74); a study by Leon Appelbaum that showed high officer turnover in ninety-four union locals in the Milwaukee area during 1960–62;
and opinion surveys showing that a majority of union members were
satisfied with union operations. They also cite academic authorities
like Derek Bok and John Dunlop who stress the honesty of most labor
leaders (p. 90). Freeman and Medoff also claim that "much union
political muscle has been devoted to promoting legislation that would
be of no obvious material gain to unionized workers—except as members of the overall working population" (p. 91).

The Deficiencies

The analysis of Freeman and Medoff deserves careful examination,
not only on its own merits but also because of the wide attention it has
received, especially among unionists. For example, Norman Hill, president of the A. Philip Randolph Institute, wrote:

> Richard B. Freeman and James L. Medoff, two highly respected
> members of Harvard University's Economics Department...
> published in *The Public Interest*, the conservative quarterly edited
> by Irving Kristol, a member of *The Wall Street Journal*'s board of
> contributors....The Harvard economists attributed the higher
> productivity levels, which, in some cases, were as large as 30%, to
> several factors, including lower turnover rates and greater worker
> satisfaction. They also noted that strikes aren't nearly as costly or
> as disruptive as many people might think.[11]

The problem of the "legitimacy" and respectability of unionism never
disappears, and it makes the economic and political stakes in reliable
analysis much greater than in most social research.

Although Freeman and Medoff are not wrong about everything,
their overall conclusions are either misleading, demonstrably wrong,
or, at best, based on doubtful evidence. The impact of unionism on
wage dispersion is an example of doubtful evidence, while their
analysis of the other aspects of unionism is misleading and/or wrong.

Consider their basic model of the union as an institution. Their approach is common in the economics profession in other contexts but
has a certain novelty when applied to unions. Conventional economic
analysis, based on the theory of public goods and external effects,
often is used to justify governmental intervention. The theory deals
with cases where voluntary exchange is impeded by the high cost of

negotiating and enforcing exchanges that otherwise would result in mutual gains for the parties involved.

If high costs of exchange impede trade, we have no general guarantee that resources are allocated efficiently through voluntary transactions, and inefficient equilibria are called "market failures." In other words, the actual operation of the market can differ from its ideal operation, primarily because of costly information and poorly specified property rights. This opens the door to the possibility that government can intervene to overcome transactions costs by directly changing the allocation of resources to the mutual advantage of all concerned. Unfortunately the theory does not go on to tell government officials where the market process specifically fails, or why we should confidently expect government officials to be motivated to improve efficiency, or whether actual interventions have the efficiency effects hoped for by economists. Economists of diverse persuasions now recognize that the theoretical existence of market failure is hardly sufficient to recommend real government intervention on efficiency grounds. To illustrate the naivete of many economists, George Stigler tells a story about a director of a play who had two singers auditioning for a role. After hearing the first singer, the director awarded the role to the second singer. Presumably the relevant comparison is between the actual performance of singers or the actual performance of markets and government in economic matters.

The externality argument is used to rationalize almost every conceivable intervention, and it is also the basis for the new rationale of unionism. Freeman and Medoff claim that many aspects of industrial production are public goods or external effects that might be corrected by collective action. A second reason for collective action is supposedly "fear" on the part of employees who might otherwise voice their opinion. It is not clear whether Freeman and Medoff propose public goods and externality arguments as scientific models or simply as normative hopes, but we have every right to treat them as serious explanations for the existence of unions, as a competitor to the monopoly model.

The fear argument can be dismissed out of hand. There is certainly nothing new about the familiar helpless individual who has dominated the study of labor problems, and nearly all social research, since the dawn of the industrial revolution.[12] The proposition that free markets confer an awesome power on the boss, who uses it to impoverish employees, is completely false, despite the need of so many to believe it. The argument always has had a Marxist ring to it because of its basis in the conflict view of the enterprise rather than in the view of businesses as legal entities in which employees, managers, and investors voluntarily communicate and cooperate to their mutual advantage, and ultimately to consumers' advantage as well. Exchanges uncoerced by either party, including exchanges for labor services, involve mutual agreement on and accommodation to the terms of trade. Voluntary trades satisfy both buyer and seller; otherwise they do not occur. An eyes-open look at virtually any nonunion work place, past or present, shows the overpowering extent of mutual cooperation in the productive effort, despite fantasies about slave-driven, frightened workers under the heel of voracious capitalists. Perhaps Freeman and Medoff someday will supply evidence of the "fear" that pervades nonunion mechanics, truck drivers, loggers, machinists, laborers, and dockworkers, but currrently we have absolutely no evidence that free markets produce workers who are afraid of their bosses. Both logic and the evidence indicate that the reverse is true. The options available to workers in free markets heighten individual confidence, whereas a system of unionized labor markets ruled by "union democracies" sharply restricts the freedom of each individual.

There is a possibility that a political mechanism could correct some public goods, externality, and exchange failures at the work place. This sounds plausible to many ears, especially those of the many economists who wish to avoid the free trade or laissez-faire labels and who want to endorse intervention under most circumstances. Collectivist measures to correct market failure cannot be rejected on a priori logical grounds. Unions might be service agencies that are responsive to the collective wishes of members, thereby correcting failures.

This optimistic picture of unionism is naive. First, managers do not need collective bargaining to "learn about the work place and the production process," because they are paid to know the production process and have every incentive to lower the costs of production through improvements. Managers who do not learn about the work place cannot survive in free markets. Nor are supervisory judgments "arbitrary." The essence of successful personnel management is assignment by merit, not by seniority, with consistent, uniform application of fair policies. Second, the extent of public-goods problems that can be resolved only by the intervention of outside, coercive agents like unions or government must be close to zero. Work places ordinarily involve small numbers of people in common working environments. Solutions in such situations are inexpensive and can be achieved by discussion among those directly concerned. Third, there is no evidence that unions, on average, adjust conditions closer to or farther from optimal public-goods solutions. As Bertrand Russell said, "It is undesirable to believe a proposition when there is no ground whatever for supposing it true." Freeman and Medoff hold a version of the free-market singer audition and award the prize to unions.

The Freeman-Medoff picture is in glaring contradiction to observed facts about the structure of unionism in the United States—in particular, the immense national unions that dominate the labor-representation industry. Effective service organizations are local, not national, in scope. Locals are close to the membership in a plant, company, or area, making it easier to discover and act on their constituents' desires. Beyond the local level, the collective character of common working conditions virtually disappears. How much do steelworkers in Alabama care about working conditions in Pittsburgh? Or do teachers in Portland care about teachers in Orlando?

Independent unions, which engage almost exclusively in local-level bargaining, fit the description of the service role of unions. They generally do not use economic force or take to the streets, but these organizations long ago were derided as company unions by "legitimate," bona fide trade unionists. Section 8(a)(2) of the Wagner Act prohibits employer participation or financial support of any labor organization, spelling the end of most company unions and relieving national unions of effective competitors. Some employees would prefer an employees' association based on the notion of mutual cooperation with an employer, rather than the union model of conflict between capital and labor. Of course, if a nonunion employer is nice to his employees, unionists and academics consider his behavior "paternalistic," and if an employer is nice to his employees and they unanimously oppose representation by national unions, the employer is termed "antilabor."

In 1935 during the Senate hearings on the Wagner Act, numerous witnesses who were members of company unions argued that the act would eliminate successful working relationships. Senator Wagner effectively deflated their testimony whenever he asked them where they got the funds to come to Washington. They answered, "From the company." Today more than 90% of union membership is in fewer than fifty industry-wide unions with over 100,000 members each. Independent (company) unions are insignificant.

Collective bargaining is industry-wide, and decision-making power is vested in national officials in industrial unions. As William Leiserson wrote:

> the basic unit of union government is the national union, and not the local as is often supposed. . . . All sovereign powers are in these national unions. Their governments are supreme over all members,

local unions, and other subordinate bodies. . . . In terms of citizenship a union member is a citizen under the government of his national or international union. . . . Local unions are mere subdivisions of the national organization whose constitutions provide for their government as a state does for its counties, cities, towns, and villages. . . . National laws provide for the suspension, merging, and abolition of local unions. Local officers may be removed by the national executives who may appoint administrators to manage their affairs, sometimes without the consent of the local members.[13]

This description is consistent with a monopoly interpretation of national unions. If unions raise labor costs in one area, and enterprises threaten to move away, the union must organize workers and raise labor costs in the new area to thwart relocation of work away from the original membership. The monopoly model also explains the tendency for economic power in craft unions, especially the building trades, to concentrate in the hands of the ten thousand or so local business agents. Markets are local, which means that "industry-wide" bargaining must be only area-wide to achieve effective monopoly in the supply of labor. Construction basically remains an industry in which each unit is custom built on site.

Union practices and policies—tariffs and quotas, opposition to investment overseas, higher minimum wages, building codes, long apprenticeships, closed shops, and licensing requirements—restrict trade and are consistent with monopoly theory, not with the Harvard-NBER interpretation of collective voice. When scientists construct a model to explain existing data, they continue to test its truth against new facts, new data. Are the new facts consistent with the theory or not? It is no different with political or economic theories. The monopoly model of unionism explains these wide-ranging facts about union behavior, and the Freeman-Medoff model does not.

Freeman and Medoff claim that "unions typically come into existence as a result of management's mistakes in dealing with its workforce" (p. 92). Managements certainly do make mistakes, some more than others, and those that make a lot are displaced over time because of market pressures for efficiency. People who continuously diminish the value of resources do not survive in managerial decision-making. Freeman and Medoff assert much more, though, because the implication of their remark is that the number of management mistakes (unmeasured) is greater in some industries than in others and is responsible for unionization of their work forces. This paints a picture of indigenous demand for and production by unionization by workers on the job that cannot withstand examination. Professional unionists organized industries that met the two-fold conditions for profitable unionization;

namely, rewards to organizing were higher in certain sectors of the economy, and costs were lower. Before the commitment of the federal government to unionize the labor force through legislation in the 1930s, unions consisted almost exclusively of groups of craftsmen, because these groups met two conditions: (1) they offered large potential gains in wages because of inelastic demand for craft services, and (2) they could be organized at a low cost because of the small numbers of workers, the low turnover rates, and employers who were few in number or geographically concentrated. After fifty years of favorable governmental regulation, unions are still primarily found in crafts and industries where the labor market is highly concentrated. This explains the high degree of unionization in mining, railroads, airlines, the building trades, printing, and public utilities. Industrial unions are largely found in industries with relatively few firms—transportation equipment, primary metals, electrical machinery, and petroleum refining. Unions have not had to overcome the tremendous costs of organizing many small employers in these industries, which traditionally have limited unionization in sectors like wholesale and retail trade, the services, and agriculture. A large nonunion sector in an industry always limits union wage increases to small amounts anyway, even if some firms are unionized.

Freeman and Medoff suggest that the effect of unionism depends on the management response. In a sense, this is correct. If someone sticks a gun in your ribs and tells you to hand over your money, the effect of this act of aggression definitely depends on what you do next. Freeman and Medoff say that "if the management reacts negatively to collective bargaining. . .unionism can have a negative effect on the performance of the firm." Yes, true, but notice how close it is to saying, "If you cooperate with us. . .however, if you do not. . ." One of the prominent features of Freeman and Medoff's language, in this instance and others, is a hesitancy to be truly definite about anything. Their use of expressions like "can have," "possibly," "likely," "tend to be," "appears to," "do not seem to," "suggests," and "may be" goes far beyond the limits of scientific caution. The collective voice model has the aura of reason but no well-defined structure with logically derived, verifiable implications about observable behavior. It is simply a collection of unrelated hypotheses that share one trait: a favorable view of labor unions.

Productivity Again

The so-called new view claims that unionism, on balance, induces socially beneficial increases in productivity by reducing labor mobility, enhancing worker morale and cooperation, and pressuring management into stricter efficiency. Standard economic analysis, on the other hand, always emphasized the misallocation and efficiency losses due to the wage effects of unionism. Union wages are forced up, distorting the composition of output and investment and raising unemployment as unionists price themselves out of jobs and nonunion workers price themselves in. Freeman and Medoff do not deny the existence of these losses; they simply dismiss them as "minuscule" based on Rees's estimate of the loss at 0.3% of GNP, or $10 billion in a $3.5-trillion economy.[14] Freeman and Medoff believe that the favorable non-wage effects of collective voice more than offset these losses.

Their view is surely mistaken. First, Freeman and Medoff ignore the direct restrictions on output imposed by unions, frequently referred to as featherbedding in the United States and as overmanning in Britain. Examples are legion: locals of the International Brotherhood of Electrical Workers have refused to install electrical switchboards unless factory wiring was torn out and rewired by IBEW members; the International Typographical Union has insisted on resetting existing plates of newspaper advertising; stagehands' unions require minimum crew size for theatrical performances; musicians' locals insist on standby orchestras; and motion picture projectors have compelled theaters to employ two operators for each projection machine in some cities. In a flagrant example of featherbedding, the Operating Engineers' union requires that one of its members operate each machine or engine on construction sites, even if only one switch must be turned on for an entire day's work. On one construction site, several small gasoline generators were used, and unions required each machine to be watched by an operating engineer who started the gas engine once or twice a day, an electrician who pushed wire plugs into sockets if they were moved, and a pipefitter who was there "just in case."[15]

Some longshoremen refuse to shift from ship to dock work, thus compelling the use of multiple crews. Union work rules frequently prohibit supervisors or foremen from helping or working at the trade under any circumstances, sometimes require craftsmen to do unskilled work like operating automatic elevators or handling materials, and prohibit drivers (teamsters) from assisting helpers, who are members of the same union. Over the years, perhaps the railroad unions were the most successful in promoting a labyrinth of restrictive practices, from compelling the use of firemen on diesel locomotives to imposing full-crew laws and train-limit laws. The motto is Here today, here forever.

Unions consistently resist the introduction of new labor-saving technology and equipment. Painters' locals prohibited the use of spray guns and restricted brush widths; hod carriers fought ready-mixed concrete; plumbers resisted plastic pipe; and print unions opposed computer typesetting. In 1975 pressmen did a million dollars' worth of damage to computerized presses at *The Washington Post*. *The Times* of London was shut down for fifty weeks beginning 1 December 1978 because management wanted to introduce "new" print technology— equipment that had been in common use in the United States and other parts of the world for 15 years and that allowed an average worker to increase output from 3,000 to 18,000 characters per hour. Eventually a satisfactory settlement was reached, but the unionists still refused to cooperate. Unions imposed the equivalent of a weekly pay rate (including overtime) of £500 to £600 per week, which was more than the prime minister of England was paid. Fleet Street newspapers continue to be forced to pay these monopolistic rates for one-sixth the hourly output of a comparable German or American worker.[16]

Paul Hartman studied the West Coast longshoring agreement of 1960 in which the union agreed to eliminate work rules requiring multiple handling of goods, redundant crews, and other restrictions on productivity in exchange for higher pay.[17] Hartman found that, after unionization in the mid-1930s, productivity dropped and then remained fairly constant but grew by 40% in the five years after the 1960 agreement. Longshoremen earned higher pay, no fewer longshoremen were employed, and the industry received higher volume at lower cost.

Examples of union restrictions and industry studies could be multiplied indefinitely, but they can be dismissed by skeptics as mere anecdotes. Everyone condemns restrictions as obviously wasteful, but what do they add up to? No one really knows, although most businessmen complain that the work restrictions of unions cost more than union wages. Rees concluded that "losses of this kind—deadweight losses—probably exceed the social losses from relative wage effects."[18] It is hard to believe that the benign effects of unions can offset these losses, especially since unions continue to denounce "speedups," "sweatshops," and "rate-busters." The job security and protection afforded union members induces more absenteeism, discipline problems, and petty grievances, while compression of wage-rate structure and emphasis on seniority reduce each individual's incentive to excel in production.

Furthermore, the lack of clear-cut examples of union improvements of productivity puts a heavy burden on econometric techniques to support the Freeman-Medoff view.[19] The theoretical problem is that the collective-voice model does not differ substantially from the conventional monopoly model about productivity. Unionized firms respond to union wages by altering combinations of inputs so that the marginal productivity of labor matches the higher wages. Therefore, it is hard to tell if empirical studies adequately control for the higher quantity and quality of capital per unit labor, higher quantity and quality of management per unit of labor, and the higher quality of labor employed due to artificially expensive labor. Union and nonunion productivity differences that remain after statistically controlling for measured differences might be due to benign effects of unionization per se, but they are more likely due to unmeasured factors or poorly measured variables, especially capital per worker and managerial quality. These estimations are a tricky business, much like the interpretation of the earnings gap between blacks and whites, commonly attributed to discrimination if earnings differences remain after statistical controls for characteristics like schooling, age, and marital status. Yet, strictly speaking, we can say only that any earnings (productivity) differences that remain are unexplained or unaccounted for by variation in measured characteristics.

An indirect statistical approach to the productivity hypothesis is to analyze the change in the equity value of enterprises as they unionize or deunionize. If unions actually raise production more than they raise labor expenses, then labor costs per unit of output fall, efficiency and profits increase, and the prices of equity shares will reflect the newly improved earnings of the firm. The reverse occurs if unions raise costs more than they raise production. Using this approach, a preliminary study arrived at inconclusive results.[20] Thomas Beecroft examined the 53,000 union-representation elections conducted by the NLRB from December 1971 to April 1977 and found only a dozen that met the dual criteria for useful results: (1) an election that included a major share of the company's work force, and (2) corporate shares traded on a major exchange to get an accurate daily measure of the company's market value. Six firms were studied in detail, and their two-month equity prices were compared with those of other firms in the industry to control for nonunion events affecting the value of firms in the industry.

The value of one firm moved in favor of positive productivity effects for unions, two moved in the opposite direction, and three had no significant movement. The overall results were insignificant by standard criteria. The problems included small percentages (8% to 72%) and questions about whether union elections are synonymous with union contracts and higher labor costs. Nevertheless, this approach is promising and may bear fruit in the future.[21]

There are, however, many other reasons to believe that the allegedly favorable effects of unionism on productivity do not offset their unfavorable effects. How else, if unionized enterprises are efficient and competitive, can we explain why unions invest so much effort in promoting new regulations and imposing more costs on nonunion enterprises? Also, profit-seekers would seek out unions if unions had such effects on enterprises, yet many owners of firms, who presumably want to increase their incomes, deliberately spend substantial sums to avoid or displace unions. The Freeman-Medoff answer is that managers are not trying to maximize the value of the firm but are preserving their decision-making power at the expense of profits. They also say that unionization is risky because unions don't *always* offset their negative effects with higher production.

The ultimate problem with union productivity claims is that managers, investors, and employees in nonunion firms have every financial and personal incentive to discover and adopt any techniques that produce large gains in production. Imagine two assembly plants producing the same goods in the same town. Suppose that the employees, managers, and equipment are identical in every respect except that one plant has a union and the other does not. How could the union plant sustain a 20% productivity advantage? It couldn't. If there were a magic morale booster, a means of lowering quit rates, and work rules that more than paid for themselves, the nonunion plant would quickly adopt the new procedures. If managers were ignorant or refused to adopt techniques to lower production costs, the market eventually would replace them. Surely unions can take none of the credit for the fivefold increase in agricultural labor productivity since 1950, nor can they claim credit for the economy-wide gains in productivity before the 1930s when unions were a negligible factor.

Freeman and Medoff implicitly believe that abundant profit opportunities go unexploited because of a lack of union pressure. Few people —even Harvard professors—who know of abundant profit opportunities, however, can resist taking advantage of them. Given the large numbers of people daily searching for profit opportunities, it is difficult to credit Freeman and Medoff's easy assertions about profits lying around unseized simply because unionists haven't forced managers to recognize them. The argument is identical to the old "shock theory" about the impact of the minimum-wage law, which "shocked" managers into greater efficiency. Professor Hutt makes short work of this: "It is just not true that prospects of adversity stimulated managerial and technological imagination, enterprise, and effort more than the prospects of prosperity. If it were true, it would be wise for governments to impose burdens on any sector of the economy they wished to foster—taxing an industry to give it a jolt and thereby to cause it to flourish!"[22] Taxing an industry through union rules and wage rates, minimum-wage rates, more taxation, and new regulations imposes new costs and obstacles to success, just as common sense suggests.

Managers do change their behavior after unionization, as the monopoly view implies. The response to more expensive labor is to raise output per labor hour by reducing employment, hiring higher-quality workers over time, and introducing new, improved capital, new managers, and new personnel practices. Previously uneconomical production techniques become economical after the price of labor goes up, but from a social point of view this is inefficient because scarce labor and capital of high caliber are used up in producing goods that would have been produced by lower-quality labor and capital if market prices had prevailed. The whole sequence is like urban renewal, sometimes called "Negro removal," in which government destroys old neighborhoods. The old residents turn out not to be the new residents, just as the old managers, workers, and capital are not the new ones after the "shock treatment."[23]

The fallacy in the shock theory is that by economizing on labor through mechanization, because of high labor costs, capital is simply shifted around in the economy; no new capital is created. And the artificial scarcity of labor brought about by effective unions implies that capital is less efficiently employed in the economy than it could be.

Business managers are more difficult to find than are Harvard professors who believe that unions aid productivity. In a *Wall Street Journal*-Gallup survey of 782 chief executives—282 in large corporations, 300 in medium-sized companies, and owners of 200 small companies—the most commonly volunteered criticisms of unions were that they hurt productivity (30%), imposed inflexible work rules and featherbedding (17%), fostered disruptions and uncooperative attitudes

(13%), and caused inflation and price increases (12%).[24] When asked to name the "greatest positive contribution that labor unions make to your company and your industry," the most popular reply was "none" (30%); next was "communication between workers and management" (12%), "Cooperate with management" and "organize labor force" each had 10%; "don't know" finished fifth (9%); and productivity gains finished sixth (8%). Only 1% of small companies and 4% of medium-sized companies mentioned favorable productivity effects. A resounding 47% of chief executives of small companies said unions made no positive contributions; 14% said "don't know." The smaller the company, the more likely the chief was to hold a negative opinion of labor unions.

Among the most favorable comments in the survey were "unions are OK, I guess," "they cause us to pay higher wages," "they force us to find ways to improve productivity," and "they support the company in working against tariff reduction." Among negative comments were "the union tells them [nonunion student help] to slow down and not to work so much," "totally belligerent," "union forgets that a company has to be profitable," "featherbedding and work-wasting methods," "job-preserving, productivity-robbing practices," and they "make foreign competition so difficult to deal with."

Unions, it must be conceded, may have some independent productivity-enhancing effects, but they are not the dominant effects of unionism. Freeman and Medoff claim that unionism may increase productivity in some settings and decrease it in others, but unfortunately they offer no guidance about what these settings might be. From a scientific point of view, this is no theory at all; it is only implausible conjecture. Unions surely raise observed output *per union worker employed,* but this is a classic distortion of the allocation of scarce labor and capital, not something to applaud.

Earnings Differences

Perhaps the most effective response to the Freeman-Medoff claim that the overall effect of unions is to reduce earnings differences is the witty rebuttal, So what? It is statistically conceivable that the wage-compressing effects within unionized firms and industries offset the widened inequalities among comparable workers in union and non-union sectors. This would be a purely fortuitous outcome because there is no reason for it to occur again; it would be only a momentary artifact. Equality of outcome is so earnestly pursued and so fashionable in some circles that all favored institutions are believed to promote equal earnings, or at least to reduce existing differences in earnings. Never mind how these outcomes are produced—government force, unions, accident, meritocracy—the means matter little to these people. Only outcomes matter.

Troy, Koeller, and Sheflin point out that even union members do not universally applaud the tendency for unions to compress the wage structure.[25] Skilled workers in the UAW, for example, have been on the edge of secession for many years because of the egalitarian wage policies pursued by the UAW leadership. White-collar workers have never been pleased by the relative erosion of the difference between their earnings and those of skilled blue-collar union members. Middle-aged and more-educated union workers fare less well in wage gains than do the young, less educated, and unskilled in unions. Union wage policies have a series of scatter-shot effects on various individuals, effects that are in large measure arbitrary. Wage rates bear less relation to individual differences in effort, productivity, and skill under unionism, with perverse effects on efficiency. Nor are these efficiency losses offset by any significant gain in everybody's sense of fairness. Wage distortions are piled on top of one another, and some offset one another in a statistical sense. So what?

Nor is statistical evidence about the effects of unionism on the overall distribution of earnings beyond dispute. Other economists argue that the Robin Hoods of union headquarters, if anything, have a slight tendency to add to overall inequality, primarily by increasing the gap between the income of union members and that of the very poor.[26] Even if unions had the net effect of slightly diminishing *earnings* differences among the economically active, they must answer for their exclusion of the poorest from productive economic activity. The resulting status of the unskilled as wards of the state tends to widen overall income differences. More important, the process and means of unionism must figure in normative evaluations. Peter Wiles puts it well:

> It is truly amazing that anyone should suppose this crude, selfish, violent and piecemeal process to contribute to social justice. It is, when we come to think of it, incredible that the building up by some salary and wage earners of monopoly power, in greater degree here and lesser degree there, should improve the distribution of income among them all; so incredible that the supposition has only to be directly given utterance to be dismissed.[27]

Union Autocracy

Freeman and Medoff make the breathtaking claim that "the vast majority of evidence appears to support the voice view that unions generally are democratic political organizations and are responsive to the will of their members." No student of trade unions, regardless of political persuasion, has published such a sweeping absolution of American unionists before. Clark Kerr, for instance, speaks of unions as "one party governments," and Will Herberg talks of the "time-honored facade of the constitution" and the "concentration of power in the hands of the top leadership."

Freeman and Medoff suffer from the serious misconception that the union local meeting is the locus of power in national unions. The other authors cited in this book do not make that claim. The following description by Steve Early, general counsel of PROD, a dissident Teamsters' group, is not at all unusual.

> Many [American unions] are bureaucratic and undemocratic to the core, and even those which appear to be democratic in form, often are far from it in substance. . . . District and International officers in most unions today are elected at conventions heavily influenced or controlled by full-time staff, rather than in referendum votes involving the entire membership. . . . Many top officials have written their own tickets.[28]

Early describes the Steelworker bureaucracy as "the veritable army of 800 full-time staff representatives hired and fired by the International President" and the major obstacle to any rank-and-file challenge. The only exception is a palace revolt such as I. W. Abel pulled off in 1965 because the bureaucracy was evenly split and because Abel controlled the election machinery.

Locals are, by and large, still creatures of the national officers, although use of trusteeships to quell rivals apparently diminished after Landrum-Griffin. A typical incident in the steel industry illustrates who really controls union decisions. The Kaiser Steel plant in Fontana, California, lost money for four consecutive years, $39 million in 1979 alone, and the company said that if it was to remain open, it would take wage concessions.[29] Otherwise, the plant would close. Kaiser attributed the mill's problems to competition from Japanese steel, operating problems, and a depressed market for steel. Local 2869 of the Steelworkers pledged to "seek out, discuss and implement all feasible ways to . . . make Kaiser Steel Corp. more competitive." A vote among the local's membership yielded an overwhelming majority in favor of a dollar-an-hour reduction in future cost-of-living increases spread over two and a half years. Kaiser officials hailed the local's move to help the company as an important factor in the decision to keep the mill open. International officers from the United Steel-workers, however, protected their own interests by forcing Local 2869 to withdraw its offer. The adjective "united" in Steelworkers' organizational title is not always warranted, to put it mildly. The future of the mill is uncertain, and Kaiser has been trying to find a buyer. During 1980 Kaiser laid off 2,000 of its 6,000 hourly employees and cut production from 3.5 million to 2.8 million tons a year.

It is sheer romanticism to believe that organizations of more than 100,000 people are run democratically in the ordinary political sense of the term. It is possible that some leaders are responsive to member sentiment, given the truth of the old view that most members don't care how much the leaders steal as long as the members get what they are entitled to receive. Serious intramural warfare ordinarily is confined to situations in which many members feel they aren't getting their due. Ultimately, however, any bureaucratic organization without a well-defined purpose or substantial competitive checks on its behavior becomes a vehicle for unaccountable power, pure and simple. This issue receives more attention in Chapter 10, but for the moment Arthur Shenfield provides an apt summary of the mechanics of union organization: "The truth is that they [unions] are power structures, the maintenance and expansion of whose power becomes more and more their purpose, irrespective of benefit or detriment to their members.... By way of promise of benefit to their members they first climb on the workers' back, and from that point of vantage they seek to climb upon the back of the whole society."[30]

5
Old Unionism and Governmental Support

If, indeed, the current power of unions is in no small measure based upon positive acts of assistance by political authorities, the mere removal of these acts of assistance without the addition of any punitive or repressive measures might prevent any further extension of the influence of unions on the allocation of resources, and perhaps start a slow trend in the opposite direction.
—Milton Friedman, 1951

How did American trade unions grow so large? Government intervention has been the crucial ingredient. America historically was harsh ground for unionism because Americans lacked a collectivist, class mentality, and governmental intervention therefore played a much larger role in the development of unionism in the United States than it did in Europe. The importance of the American legal system in establishing and encouraging trade unions can hardly be overemphasized, a view widely adopted by observers of different political persuasions.

Economists have been relatively silent about the legislation from the 1930s that supports unionism and collective bargaining in the United States. A failure to apply economic analysis to the Norris–La Guardia and Wagner acts has allowed a consensus about this legislation to develop among labor writers, basically by default. Expressed in terms of established economic theory, most accounts appear to rest on two central propositions: (1) employees and employers are natural antagonists, and employers have a powerful advantage over employees (labor monopsony), and (2) public policy ought to promote unions and collective bargaining in order to offset this inequality (bilateral monopoly). Even if the first proposition (which many economists would reject) were accepted as factually correct, acceptance of the second proposition would not follow, because it would have to be compared with alternative measures—for instance, with policies intended to encourage more competitive bidding for labor services.

Most labor scholars have approved of the labor legislation of the 1930s, although they differ in detail and sometimes express disappointment at the administrative evolution of the laws.[1] The questions that labor writers ask and the data that they use have been sharply limited by their implicit acceptance of the monopsony model and their shared conviction that greater involvement by government and labor unions in determining wage rates and working conditions was a favorable departure from the status quo ante.

On the other side of the issue, one of the few economists to comment explicitly on the legislation has been W. H. Hutt: "The Norris–La Guardia and Wagner acts will, I predict, come to be regarded by future historians as economic blunders of the first magnitude. They were worked for and acquiesced to under motivations of almost unparalleled sordidness and cynicism combined with the highest, misguided idealism."[2]

Hutt's provocative characterization cannot be confidently accepted or rejected presently because we lack a major analysis of the legislation within the framework of accepted economic theory and public-choice analysis. The purpose of this chapter is to remedy this deficiency. Specifically, my aim is (1) to describe the main features of the Norris–La Guardia and Wagner acts in terms of standard economic theory and the emerging theory of regulation, (2) to analyze the direct effects of the laws, and (3) to explain why the legislation passed when it did.

The basic contention, reduced to its core, is that the evidence is consistent with the view that self-interested political activists—unionists, academics, bureaucrats, politicians, and a minority of big businessmen—played major roles in fostering a major expansion in the labor-representation industry, a development that was essentially in their financial and nonfinancial interests. Some proponents genuinely, even altruistically, believed that unionism was the right method to raise the standard of living in this country. But the labor literature generally posits political idealism as the sole motive of unionists and their political allies, uncritically accepting their good intentions at face value. The same view is rejected for political opponents of the legislation, who generally are viewed as motivated by self-evident financial gain rather than deep ideological commitment. The asymmetric treatment has left the possible evidence for academic and political profits from the labor-representation industry largely untouched. I propose to apply the theory of self-interest and pressure groups in the search for the causes and effects of the Norris–La Guardia and Wagner acts.

The Background

Labor unions historically were difficult to organize and sustain in the United States. Common obstacles to forming any private combination designed to raise price or restrict supply intruded. The difficulties were especially severe in U.S. markets for labor services, characterized by large numbers of buyers and sellers, ease of entry and exit, high turnover, high mobility, geographic dispersion, active resistance among buyers, and differences of opinion about collectivism and the use of force. The courts also tended to restrict union tactics such as threats, violence, and interference with voluntary trade; unionists, therefore, prominently demanded governmental privilege and mounted persistent and intensive political campaigns for favorable legislation.

Prior to World War I, unionists had relatively little to show for their political investments. From 1842 onward unions had the clear legal right to exist, and workers could join such self-help organizations, but employers were under no legal obligation to deal with these unions. The courts also tended to make little distinction between union and business restraints on competition. They ruled, for example, that union actions in a boycott organized by the United Hatters of Danbury, Connecticut, against the products of D. E. Loewe and Company (1908) violated the Sherman Anti-Trust Act of 1890. The boycott was held to be in restraint of trade, and individual members were held responsible for the union's acts and assessed damages and costs totaling $252,000.

In 1912 Congress supplied some union assistance with the Lloyd–La Follette Act, which encouraged postal workers to unionize and compelled bargaining by the post office. Then in 1914 Congress attempted to supply a very broad range of favors on unions by passing the Clayton Act. This legislation exempted unions from the 1890 Sherman Anti-Trust Act, restricted the use of injunctions in labor disputes, and stated that picketing and similar union activities were not unlawful. Samuel Gompers optimistically hailed the Clayton Act as labor's Magna Carta, but subsequent judicial rulings quickly neutralized the prounion provisions.

The national emergency of World War I provided much of the experience and precedent for subsequent labor legislation, as well as other cartel-like economic policies. Historian William E. Leuchtenburg, for instance, points out that "The panoply of procedures developed by the War Labor Board and the War Labor Policies Board provided the basis in later years for a series of enactments culminating in the Wagner National Labor Relations Act of 1935."[3] The War Labor Board and the War Labor Policies Board, the latter led by Felix Frankfurter and modeled on a directive by Franklin D. Roosevelt, who represented the U.S. Navy on the board, proclaimed governmental support of unions and enforced pro-union measures on industry.[4] The boards, for instance, ordered the establishment of "work councils" composed of employee representatives and seized defiant enterprises. In one instance the government actually created a union, the Loyal Legion of Loggers and Lumbermen, and forced lumbermen to join as part of the battle against the International Workers of the World (IWW). The Loyal Legion collapsed after World War I despite government efforts to keep it alive. Just as the War Industries Board, led by Bernard M. Baruch and General Hugh S. Johnson, was the forerunner of the 1933–35 National Industrial Recovery Act (NIRA), headed by Johnson, the War Labor Boards were predecessors to Section (7a) of the NIRA and the National Labor Relations Act of 1935.

Leuchtenburg supports the contention that the war gave new influence and power to professors who, for the first time, swarmed into Washington with something to do.[5] Leuchtenburg claims that by the 1930s professors and other university-trained intellectuals played crucial parts in shaping legislation and manning the new agencies that their legislation developed:

> The passage of the Wagner Act in 1935, for example, resulted less from such traditional elements as presidential initiative or the play of "social forces" than from the conjunction of university trained administrators like Lloyd Garrison within the New Deal bureaucracy with their counterparts like Leon Keyserling in Senator Wagner's office. This new class of administrators, and the social theorists who had been advocating a rationally planned economy, found the war an exciting adventure.[6]

The first durable help for unions was the Railway Labor Act of 1926. The labor disputes that periodically erupted on the railroads were highly visible, violent, and politically unpopular. Although the interstate commerce clause of the U.S. Constitution (as interpreted then) restricted the ability of the national government to intervene in most economic affairs, Congress had the unchallenged power to regulate interstate commerce. A sequence of federal laws regulated railway labor beginning in 1888, and the 1926 law was passed by Congress almost in the identical form agreed on by the railroad unions and the major railroads. The act, with an amendment in 1934, basically mandated collective bargaining for all interstate railroads and set up machinery for governmental intervention in labor disputes.

This was an obvious example of government enforcement of monopoly arrangements in an industry. The already unionized railroads found it comfortable to impose compulsory collective bargaining on *all* interstate railroads, some of which resisted union pressure better than others. The Interstate Commerce Commission, in turn, fixed freight rates for railroads based on costs, which were higher because of unions. Thus, railroad wage and price determinations were effectively transferred from the economic marketplace to the political marketplace.

During the confusion of the Great Depression, Congress supplied six major pieces of labor legislation favored by unionists: Davis-Bacon, Norris–La Guardia, National Industrial Recovery Act, National Labor Relations (Wagner) Act, Walsh-Healey, and Fair Labor Standards Act. Three of the bills (Davis-Bacon, Walsh-Healey, and Fair Labor) authorized direct federal regulation of wages, hours, and working conditions in various sectors of the economy, and I will say no more about them here.[7]

NIRA was a system of industry codes or cartel agreements sanctioned by the national government in 1933 and intended to push up prices throughout the economy. The rationale was that falling prices were causing the depression and a reversal of "excessive" competition would hasten recovery. Although short-lived, the act included Section 7(a), which broke important ground for national labor policy by declaring "the right [of employees] to bargain collectively through representatives of their own choosing without interference, coercion or restraint on the part of the employer."[8] The favored theory was that falling wage rates caused purchasing power to decline and powerful unions would reverse it. This theory ignores the fact that higher prices for labor services, other things being equal, reduce employment and thereby reduce output (real income).

In contrast to the wide scope of NIRA, the Norris–La Guardia and Wagner acts were limited to promoting labor cartels and cartel-type bargaining in labor markets. The ability of unionists to interfere with trade or, to adopt the expression of the labor literature, use the weapons of labor, rests largely on immunities from damage suits and equity relief granted by Norris–La Guardia and, more important, on government machinery set up by the Wagner Act to impose labor representation and collective-bargaining procedures on those employees and enterprises who would otherwise refuse to accept and participate with unions in collective bargaining. These laws have proven effective and durable, even though falling nominal wages and nominal purchasing power have not been notable problems for many years. It is no exaggeration to assert that American experience with nationwide labor representation is only fifty years old and owes its existence mostly to Norris–La Guardia and Wagner.[9]

The Norris–La Guardia Act

President Hoover signed the Norris-La Guardia Anti-Injunction Act on 23 March 1932, after it had passed the House by a vote of 363 to 13 and the Senate by 75 to 5. This was the culmination of a fifty-year campaign by trade unionists and their allies in the academic community against "government by injunction." The act had three purposes:

1. to declare nonunion oaths (yellow-dog contracts) unenforceable in U.S. courts (Section 3)
2. to relieve labor organizations from liability for wrongful acts under antitrust law (Sections 4, 5)
3. to nullify the equity powers of federal courts in labor disputes (Sections 7–12).[10]

A yellow-dog contract made nonunion status a condition of employment. Unionists labeled nonunion pledges "yellow dog" because they regarded anyone who disagreed with union policies or was willing to pledge nonunion status for other reasons as a cowardly, yellow cur with its tail between its legs. Norris–La Guardia neither outlawed the existence of nonunion pledges as a condition of employment nor prevented employers from firing employees who joined a union, but it did make the oaths unenforceable in U.S. courts. Benjamin Aaron claims that there is no record of any legal action by an employer against an employee for breaching a yellow-dog contract.[11] Within three years, however, the Wagner Act went beyond Norris–La Guardia to make it an unfair labor practice for an employer to dismiss or discriminate against an employee because he or she was a union member or had participated in union activity.

Most writers use the terminology of unionists to describe people who signed nonunion pledges; they also accept the union explanation of why employees signed pledges. Almost all textbooks and articles that discuss the issue refer to antiunion employers who "exacted" and "forced" the "infamous" yellow-dog contracts from employees.[12] The well-known case of *Hitchman Coal & Coke Co.* v. *Mitchell* (245 U.S. 229 [1917]) usually is cited as the prime example. The facts, however, do not support the conventional interpretation. The bituminous coal mining cartel, located in western Pennsylvania, Ohio, Indiana, and Illinois, hired only UMW miners under a closed-shop regime, although pay was no higher than in the nonunion, competitive part of the industry, located mostly in West Virginia and parts of Pennsylvania.[13] The UMW acted against nonunion mines because nonunion coal was underpricing cartel coal, especially in periods of slack demand.

The Hitchman mine in West Virginia opened in 1902 and operated as a nonunion mine until 1 April 1903, when the owners recognized the UMW after union officials threatened to shut down a unionized mine in Ohio operated by the same owners. A two-month strike for higher pay followed the next day. National officials of the United Mine Workers called a two-month strike again in the spring of 1904, imposing additional financial losses. The company operated on union terms until the UMW called another strike in 1906. When the company could not resolve the strike after two months, Hitchman reopened as a nonunion mine.

The ironic truth is that employees at Hitchman were as eager as the owners to have the yellow dog. Many nonunion miners were (and are) fiercely antiunion, more antiunion than their employers. Hoping to avoid the disruptive union tactics that had already cost them so dearly in sacrificed wages, employees at Hitchman agreed to refrain from joining the union in exchange for assurance that the company would refuse to deal with the national union. The employees accepted nonunion pledges, as did newly hired workers, in order to resume their production and earnings.[14]

Why all the political agitation over yellow-dog contracts? They added nothing to the acknowledged legal right of employers to discharge workers for any reason, including union activity. In the absence of agreements to the contrary, employment relationships were "at will" and could be terminated by either party at any time in that era. The few writers who raise this question conjecture that the yellow-dog contract gave employers a psychological edge, intimidated some workers, deluded workers into believing that they had a moral obligation to abide by a contract, or that the tactic discredited unionists.[15]

Although these explanations may be based in truth, they are rather vague and difficult to verify. These writers assume a continuing failure of workers to learn from experience, and they apparently accept a quasi-Marxist belief in a natural antagonism between those two great abstractions, labor and capital. Furthermore, the proposed explanations do not explain the apparent time-series pattern (or periodic appearance) of yellow-dog contracts. Although systematic data do not currently exist, waves of nonunion oaths appeared to follow outbreaks of destructive strikes and boycotts—for example, during the widespread violence by railroad workers, coal miners, and garment workers unions that triggered antiunion sentiment across the country in the 1920s. Since written, signed yellow-dog agreements did not enhance an employer's direct advantages under the law, the explanation for their ebb and flow must lie elsewhere.

A plausible hypothesis is that the agreements were in the mutual interest of employers and employees who accepted them, just as other aspects of an employment relationship are determined by mutual agreement in free markets. More employees would want oaths during periods of union violence because pledges could enhance the attractiveness of working conditions for those fearful of union-related conflict and violence. By this thesis, pledges could effectively reduce an employee's chances of becoming involved in a union dispute. From an employer's point of view, the contracts were a form of full disclosure about working conditions and an economical means of improving working conditions for employees who wanted nothing to do with unions; nonunion requirements would reduce a firm's labor costs if they were popular with a substantial number of workers.

The *Hitchman* decision supports this hypothesis about the gains from nonunion oaths. In a lower court opinion in September 1909, Judge Alston G. Dayton wrote: "there was no controversy between the plaintiff and his employees. . . .there was between them a contract to maintain an 'open shop,' and no strike was desired or threatened by them, [which] removed this case from the field of controversy affecting the rights of members of unions. It is not a case where the labor union has any longer any legitimate interest or concern."[16] In the 6–3 Supreme Court decision (1917), Justice Mahlon Pitney wrote for the majority:

> In short, plaintiff was and is entitled to the good will of its employees. . . .The value of the relation lies in the reasonable probability that by properly treating its employees, and paying them fair

wages, and avoiding reasonable grounds of complaint, it will be able to retain them in its employ, and to fill vacancies occurring from time to time by the employment of other men on the same terms. The pecuniary value of such reasonable probabilities is incalculably great, and is recognized by the law in a variety of relations.[17]

Conversely, nonunion pledges would make organizing workers more difficult for unionists since people who wanted to avoid union conflict and involvement could claim contractual obligations to remain nonunion.[18] Yellow-dog contracts, by this view, were the result of government's frequent failure to protect people from union coercion and violence in labor disputes; they were not due to vicious employers.

The second purpose of Norris–La Guardia was to exempt labor unions from antitrust laws. Norris–La Guardia effectively repealed the Sherman Act for labor unionists for all practical purposes, even in cases of aggressive violence to obstruct trade. Legitimate or bona fide unionists are immune from the laws prohibiting combinations and agreements in restraint of trade; they also have an effective writ to interfere actively with commerce while remaining immune from the equity injunction.[19] Direct and intentional prevention of shipment or delivery of goods in interstate commerce by labor unions was held *not* in restraint of trade in *Apex Hosiery* v. *Leader* (310 U.S. 469 [1940]). Secondary boycotts by unions in order to keep nonunion goods or goods produced by members of other unions out of the market were held immune from the Sherman Act in *U.S.* v. *Hutcheson* (312 U.S. 219 [1941]), provided the union acted in its self-interest and did not conspire with nonlabor groups. In *Hunt* v. *Crumboch* (325 U.S. 821 [1945]) the Supreme Court adopted total immunity by a 5–4 vote. In this case an employer had antagonized union officials, and they responded by refusing to supply him with labor. In his dissent, Justice Robert H. Jackson wrote, "The Court now sustains the claim of a union to the right to deny participation in the economic world to any employer simply because the union dislikes him."

This evolution of union power illustrates a double standard that has developed since 1932 in antitrust. Nonviolent and relatively ineffective price-fixing by businessmen, based on arguable evidence and economic theories, is vigorously prosecuted by the Department of Justice, the Federal Trade Commission, state agencies, and private plaintiffs, while industry-wide price-fixing by unionists, often accompanied by violence, is exempt from law, if not actually encouraged by government policy. Prior to Norris–La Guardia there was little distinction in the legal treatment of union-versus-business restraints on competition.[20] After Norris–La Guardia was passed and its constitutionality confirmed by the Supreme Court, the courts basically were forced to permit worker cartels that fixed terms of employment; then they could try to regulate the cartels' behavior.

The third purpose and main object of Norris–La Guardia was to eliminate equity relief by U.S. courts in labor disputes. The importance of equity relief derived from the fact that unionists used force to pursue their objectives, and others consequently suffered damage. For example, Archibald Cox and Derek Bok, as quoted in Chapter 3, write in their textbook on labor law that "counter-attack lay in concerted activities designed to injure the employer's business until he came to terms....the strike, boycott and picket line were indispensable weapons."[21]

Repeated trespass on an individual's land ordinarily can be halted by injunction in courts of equity, an important remedy in the case of picketing and strikes whose purpose is to cut off public access to the business and thereby inflict economic losses on the owner. Until the 1880s four legal remedies were available to a private plaintiff who claimed to be a victim of union-induced damages: criminal conspiracy, tort law, criminal proceedings, and equity injunctions.

Employers could not expect redress through criminal conspiracy charges because unionists were never convicted simply for acting in concert unless their actions involved physical coercion. There were only eighteen convictions of unionists on conspiracy charges in the United States from 1806 to 1846 when the doctrine was at its peak.[22] In addition, relief did not arrive swiftly.

Tort law suffered from delays, difficulty in quantifying the monetary value of union damages, and the uncertain legal status of unions. Repeated suits for damages generally did not provide reasonable protection for owners of businesses because unions never incorporated, with the result that unions in most jurisdictions were private associations without legal standing to sue or be sued for damages. The evidence suggests that unions deliberately avoided incorporation to avoid legal responsibility for their actions.[23] Union treasuries and assets also were small relative to damages, further diminishing tort law as a remedy for union-caused damages.

Criminal prosecution too, was deficient as a legal remedy. Since crimes are offenses committed against the state, private individuals must rely on local public authorities to investigate and prosecute offenders efficiently. An obvious problem was that public employees were uninterested and inefficient whereas private parties took a strong interest in the outcome. This general tendency to do as little as possible was heightened in labor cases because some officials had a sentimental attitude toward labor and others were reluctant to intervene in labor brawls because they involved immigrants and other "low characters." In many instances mass assemblies of angry union members left outnumbered police forces little choice but to back down. In other instances unions had already secured political compliance by donating money to help elect a sheriff or mayor. Even if unionists were convicted under criminal law, victims could expect no compensation.

Under these circumstances, the injunction had obvious advantages as a legal remedy for labor disputes. Equity courts had built a centuries-old common-law tradition for nonlabor cases when retroactive money damages did not seem suitable, or when "the remedy at law would be inadequate." The injunction developed because it was timely and effective. Scholars do not completely agree on the date of the first injunction issued in an American labor dispute, but Edwin Witte counted 28 during the 1880s. During the 1890s he found 122; in the next two decades there were 328 and 446; and he counted 921 in the 1920s.[24] The equity injunction gradually emerged as the primary legal remedy for victims of union violence during this period because it was timely and effective, just as it was in many nonlabor disputes. An injunction temporarily restrained union actions pending a trial, and this explains the intense union campaign against the use of injunctions in labor disputes because once violent strikes had been enjoined for a few days, they were difficult to revive, reorganize, and rekindle.

Most labor scholars refer to the "injunction abuse," as did many politicians of the era. Irving Bernstein, for example, refers to "the cancerous mass of procedural abuse that the courts had spread with the labor injunction."[25] Sylvester Petro, however, could not find any evidence for abuse in the only detailed examination of cases since the fragmentary study of Frankfurter and Greene in 1930.[26] Petro's examination shows that the courts were circumspect, careful, and reluctant to issue injunctions in labor disputes. Petro analyzed all 524 reported federal and state injunction cases from 1880 to 1932 (a case usually went unreported if there was no subsequent legal action) and found that no primary strike for better terms and conditions of employment was ever enjoined as such. Nearly the same was true of peaceable primary picketing by employees of the picketed establishment and of peaceable persuasion, except where it was part of a violent conspiracy.

Academic discussions usually fail to describe the violence, property destruction, and intimidation that prompted the issuance of injunctions by courts of equity in labor disputes. In virtually every dispute, unionists were the aggressors; those beaten, bombed, and besieged were nonunion, antiunion, and rival union employees, and the property of investors was damaged. Here, from the court transcript, is a 1902 example of union aggression:

> As Caldwell and Ball approached the point named they saw five or six men. Most of them they recognized as strikers. Ball believed there was to be trouble, but Caldwell thought not. The pickets stopped them, and asked them where they were going. Caldwell said, "To the shops." Then Caldwell said, "I tell you, boys, we don't want any trouble. Now, I just come last Thursday, and as soon as I get money enough I will go back to Chicago." Immediately Caldwell was struck in the jaw, knocking him into the ditch. Ball started to assist Caldwell, when two men jumped on him. He got loose, and started to run, and fell down, when he was hit with a club. He finally got away, and threatened to shoot the assailants, but ran away, and then he was stoned. After Caldwell was down, he was either struck or struck at with a club. Caldwell got up, walked inside the gates, and in a few minutes was dead; murdered.[27]

Unionists do not entirely deny that they have used violence through the years. In fact, violence is a central feature of the legend of "labor's bitter struggle," and labor's martyrs were, for the most part, violent men. Unionists claim, though, that employers were guiltier than unions. Undoubtedly, many employers were guilty of resistance to the demands of unionists, but if employers were as guilty of unlawful actions as unionists were, both unionists and labor scholars must explain why unions rarely sought, much less gained, equitable relief in the courts against the alleged depredations of employers.[28] The common answer is that judges were biased against unions by virtue of their education, their upper-class background, and their association with the "employer class." Such uniformity of temperament and complete absence of fair-minded individuals would be surprising in any occupational group, much less the judiciary, many members of which were schooled in the rule of law and the importance of impartiality. The real answer is that union suits for equitable relief simply could not meet the standard legal criteria for issuance. In virtually all labor disputes, unions, as the aggressors, could not hope to demonstrate (1) unlawful conduct by employers, (2) threat of irreparable injury, (3) lack of alternative, adequate remedies at law—nor did unions have clean enough hands to be granted equity relief.

The association between unionism and violence is clearly accounted for by basic economics. In order to push the prices of their members' services above open-market wage rates, labor unions must restrict (cut off) the supply of labor to struck enterprises. The only effective way they can do this is through threats and violence, because many U.S. workers are willing to cross picket lines and accept wages and working conditions below those demanded by unionists. As Henry George wrote in the nineteenth century, "Those who tell you of trade-unions bent on raising wages by moral suasion alone are like people who tell you of tigers that live on oranges."[29] The employer's (and consumer's) interest, by contrast, is to preserve access to a free labor market and maintain peaceful conditions so that work and production can proceed smoothly and economically.

Labor scholars assert that unions continually faced injunctions to restrain their strikes and gatherings, injunctions supposedly readily granted by compliant judges. The data show otherwise. During the years 1881 to 1905, and from 1914 to the present, the U.S. Bureau of Labor Statistics recorded a number of work stoppages by examining the daily press and trade press. They followed up this study by questioning the parties involved.[30] Between the years 1881 and 1932, excluding 1906–13 when reporting was discontinued, there were 72,888 reported work stoppages, virtually all of them union-organized strikes. There were 182 reported federal labor-injunction cases from 1881 to 1932, or an average of 3.5 per year. Edwin Witte also compiled 508 examples of unreported federal labor-injunction cases between 1894 and 1932, substantially overlapping reported cases.[31] An equity decision goes unreported if the original order meets no objection and no appeal is filed by either party. Therefore, less than 1% of reported work stoppages (690 divided by 72,888) became federal labor-injunction cases between 1881 and 1932. This is an upper estimate because 25% to 50% of all federal labor injunctions were issued in the railway shopcraft strike of 1922, which had 1,500 cases of violent assault to kill, 51 cases of dynamiting and burning railroad bridges, 65 reported kidnappings, and so on. To conclude that less than 1% faced injunctions one must ignore injunctions granted by state courts; Edwin Witte claimed that 1,364 labor injunctions were issued on application by employers prior to 1 May 1931 in state courts, or less than 2% of all reported work stoppages. Therefore, fewer than 3% of all work stoppages resulted in injunctions by all courts against union actions, probably a modest figure relative to the impression conveyed by labor scholars and the potentially large number of labor disputes where private coercion and mob violence might have justified an injunction.

The Norris–La Guardia Act also reinforced the one-sidedness of collective bargains by prohibiting injunctions against unions for breach of contract. Prior to the Taft-Hartley Act in 1947, a contract between an enterprise and a union was really binding only on the enterprise (if it was binding on anyone), because unions could not be sued for breach of contract (or anything else, for that matter), a phenomenon that Taft-Hartley has changed very little. Unions cannot really breach a collective contract because unions do not agree to deliver anything of value. The only exception is if an agreement contains a no-strike clause. To illustrate the continuing immunities of unions from damage suits, the Supreme Court ruled in the 1970s that a union that violates its statutory duty to represent a member fairly in a grievance cannot be required to pay punitive damages.[32] A jury had awarded $75,000 in punitive damages to a member of the International Brotherhood of Electrical Workers because the union had failed to process the employee's unfair dismissal grievance before a crucial deadline, thus depriving him of an opportunity to appeal (*IBEW* v. *Fouts,* US 60 L Ed 2d 698 [1979]). In reversing the judgment, Justice Thurgood Marshall wrote for the high court that any remedy for victims of union misconduct must be consistent with the "overarching legislative goal" of the National Labor Relations Act, namely, "to facilitate collective bargaining and to achieve industrial peace." Punitive damage awards would not "comport with national labor policy" because they could "deplete union treasuries, thereby impairing the effectiveness of unions as collective bargaining agents," might curtail the broad discretion afforded unions in handling grievances, and could "disrupt the responsible decision-making essential to peaceful labor relations." In plainer language, unions are beyond the law that applies to everyone else in damage suits.

The Wagner Act

After the NIRA was struck down by the Supreme Court in the Schechter Poultry case of 1935 on the grounds that the act delegated virtually unlimited legislative power to the president, almost identical labor regulations were adopted by the Congress, piecemeal, in surviving legislation like Walsh-Healey and Fair Labor Standards. But the most famous and important legislation was the Wagner Act, which passed the Senate by a 63–12 vote, and by an unrecorded voice vote in the House, and was signed by President Roosevelt on 5 July 1935. Roosevelt gave pens to Senator Wagner and William Green, president of the American Federation of Labor, whereupon Green declared that the legislation would prove to be the "Magna Carta of Labor of the United States," echoing Gompers's ill-fated statement about the Clayton Act twenty-one years earlier. Green, however, proved to be right in the sense that the legislation turned out to be the primary source of economic power for U.S. unionism, indeed of most unions' existence.

The act declares that the policy of the United States government is to encourage the practice and procedure of collective bargaining, as well as to protect worker designation of representatives to negotiate terms and conditions of employment. The Wagner Act supplied six principal services to unionists:

1. creation of a political board, the National Labor Relations Board (NLRB), to enforce the act
2. limiting buyer resistance to unionization by specifying "unfair labor practices" by employers
3. NLRB enforcement of majority elections for union representation
4. NLRB determination of eligible voters
5. NLRB enforcement of exclusive (monopoly) bargaining rights for certified labor representatives
6. NLRB enforcement of union pay scales for all represented employees, whether union members or not

The basic technique of the Wagner Act was to reduce drastically the cost of imposing labor representatives on enterprises and employees. Subsequent federal legislation modifying the Wagner Act (Taft-Hartley in 1947 and Landrum-Griffin in 1959) has not been so favorable to unions, but this can be easily exaggerated. Neither Taft-Hartley nor Landrum-Griffin tampered with the basic government services supplied to labor organizations. These amendments simply added regulations that expand government intervention to deal with effects of union power in the labor market. This is a familiar pattern in regulatory behavior because, once monopoly rents (i.e., transfers of income caused by government intervention) are created and enforced by government (through tariffs, marketing orders, licensing, and a wide variety of redistributions), there is a tendency to dissipate rents in response to pressures by other interested groups.

The key characteristic of the NLRB is discretion. Its members (expanded from three to five in 1947 by Taft-Hartley) are appointed by the president to five-year terms and approved by the Senate. The board decides who votes in representation elections, investigates and decides complaints, has exclusive jurisdiction over unfair labor practices, pre-empts direct access to the courts in labor disputes, makes findings about facts that are conclusive in the event of appeals in the courts, issues cease-and-desist orders, reinstates employees with back pay, orders periodic reporting to the board, has power of subpoena for evidence and investigation, can reverse or modify its previous orders at will, and at board hearings "the rules of evidence prevailing in courts of law or equity shall not be controlling." Such administrative flexibility was desired by union lobbyists who wanted a political board that would be more sensitive to union political pressure than the courts were. The result has been an extraordinary series of reversals and changes in NLRB policies, especially with changes in Republican and Democratic administrations.[33]

The term "unfair labor practice" means any of five employer activities made unlawful under the Wagner Act (Taft-Hartley added a like number, though not equivalent, of unfair union activities). Essentially it was illegal for employers to resist unionization of their enterprises. The NLRB handles more than ten thousand of these complaints each year. The theory is that unfair practices are akin to common-law torts: an invasion of publicly declared rights or, more strictly speaking, behavior contrary to declared public policy. The notion is that the act created public rights and duties and, therefore, enforcement was left to public agencies rather than to private parties.

An election in a bargaining unit is normally held under terms of the National Labor Relations Act to determine "collective bargaining representation." If a union organization wins a simple majority of the valid votes cast in the final round, the victorious unionists become the exclusive agent for *all* employees in the unit, even if a majority does not vote for the union. The term "bargaining unit" is a misnomer because it is only a voting unit for purposes of "certification" of labor representatives. Bargaining units are made up of many such groups to make monopoly gains feasible for labor representatives and/or members. The NLRB is not very restricted by the vague language of the act in determining an appropriate unit, and the word "gerrymander" illustrates how important the exact boundaries of election districts can be in political competition. In recent years, managements and unions agreed on voting boundaries (eligible voters) in about 75% of cases, and the board determined the voting unit in the remaining two thousand cases per year. In earlier years, the NLRB consistently used its authority to help CIO industrial unions win representation elections, much to the distress of the AFL. NLRB policies continue to favor unionization consistent with the policy statement of the act. Techniques that the NLRB uses to the advantages of unionism include overturning union defeats due to "unfair" election tactics by employers, as defined by the NLRB, and disqualifying voters challenged by union officials—for example, part-time employees, if a majority of them are known to be antiunion.

Direct parallels between federal formation of cartels in agricultural and labor markets illuminate NLRB techniques. In milk markets, for example, federal control was authorized by the Agricultural Adjustment Act of 1937, which, like the Wagner Act, replaced legislation passed in 1933.[34] The law allows dairy farmers to force marketing controls on bottlers or dairies, called "handlers" in the industry. Before the legislation, dairy farmers often tried to impose monopoly pricing through cooperatives, but independent competition kept breaking out, despite milk strikes and violence among dairy farmers. Much like unionists, they argued that strikes, associated violence, and price instability were the undesirable consequences of competition and resistance by buyers.

Under the 1937 act, a proposed marketing order is presented to relevant handlers for their voluntary signatures. Naturally they refuse, because signing restricts them to dealing with a monopoly supplier, but the order is enforced by government if two-thirds of the milk producers or producers of two-thirds of the output sold within the market area vote for the proposal in a U.S. Department of Agriculture election. Fluid milk prices are estimated at 7% to 15% above competitive levels due to this scheme.[35]

Federal officials determine monthly price under a market order, in contrast to unionists, who are permitted privately to negotiate virtually any wages and working conditions they wish. Dairy producers, however, are allowed to negotiate prices, called a superpool premium, above those set by the federal administrator. Another difference is that the federal costs of administering a market order are paid through a tax on handlers. Since these costs must be covered by receipts in the long run, consumers of dairy products basically pay the cost of administering dairy cartels. NLRB costs for elections and enforcement, on the other hand, basically are paid by federal taxpayers rather than by consumers of union-made goods.

The Wagner Act does not expressly compel employers to reach an agreement with a certified labor representative, but the right to refuse is attenuated by the fact that employers are obligated to bargain in "good faith" with union officials, a phrase interpreted by the political appointees of the board. To illustrate how the statute operates in practice, the Supreme Court recently ruled that in-plant food prices and services are mandatory subjects of bargaining, even if the food operation is operated by a third party (*Ford Motor* v. *NLRB,* U.S. 60 L Ed 2d 420 [1979]). Justice Byron White, writing for the Court, said that even though he anticipated that "disputes over food prices are likely to be frequent and intense," national labor policy supported the conclusion that "more, not less, collective bargaining is the remedy."[36]

In addition to fixing voting units and conducting elections for unionists, the NLRB enforces exclusive bargaining rights under the Natonal Labor Relations Act. This is the minimum guarantee of union security because union officials are safe from rival unionists or employee decertification efforts for at least one year after a previous decertification vote. This legal situation is much like the historical meaning of the word "monopoly," a grant from the state of the exclusive right to sell some good. Exclusive bargaining is a legal barrier to entry in the labor representation industry, protecting incumbent unionists by raising the costs to rival unionists interested in competing for greater membership (called "raiding," one of many military terms in the vocabulary of unionism).

Exclusive bargaining delivers another service to unionists because the collective bargaining agreement must apply to all employees in a unit whether or not they are union members. A union's monopoly power would erode rapidly if individuals and their employers were free to reach individual agreements that departed from union terms.[37] Some employees would agree to work for less than union wages or produce more output at union wages, and an employer would hire more of these employees and fewer union members. Unions also discipline employees who tend toward "excessive production" by informal social pressure, as well as by formal work rules backed up by the union's disciplinary powers—which, in turn, are effective only against its members, hence the importance to the union of compulsory membership. Government enforcement of collective conditions on all employees in a bargaining unit relieves unionists of these dangers to their survival. The legislative history of the Railway Labor Act and the National Labor Relations Act shows that union officials favored "exclusive representation" in the law. For instance, William Green, then president of the AFL, offered an accurate analogy between exclusive union representation and the adoption of NIRA codes by majority vote in industry cartels.[38] In 1976 officials of the large postal unions denounced HR 5023, a bill designed to relieve postal unions of the obligation to represent nonmembers in grievance proceedings.

The Effects of the Norris–La Guardia and Wagner Acts

Any one of, or any combination of, three general results can occur when government intervenes in economic affairs: (1) no substantive impact, (2) perverse or unintended effects, and (3) intended effects. Norris–La Guardia and Wagner basically fall into the last class as extremely effective, an assertion I will establish below.

Directly Visible Effects (Means)

Direct effects of the legislation are easily established. Norris–La Guardia passed its constitutionality test as a proper legislative restraint on the federal courts.[39] Yellow-dog contracts totally disappeared after 1932, although the NLRB continues to handle unfair labor practice complaints about discrimination in employment because of union activity. By 1941, nineteen states also had passed anti-yellow dog acts. The antitrust exemption of unionists is well established.[40] With respect to labor injunctions, Norris–La Guardia succeeded in making it virtually impossible for private plaintiffs to obtain equity relief from federal courts in labor disputes, and nearly so in state courts as well.[41] Scattered data show the number of injunctions granted by the courts to private plaintiffs fell precipitously after Norris–La Guardia.[42] And by 1941, 24 states had their own anti-injunction laws to restrict injunctions in state courts.[43] These courts are not directly bound by Norris–La Guardia, but an action in state courts may, on petition of the party against whom the injunction is sought, be removed to a federal court that has original jurisdiction and may be dismissed there because such courts lack authority to grant equity relief. The major plaintiff seeking labor injunctions against union actions is now the U.S. government.[44]

The main direct effect of the Wagner Act was to create a regulatory board to enforce the broad mandate of the bill, and there is little doubt about the board's active existence. In fiscal year 1936, its first year of operation, the NLRB had 140 employees, drew on a budget of $620,000, and conducted 31 representation elections with 7,734 voters participating; by fiscal 1980 the numbers had grown to 2,900 employees, a budget of $108 million, and supervision of 8,531 elections with 458,114 votes cast. On 2 March 1977 the board celebrated the thirty millionth vote in NLRB elections. Among regular publications of the board is *Decisions and Orders of the National Labor Relations Board,* a series occupying 50 feet of shelf space. Volume 1 covers a six-month period from 7 December 1935 to 1 July 1936, while a recent volume, number 256, covers a nine-week period from 14 May 1981 to 20 July 1981. The board has issued over 400,000 pages of decisions and orders in the published series. The NLRB's *Annual Report* for fiscal 1979 modestly understates the situation by saying, "The uninterrupted growth of the NLRB case load underscores that the field of labor relations in the United States remains controversial and volatile, an area of national importance and concern, forty-four years after the labor relations statute was enacted and the Labor Board was established" (p. 1).

Other Effects (Ends)

The purpose of the Norris–La Guardia Act was to give unionists greater freedom to use their tactics, and the Wagner Act's purpose was to spread the practices of collective bargaining and labor representation. Have they succeeded? The time-series evidence is consistent with a positive answer, although other hypotheses might also explain the expansion of unionism and collective bargaining during the 1930s and 1940s. I intend to show that the observed expansion of the labor-representation industry can be explained *only* by recourse to these two labor laws. Norris–La Guardia and Wagner sharply reversed an ongoing contraction of the labor-representation industry be creating abundant profit opportunities, a reliable way to attract new entrants, innovation, and new competition. Here I am concerned *only* with the pattern of expansion in the employee-representation industry, as measured by indexes like the amount of strike activity, number of unions, union customers (membership), union revenues, full-time bureaucracy, and number of contracts. Consideration of the larger economic effects of unionism on the level of national income, labor's share of income, unemployment rates, inflation, working conditions, and other variables is ignored here in order to limit the analysis.

Strikes

The legislation clearly did not accomplish the announced purpose of ushering in an era of "industrial peace," because Norris–La Guardia allowed unionists more latitude to use their aggressive tactics, while Wagner promoted unionism. Statistics on industrial conflict support this interpretation. Between 1922 and 1932 there was an average of 980 work stoppages a year, as shown in Table 5-1. After Norris–La Guardia passed in 1932, the number of strikes doubled in 1933 to 1,695 and continued to climb to a peak of 4,740 in 1937, the same year that the Supreme Court, by a 5–4 vote in April, declared the Wagner Act constitutional (the stitch in time that saved nine), thereby "certifying" the Wagner Act and the NLRB. During the 1970s, strikes averaged 5,300 per year, or 20 new strikes each business day, but strikes fell off sharply in the early 1980s.

Number of Unions

Expanding industries attract new firms and innovators, a characteristic of unionism in the 1930s. Table 5-2 shows the number of unions founded and dissolved by decade, beginning in 1830. These figures are calculated from an encyclopedia of trade unions that contains biographical sketches of more than two hundred national unions. Although not comprehensive, the volume contains information on every national union of any significance and others as well. The 1930s witnessed the appearance of forty-two new unions, the most prolific decade in U.S. unionism, edging out the 1890s, which saw the emergence of forty new unions. The net gain during the 1930s was thirty-four unions, since eight failed or merged, while eleven failed in the 1890s for a net gain of twenty-nine organizations. The 1880s to early 1900s was a period when the formula of business unionism along craft lines finally proved successful, after a series of failed experiments in unionism. At the turn of the century, unionism was substantial only in coal mining, contract construction, printing, railroads, local transit, and the postal service, and only a dozen unions claimed more than ten thousand members.

The 1930s also were characterized by innovation in unionism. In 1931 and 1932 the AFL appeared to be a moribund group of declining organizations. Morale and funds to organize were lacking, and union leaders basically were concerned about preserving their existing hold on crafts. Most of their time and energy involved jurisdictional feuds with other craft unionists. Mass-production blue-collar industries were unorganized and appeared unorganizable by feuding craft unions. Another national federation appeared, the Congress of Industrial Organization (CIO), and CIO-type unions entered the organizing in-

Table 5-1

Reported Work Stoppages in the United States, Selected Years, 1922–81

Year	Work Stoppages
1922	1,112
1923	1,553
1924	1,249
1925	1,301
1926	1,035
1927	707
1928	604
1929	921
1930	637
1931	810
1932	841
1933	1,695
1934	1,856
1935	2,014
1936	2,172
1937	4,740
1938	2,772
1939	2,613
1940	2,508
1941	4,288
1942	2,968
1943	3,752
1944	4,956
1945	4,750
1946	4,985
1950	4,843
1960	3,333
1970	5,716
1977	5,506
1978	4,230
1979	4,827
1980	3,885
1981	2,577

Sources: U.S. Bureau of Labor Statistics, *Handbook of Labor Statistics,* (Washington, D.C.: U.S. Government Printing Ofifce, 1972);*Analysis of Work Stoppages, 1980,* Bulletin 2120, March 1982; *Monthly Labor Review,* March 1982, p. 5.

Table 5-2

Number of National Unions Originated and Dissolved, by Decade, 1830–1979

Decade	Number of Unions Originated	Number of Unions Dissolved, Merged, or Terminated	Net Gain or Loss in Unions
1830–39	2	2	0
1840–49	1	1	0
1850–59	3	0	3
1860–69	12	2	10
1870–79	7	7	0
1880–89	26	3	23
1890–99	40	11	29
1900–09	24	6	18
1910–19	24	6	18
1920–29	9	4	5
1930–39	42	8	34
1940–49	18	10	8
1950–59	11	22	−11
1960–69	7	15	−8
1970–79	5	20	−15

Source: Calculated from Chronology, Appendix 2, in *Labor Unions, The Greenwood Encyclopedia of American Institutions*, ed. Gary M. Fink (Westport, Conn.: Greenwood Press, 1977).

---

dustry to compete with AFL unions for membership, successfully organizing much of manufacturing. Some of the major unions formed during this period included the United Auto Workers in 1936, United Steel Workers in 1942 (officially), Communications Workers in 1939, and Rubber Workers in 1934.

Membership

The number of union customers (i.e., dues-paying members) fell throughout the 1920s from a reported peak of 5 million in 1920 to fewer than 3 million in 1933. According to NBER figures, membership rose sharply to 7.2 million by 1940, then to 13.2 million by 1945, and 14.8 million by 1950. Figure 5-1 shows the pattern of membership from 1900 to 1951, a time span that includes the periods of union growth in the twentieth century. The boost in membership is apparent during World War I and World War II, when government labor boards

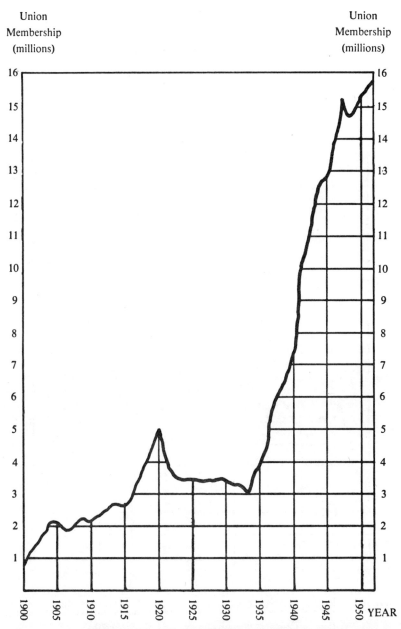

Figure 5-1. Union Membership, 1900–51, NBER figures (Canadian membership included). (Source: U.S. Bureau of the Census, *Historical Statistics of the United States, Colonial Times to 1970,* pp. 176–77.)

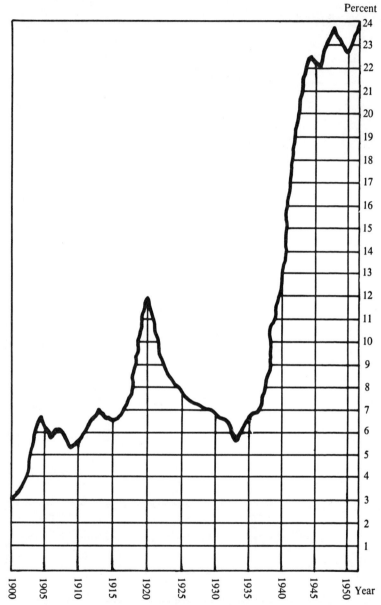

Figure 5-2. Union Membership as a Share of the Civilian Labor Force. (Source: *Historical Statistics,* pp. 126–27, 1976–77. Union membership in NBER figures; Canadian membership included prior to 1930.)

operated to advance unionization, but the sharp increase in the 1930s also is apparent.[45] The erosion in membership that followed World War I did not repeat itself after World War II.

Figure 5-2 presents the same membership data as a share of the civilian labor force, and the data follow a pattern similar to that in Figure 5-1. Between 1933 and 1945 the fraction of the civilian labor force in unions rose fourfold from 5.7% to 22.4%. The proportion stayed around 25% during the 1950s and then gradually receded to its current 20%.

Union Revenues, Staff, and Collective Contracts

There are no published estimates of union revenues during the 1930s, but reasonable estimates can be derived. There is substantial anecdotal evidence that a number of labor unions were close to financial collapse in the early 1930s. The 1933 AFL convention reported that unemployment among members of its affiliated unions rose from 8% in 1929 to 25% in 1933, and another 20% worked part-time. Irving Bernstein reports that the financial position of the United Mine Workers union was critical and most of the district organizations went under. The International Ladies Garment Workers Union was heavily in debt, only skeleton organizations remained in many trades, and contracts were disappearing. Members' earnings in the Typographical Union dropped from $180 million in 1929 to $123 million in 1933. Share-the-work devices were used, and employed members were taxed as much as 18% to 20% of earnings to pay benefits to unemployed members.[46]

Membership dues are the primary source of revenue for unions, although they also collect initiation fees, fines, and assessments. The structure of dues varies widely across unions, but 1% of members' earnings is a reasonable estimate of union revenues from dues—that is, between one and two hours' wages per month.[47] Average annual earnings in manufacturing in 1933 were $1,086. Although many union members certainly enjoyed higher hourly wage rates, in view of heavy unemployment and part-time employment, this is probably an approximate average figure for members' annual earnings. With membership of 3 million and a union tax rate of 1%, union revenue from dues was about $32 million in 1933, down from $54 million in 1929. Union membership rose to 7.3 million by 1940 and average annual earnings to $1,432, which would yield $104 million in union dues, more than a threefold increase in the seven-year period from 1933 to 1940. Union revenues had tripled again by 1945, rising to $332 million based on the same calculation, a tenfold increase in the twelve-year period since 1933.[48]

The number of full-time paid union officers, staff, and organizers probably increased as membership grew in the 1930s and 1940s, but there are no published estimates. According to Florence Peterson, "In general, the paid organizers and enforcement officers [constitute] the bulk of the unions' staffs. On average, there is probably one full-time paid representative for each 1,000 members."[49] Using this ratio, there were an estimated 3,000 union officials in 1933, then 7,300 in 1940, and 13,200 in 1945. The ratio of unionists to members would fluctuate over time and across unions, however. Peterson reported that reduced union funds forced many a union to "lay off many of its organizers" in 1938. She also reported that as members were reemployed, unionists "carried on intensive campaigns to induce former members to resume payment of union dues."[50]

Information about employment in labor unions improved after 1959 because of mandatory reporting under the Landrum-Griffin Act, but there still is no estimate of total employment. Table 5–3 shows that 6,800 employees worked in the national offices of the ten largest unions in 1979. Total membership was over 10 million, or one national staff employee for every 1,600 members. There are 71,000 local unions ranging in size from 5 to 40,000 members, and not all have a full-time union employee, but many do. The Teamsters, for example, reportedly have 7,000 officers and business agents in their 742 locals, far in excess of the 305 employees shown in Table 5–3 for the national office alone.[51] A reasonable guess for total employment among union staff and officers in the country is between 30,000 and 40,000, or one staff member for approximately every 800 employees represented by unions.[52]

The Wagner Act "had a simple, unified purpose: it was designed to promote collective bargaining."[53] Unfortunately, however, there are no published statistics on the number of collective contracts in the United States during the 1930s and 1940s that would be a direct measure of the effect of the Wagner Act. The spread of collective contracts during the 1930s is not in doubt, though. The Bureau of Labor Statistics (BLS) said in 1938, "In less than five years the picture of employer-employee relations has markedly changed.... collective bargaining through trade union agreements has grown to the point where it has now become the accepted procedure in establishing wages, hours, and

Table 5-3
Membership and National Staff of Ten Largest Unions, 1979

	Union Membership (in thousands)[1]	National Officers and Staff[2]	Union Members per Staff Employee[3]
Teamsters	1,889	305	6,193
NEA	1,600	553	2,893
Auto Workers	1,358	1,579	860
Steel Workers	1,300	1,630	797
Electrical (IBEW)	924	504	1,833
Machinists[4]	917	936	980
Carpenters	820	263	3,118
State, County, Municipal	750	417	1,799
Retail Clerks	651	380	1,713
Laborers	650	239	2,720
Totals	10,859	6,806	1,600

1. Calculated from U.S. Bureau of Labor Statistics, *Directory of National Unions and Employee Associations,* 1977, Bulletin 2044, December 1979.
2. Excludes officers and staff of local unions. Calculated from U.S. Department of Labor, *Labor Organization Annual Reports,* Form LM-2, filed under the Labor-Management Reporting and Disclosure Act of 1959, as amended.
3. Column 1 divided by column 2.
4. Staff data, 1976.

working conditions in a considerable part of American industry."[54] The BLS described it as "an expansion in collective bargaining unparalleled in the history of the United States."[55] No complete survey of collective coverage exists, but individual unions claimed new contracts by the score in 1937. The Machinists, for instance, claimed 2,000 new contracts; the Auto Workers claimed all auto manufacturers, except Ford, and 300 auto parts suppliers; the Steel Workers Organizing Committee claimed 431 new contracts; Rubber Workers, 100 new contracts; Textile Workers Organizing Committee, over 900 new contracts; and the nonoperating railroad unions, 200 new contracts.[56] By 1976 there were an estimated 200,000 collective contracts.[57]

The number of pages in collective contracts expanded even more rapidly than the number of agreements. As Charles Killingsworth put it, "In one typical relationship, the initial agreement in 1937 was two typewritten pages; the current agreement runs to 186 printed pages plus a separate pension agreement."[58] The *Labor Relations Reference Manual* of 1938 printed nine contracts, which averaged only three pages each.

Cross-Section Evidence

The expansion of unionism in the 1930s and 1940s is well known, but was it caused primarily by the Norris–La Guardia and Wagner legislation or were they only contributing factors? More general theories about the growth of union membership suggest a number of other factors, including the degree of worker discontent, the stock of grievances, the general climate of public opinion, intellectual revulsion against free markets, the business cycle, composition of Congress, the percentage of industry already unionized, rates of inflation, and unemployment.[59] Although these factors may be important as background, precipitating variables, the permanent gains of unionism can be attributed only to Norris–La Guardia and Wagner, especially the latter. Evidence follows.

The Public Sector

The Wagner Act specifically excluded government employees from its coverage, and there was no spurt in unionism comparable to that in the private sector during the 1930s and 1940s. Since 1960, however, union membership in the public sector has increased from less than 1 million, mostly in postal unions, to more than 6 million. Unionization increased from 11% to nearly 50%, a replay of the experience in the private sector during the Depression and World War II.

The explanation is close at hand. President Kennedy signed Executive Order 10988 in January 1962 to promote unionism in the federal bureaucracy. It was based on the National Labor Relations Act but was less generous because it prohibited both strikes and compulsory union membership (union shop), established no separate NLRB-type agency (the Federal Labor Relations Service was established later), required agreements to conform to civil service regulations, and demanded a statement of management rights in every agreement. The state of Wisconsin had earlier (1959) enacted bargaining legislation to cover employees of local governments, but Kennedy's executive order triggered a series of bargaining laws in states like Michigan, New York, Washington, and Pennsylvania, where unions traditionally played a large role in the political process. At last count, only a dozen states, mostly in the South and West, did not have some kind of mandatory bargaining law to promote public sector unions. North Carolina is the only state specifically to prohibit all public-sector bargaining by legislation (although the Supreme Court of the State of Virginia ruled in 1977 that a public employer cannot be forced to bargain with labor representatives without enabling legislation), and other states prohibit collective bargaining for some segments of the public sector, especially police and fire protection.

Union lobbyists continue to push for more favorable legislation because the laws vary across states and none, including federal, is as favorable toward unionists as the Wagner Act is. The National Education Association and the American Federation of State, County, and Municipal employees continue to pressure Congress for legislation like the Clay Bill, which goes beyond the Wagner Act to order every governmental unit in the United States to obey an NLRB-like board that would enforce a national bargaining law authorizing a long list of union privileges, including monopoly status for union representatives without secret-ballot elections, strikes for public-sector employees, and so forth. Constitutionally it would be questionable under the general precedent of *National League of Cities* v. *Usery* (97 S. Ct. 2465 [1976]), in which the high court found that Congress violated the federal principle by subjecting state and municipal governments to Fair Labor Standard–type coverage in 1974. However, the Wagner Act also was widely believed to be unconstitutional until April 1937.

Agriculture

The Wagner Act excluded the agricultural sector from coverage, and no burst of unionism occurred. A Southern Tenant Farmers Union was formed in July 1934, under the impetus of the Agricultural Adjustment Act, but this labor cartel quickly failed without government machinery to support it. In recent years, however, state boards for labor relations in agriculture were created in California and Arizona, after pressure from Cesar Chavez, his United Farm Workers' Union, and his political allies. There is evidence that the California Board has promoted unionization in agriculture.[60]

Foremen

The short history of the Foreman's Association of America graphically illustrates the importance of NLRB enforcement of unionism. Formed by first-line supervisors at the Ford Motor Company in 1941, it quickly grew to a membership of 5,000 and, before its first anniversary, a strike forced Ford to reinstate discharged foremen and sign an agreement. In the 1943 *Maryland Drydock* case, however, the NLRB declared that supervisory personnel were not an appropriate unit for collective bargaining under the NLRA. The Ford Motor Company immediately withdrew its recognition of the Foreman's Association. Without certification under NLRA and without the voluntary cooperation of employers in bargaining, the Foreman's Association managed to stay together and stage more than thirty strikes in 1944. Although the National War Labor Board denounced the union and its tactics, it succeeded in gaining some contracts, and Ford signed again in May 1944.

In 1945 the NLRB reversed its previous position in the *Packard Motor* decision and declared foremen an appropriate bargaining unit. The Foreman's Assocation grew rapidly, exceeding 28,000, until Taft-Hartley was passed in 1947, and Section 2(3) specifically excluded supervisors from existing bargaining legislation. Employers withdrew recognition from the union, and it disintegrated within a few years.[61]

Plant Guard Workers

Automobile plant guards emulated the unionism of automobile workers during the late 1930s. Management put up strong resistance, since guards are hired to protect the owners' investment. After considerable indecision, the NLRB, after World War II, ruled favorably on guard locals as appropriate units and ordered managements to bargain with them. A series of guard strikes succeeded in securing agreements after many unionized production workers honored guard picket lines.

Most plant guard local unions were organized as branches of industrial unions, essentially the UAW, but under Section 9(B)(3) of the Taft-Hartley Act it became illegal for protective employees to organize in the same unions as production workers. In February 1948 the CIO set up the Plant Guards Organizing Committee, but the NLRB ruled that the new union was indirectly affiliated with production unions in the CIO. An independent union, the United Plant Guard Workers of America (UPGWA), was quickly formed, and it successfully struck the Briggs Manufacturing Company after UAW workers refused to cross picket lines. Today the UPGWA is an independent union of some 20,000 members.[62]

None of this evidence means that unionism would wholly disappear without regulation on its behalf. However, these cases verify the strong correspondence between labor regulations and the success and form that unionism takes.

Despite all the talk and writing that claims that unionization depends on worker resentment, revulsion against capitalism, the rate of inflation, and other economy-wide influences, the *sine qua non* for permanent union gains in the United States has been government intervention. The differential pattern in collectivizing the labor force across industries in the 1930s and 1940s cannot be explained in any other way.

Why the Legislation Passed

Every piece of legislation has its unique history, circumstances, and personalities, and these have been described for the Norris–La Guardia and the Wagner acts.[63] What has been ignored is an explicit analysis of the beneficiaries of the legislation, including benefits supplied to the academic community.

Individuals support legislation if they expect the personal rewards to exceed the personal costs.[64] Rewards can be pecuniary and/or non-pecuniary. Legislation passes if promoters can assemble a majority coalition, which, in turn, depends on the initial strength of the opposition. In the political market for labor regulation in the 1930s, people from four primary groups maneuvered Norris–La Guardia and Wagner to passage: unionists, politicians and bureaucrats, academics, and an influential minority of businessmen. Active opposition came from the business community, especially the National Association of Manufacturers, and portions of the legal community. The legislation passed in the 1930s rather than in the 1920s because the cost of voting yes had been reduced drastically for congressmen. Opponents from the business community had been discredited by the Great Depression; sympathy for unions and the unemployed was widespread; there was a general urge to "do something"; and the Democratic party rolled up large electoral gains in the 1930, 1932, and 1934 elections, for all practical purposes eliminating opposition from the Republican party.

There is a long history of intellectual support of unionism, including some support by economists—although most supporters were non-economists. These pro-union opinions generally rested on the notion of the helpless individual and never had been widely shared by the American public before the 1930s. As a result, legislation favored by unionists and their academic supporters, such as anti-injunction bills, got nowhere in Congress, state legislatures, and the courts, despite persistent effort through the 1920s. More ambitious peacetime interventions like a Wagner-type act were politically unthinkable until the onset of the Great Depression and the NIRA precedent. Even in the midst of the depression, the Wagner Act faced significant opposition and was widely believed to be unconstitutional at the time it was passed, especially after the court struck down NRA. Some senators who voted for the Wagner bill apparently wanted to avoid antagonizing the AFL at the polls and confidently expected the court to nullify the Wagner Act. Under pressure of FDR's threat to pack the court, however, the act was ratified by a 5–4 vote in *NLRB* v. *Jones and Laughlin Steel* (301 U.S. 1 [1937]). The special nature of political conditions during the 1930s also is highlighted by the swing of the political pendulum against additional legislative benefits for unionism beginning in the late 1930s. Many state legislatures began to adopt restrictive measures to control union actions, Congress passed the Hobbs amendment to include labor violence in the Anti-Racketeering Act, and Congress passed Taft-Hartley over a presidential veto only twelve years after the Wagner Act.

Benefits from the Norris–La Guardia and Wagner acts for unionists in their self-appointed role as public spokesmen for all labor are obvious. Earlier in this chapter I documented the huge expansion of the labor-representation industry produced by legislation. Organized labor had agitated for anti-injunction legislation and exemption from antitrust for half a century. As early as 1896 the Democratic party platform had a plank that denounced labor injunctions and supported restrictions on the courts. Edwin Witte described the political efforts of unionists this way: "The virtual partnership of organized labor with the Democratic party continued through the congressional elections of 1910 and the presidential elections of 1912 and led to the enactment of the Clayton Act in 1914."[65] Not all Democrats were pro-union. In House debate, Congressman James Beck, a distinguished free-market Democrat and solicitor general in the Wilson administration, described impending congressional acceptance of Norris–La Guardia as a "young lady who, wearied of the importunate solicitations of a suitor, married him to get rid of him."[66]

Politicians weigh the support to be gained or lost by advancing one cause or another. Politicians who enjoy only marginal support are sensitive to pressure groups like unions that are comparatively well organized and have campaign funds, campaign workers, in-kind resources, and members whose votes might be influenced by union leaders. These resources can be used for or against candidates. Other politicians are not marginally sensitive to unionists but have discretion to pursue their own ideology on labor affairs, or want to increase their prestige by promoting programs, agencies, new interest groups, budgets, regulations, and interventions. Successful political entrepreneurship involves innovation, the spawning and nourishment of like-minded pressure groups and programs, rather than merely passive response to the votes and money of existing political groups. Although unions seemed to be at their nadir as a pressure group in 1933, it is an understatement to say that their growth potential in votes and money was positive, especially for northern Democrats.

The entrepreneurship of Fiorello La Guardia and Robert F. Wagner is easily explained. They hailed from New York City. One-half of reported labor injunction cases in state courts took place in New York State during the years 1881-1932. New York always has been the leading state in union membership, and has more union members today than the eleven southern states combined, including Florida and Texas. Fiorello La Guardia worked as an attorney for labor unions, introduced anti-injunction bills in every session of Congress after 1924, won very close congressional races as a Republican, and, in fact, was defeated by 1,200 votes in the Roosevelt landslide of 1932.[67] Senator Wagner has been called the "decisive congressional figure in the formulation of labor policy."[68] An eloquent speaker and energetic worker, he was a Tammany Hall loyalist, chairman of the first labor board under NRA, and a strong believer in the purchasing-power doctrine of forcing up wage rates to end the Great Depression. He was narrowly elected to the Senate in 1926 when Republicans split on the prohibition issue but was handily reelected in 1932, 1938, and 1944 by margins of 400,000 votes and more. The Wagner Act, widely believed to be unconstitutional at the time, was a personal triumph for Senator Wagner rather than direct appeasement of well-formulated union demands.

The entrepreneurship of George Norris for unionism is not so easily explained. Nebraska, his home state, had no substantial union membership, although it should be pointed out that unionists can shift their money and resources across state lines to support or oppose candidates. Like William E. Borah and Robert M. La Follette, Norris was a plains state progressive, who had great latitude to promote his own causes. A *New York Times* editorial on 1 December 1924 claimed that Norris "has a sort of unwritten charter from his State to do what he pleases." Another *Times* editorial on 30 November 1930 said he carried

Nebraska "in his waistcoat for himself." Norris was elected to the House in 1904, appointed to the Senate in 1913, and reelected repeatedly until his defeat in 1942 as an independent candidate at age eighty-one. The personal glory that Senator Norris realized is indicated by the gaudy subtitles of his biographies, accounts which claim that Norris seized on unionism as a cause after being impressed by the harshness of the workingman's lot during a campaign swing through Pennsylvania.[69]

Governmental labor bureaucrats actively promoted the legislation and subsequently benefited in the form of larger bureaus, budgets, and interventionist authority. This was particularly true of the NLRB and of others also. The U.S. Department of Labor had total expenditures of $13.4 million in fiscal 1933 and expanded to $28.7 million in fiscal 1940, a slightly larger percentage expansion than occurred in the total U.S. budget. During the same period the number of commissioners of conciliation in the office of the U.S. Secretary of Labor went from 38 to 104. Under Taft-Hartley this group of commissioners became an independent agency, the Federal Mediation and Conciliation Service, which grew to 347 employees by 1960 and 556 by 1978.

Few doubt that unionists are the primary clientele of the U.S. Department of Labor and that the department depends at least partly for its size on the political effectiveness of unionists. The Department of Labor was founded originally in response to union pressure, as were state departments of labor; and in closing her address to the 1933 AFL convention, Frances Perkins, then U.S. secretary of labor, asked the delegates to regard the Department of Labor as their own department.[70] A related pressure group was the International Association of Governmental Labor Officials (IAGLO). At its twenty-third annual meeting in 1937, President A. L. Fletcher, commissioner of labor in North Carolina, asserted that the influence of the IAGLO officials was apparent in the nature of the labor legislation introduced into forty-three state legislatures during the year, "as nearly all the principal bills had been sponsored originally by our organization and painstakingly studied, drafted, and redrafted by our committees."[71]

Many important individuals in the passage of the Wagner Act came from the National Labor Board, which preceded the NLRB. Among them were Senator Wagner himself and Calvert Magruder, general counsel of the board. Others had backgrounds like Donald Richberg, an attorney for the railroad unions, codraftsman of the Norris–La Guardia Act, and later general counsel of the National Recovery Administration. There was no active bureaucratic opposition to labor legislation in the 1930s, with the exception of Frances Perkins, who supported the Wagner bill but wanted the NLRB to remain in the Department of Labor.

Another major group that pushed labor legislation was the academic community. Although labor and law professors may have been motivated primarily by political beliefs about what was best for the nation, the legislation did nothing to decrease their personal power and income, either as individuals or as members of their occupational group. Identifiable benefits took many forms: (1) drafting and testifying for legislation, (2) jobs for their students, (3) new industrial relations centers under their direction, (4) new journals, (5) more research funds, and (6) consulting income and influence through litigation, mediation, and arbitration.

Four scholars, in addition to Donald Richberg, drafted the Norris-La Guardia Act: Felix Frankfurter and Francis Sayre of the Harvard Law School, Herman Oliphant of Columbia, and Edwin Witte of Wisconsin. The four had contributed a great deal to the voluminous anti-injunction literature over the years.[72] The bill had to be carefully drafted to accomplish its purpose without destroying equity relief in general. In hearings, nearly all academic witnesses testified in favor of the bill, and the same was true with the Wagner bill, although it was drafted by Senator Wagner's office. The American Association for Labor Legislation (AALL) was organized by academics like Richard Ely, its first president; other political economists of the American Economic Association such as John R. Commons; and prominent business leaders. A key pressure group for labor legislation and Social Security between 1906 and 1945, the AALL was closely related at its outset to the National Civic Federation in spirit and practice, and almost all of its financing came from a few wealthy backers and a handful of foundations. Those who served on the council of the AALL at one time or another included Louis D. Brandeis, Bernard M. Baruch, Gerard Swope of General Electric, John D. Rockefeller, Elbert Gary of U.S. Steel, Anne Morgan (daughter of J. P. Morgan), Mrs. Madeline Astor, Thomas L. Chadbourne, longtime president of the AALL and leading Wall Street lawyer for the Guggenheim and Morgan interests, and other business leaders who supported a more cartelized and centralized economy.[73]

In 1948 Edwin Witte pointed out that John R. Commons had trained many labor economists of the day as well as many top civil servants concerned with labor problems; that a majority of members of the

American Economic Association listed labor as their major field; and that no courses on campuses were more popular than those in labor.[74] Arnold N. Tolles, chairman in 1949 of the Industrial Relations Research Association committee on teaching, said, "The dominant area of specialization within the social sciences, as taught in American colleges and universities, is now the area of labor problems and industrial relations."[75]

The first industrial relations center was the Labor Relations Section founded at Princeton in 1922. It was followed by some thirty centers during the 1930s and 1940s. By 1973 *Roberts' Dictionary of Industrial Relations* listed eighty-one such centers. Highly unionized states like Massachusetts, California, Michigan, New York, and Illinois had between five and eight labor relations centers each, while there were only four in the entire South. The announced purpose of the centers is typified by the statement of the center established at the University of Minnesota in 1945, "These [centers] were designed to cope with the pressing problems of management-labor conflict."

To gain an appreciation of the magnitude of the academic expansion in labor relations, consider the associations that grew with unionism. The Industrial Relations Research Association began in 1948 as an offshoot of the American Economic Association with 1,026 members in its first year of operation, expanded to 1,750 by 1952, and currently claims 5,000 members. The American Arbitration Association, founded in 1926 to promote private settlement of business disputes, launched an Industrial Arbitration Tribunal in 1937 as "an important first step in the development of labor arbitration, and to this day the American Arbitration Association plays a large role in this field."[76] Its panel of labor arbitrators numbered 12,353 persons in 1949 and 26,000 in 1970. The Labor Relations Law Committee of the American Bar Association is one of the ten largest sections, with more than 10,000 members. A small but prestigious group is the National Academy of Arbitrators, which was founded in 1947 with a few hundred members and numbered 350 in 1968.[77] The Federal Mediation and Conciliation Service lists 1,200 persons on its roster of arbitrators. An unknown number of other groups make up the rest of the field. They include the Association of Labor Relations Agencies (ALRA) founded in 1952 and the Society of Professionals in Dispute Resolution founded in 1973.

The arbitration process alone yields a large amount of income to academics in labor relations, in addition to income from their other services as labor experts. In the 1930s an estimated 8% to 10% of collective agreements provided for arbitration as the final step in the grievance procedure, but by 1941 the U.S. Conciliation Service found such clauses in 62% of the 1,200 contracts in its files. Almost all contracts now provide for arbitration; a standard figure cited is 96%.[78]

A questionnaire sent in mid-1974 to members of the National Academy of Arbitrators showed that 47.6% of respondents were affiliated with universities. The next largest group was practicing lawyers, at 19.5%.[79] Other inventories of arbitrators confirm the preponderance of law, economics, industrial relations, personnel, business professors, and university officials.[80] A survey by the Federal Mediation and Conciliation Service in 1978 showed that arbitrators charged an average of 3.09 days per case and $239 per diem total fees.[81] No one knows how many arbitration cases are decided in labor disputes each year. According to one estimate, at least 20,000 cases were heard in 1960.[82] The American Arbitration Association reported that a record of 8,655 labor disputes went to arbitration during the first six months of 1980.[83] These estimates are undoubtedly low because there are an estimated 200,000 collective agreements in the country. One arbitration case per contract per year would mean $143 million in income each year for arbitrators at three days per case and $239 per day. Surveys of the National Academy of Arbitration showed that its members averaged 36 arbitration cases in 1952 and 51 in 1969, the latter amounting to 17,500 cases for this small group alone. Two-thirds of members reported waiting lists.[84]

An arbitrator must maintain his acceptability to unionists and managers in order to sustain this source of income; otherwise the parties can settle their differences directly, saving the expense of arbitration, or they can choose other arbitrators. The situation is analogous to a court system in which each judge derives his income directly from the disputants and must take their reactions into account in his decision. J. A. Raffaele claims that concepts like "past practice" and "common law of the shop" were introduced so that arbitrators could decide more grievances for unionists.[85] Many employers now have a form of arbitration that they probably never expected to buy. Although arbitrators deny that they are concerned about rendering at least 50% of their decisions in favor of union grievances, it is well known that commercial organizations issue ratings on arbitrators and prospective arbitrators, basically in terms of pro- or antiunion. These incentives also help to explain the bland nature of the academic literature in industrial relations, where no one is known as antiunion.

As a point of clarification I should note that my contention is *not* that arbitrators were the crucial interest group behind the Wagner Act, the ones who subsequently benefited by institutionalization of the labor-conflict system. Arbitrators simply were too few in number and the lag in expansion of the arbitration system too long and uncertain to make this a viable interpretation. My point is similar to that of the Friedmans: "An individual who intends only to serve the public interest by fostering government intervention is 'led by an invisible hand to promote' private interests, 'which was no part of his intention.' "[86]

Academics did serve as arbitrators and dispute mediators prior to the Wagner Act, and their advocacy of Wagner-like procedures, perhaps without private financial gain as a motive, fostered a large increase in the demand for their skills, most of which was eventually supplied by new people. Thus, even if the original proponents of the Wagner Act did not personally profit from the growth spawned by the legislation, their ideological and occupational successors did.

The last group that paved the way for the labor legislation of the 1930s was an important sector of the business community. Although the Wagner Act is often viewed as a complete victory over the business community, this is not quite true because the business community was not united and determined in its opposition to unionizing legislation. Although influence is impossible to trace precisely, perhaps the most important figure among those pushing for cartelism was Gerard Swope of General Electric, but he was joined by many others. Those gathered in the Business Advisory Council of the Commerce Department included W. Averell Harriman; Thomas W. Lamont of J. P. Morgan & Co.; Sidney Weinberg of Goldman, Sachs; Louis E. Kirstein of Filene's and Federated Department Stores; and Walter J. Teagle of Standard Oil of New Jersey. Others were associated with the National Civic Federation and the American Association for Labor Legislation. J. P. Morgan's lawyer, Francis Lynde Stetson, captured the general belief among this segment of the business community when he said, "The discontent of the masses... 'is to be allayed not by a policy of stern and unbending toryism, but by flexibility.' "[87] Probably a strong majority of the business community, prominently represented by the National Association of Manufacturers, was adamantly opposed to pro-union legislation, yet an increasing number of corporate leaders grew to accept government interference in economic life as a means of solving problems during this century, culminating in the Wagner Act in this instance. The precise role of the business community in the passage of the Wagner Act deserves considerably more research, but the general thesis of George Stigler could well serve as a guide: "the larger part of the regulations that businessmen are subjected to must be of their own contriving and acceptance.... most regulatory policies have been sought by producer groups, of whom the business community is the most important and the academic community by no means the least important."[88]

Conclusion

The huge expansion of unionism in the 1930s traditionally has been interpreted as a function of worker discontent, public sympathy for unionism, revulsion against free markets, and only secondarily to enlightened labor legislation. The confusion and despair of the Great Depression dramatically reduced prevailing political constraints, and specific individuals with specific ideas seized the resulting political opportunities. This chapter argues that neither the Norris–La Guardia Act nor the Wagner Act can be accurately described as government intervention to correct previous market failures, which is a conventional academic interpretation, but that the sharp increase in size of the labor-representation industry was due to monopoly-type regulatory legislation. These developments were produced by good intentions, in part, but received major assistance from self-interest. The identifiable beneficiaries of the legislation—unionists, politicians, labor bureaucrats, their academic allies, and a minority of businessmen—were largely the same individuals who had supported the legislation (or their occupational successors), an observation consistent with economic theory but widely ignored in the literature about the period. Although labor legislation is usually cluttered with even more public-interest rhetoric than other legislation, in view of the available evidence it is difficult to see why the process of labor legislation should be modeled any differently from the normal case of intervention on behalf of an industry.

These conclusions do not exclude the possibility that participants in the legislative and regulatory process had good intentions. Frequently they did. Some activists had deep conviction. Participants probably had the usual admixture of idealism and narrow self-interest. Political activists had no more perfect foresight about their prospective gains than market participants do. Nor was there a conspiracy. Legislation always is produced by a relatively small number of people who pursue their own interests. But the mythology of labor legislation apparently is immovable. Benjamin J. Taylor and Fred Witney, for example, say, "Supporters of the legislation [Wagner Act] recognized that the modern industrial environment rendered obsolete the concept of individual bargaining as the regulator of industrial relations. Unchecked economic power lodged in a comparatively few corporate giants could lead to some form of despotism. . . . Social legislation was blocked by a Supreme Court which ignored the most obvious facts of economic life."[89]

Today a substantial number of people directly earn their livelihoods from conflicts generated year after year in our system of labor representation. Unionists collect over $5 billion in dues and fees each year; full-time union officials number more than 30,000 and are paid in excess of $1.2 billion; there are over 10,000 members of the American Bar Association's Labor Relations Section, more than 5,000 members of the Industrial Relations Research Association, more than 20,000 persons on the labor roster of the American Arbitration Association, almost 3,000 employees of the National Labor Relations Board, and so forth. The redistributive effects of unions exceed $30 billion each year.[90] Politicians seek reelection, and unions are the largest organized political group in terms of manpower and money. Each bureaucracy seeks to retain and expand its functions. The Federal Mediation and Conciliation Service, for instance, whose mandate is to "proffer its services in any labor dispute in any industry affecting commerce. . . . whenever in its judgment such dispute threatens to cause a substantial interruption in commerce," has a case load that includes a retail bakery of six employees and a tile company of eight employees.

European unions never had to spend much effort to organize workers, relying instead on class identity for allegiance. Until the 1930s, American unionists had to organize and use aggressive tactics to establish their organizations because of the diverse opinions of workingmen and employers, and the ultimate willingness of the courts to enforce the law against private coercion. In the 1930s, however, unionists gained a more or less permanent foothold in the economy as a result of legislation on their behalf. And the accompanying mediators, conciliators, fact finders, arbitrators, and crisis-solving experts of the labor-representation industry grew in stature and income along with them.

6
Federal Regulation of Wages

...the labor movement in America is one of the ornaments of our political democracy, a movement essentially pro-capitalist and a movement essentially allied to ideas that are central to business and conservative goals: pro-growth, pro-expansion, deeply suspect of environmental excess, and vigorously pro-freedom around the world.
—Ben J. Wattenberg

Certainly unions do everything they can to undermine capitalism without realizing that only under capitalism do unions have any reason for existence. In any other system they would of course be dead, but they have no conception of this and prefer instead to believe that they will actually manage whatever economy arises from the ashes of capitalism.
—Arthur Shenfield

The Norris–La Guardia Act and the National Labor Relations Act were rather obviously designed to promote unionism and collective bargaining, but not all political activism by unions is so easily recognized.

Yet a great deal of union behavior in the political arena can be explained as attempts to increase or preserve the demand for union labor by political means. Examples are the union-label campaign, support for tariffs and quotas that restrict foreign goods competing with union-made goods, laws that compel "Made in Korea" labels, building codes that compel installation of union-supplied materials and labor services, reduced student class sizes to raise the demand for unionized teachers, mass transit subsidies, and opposition to "contracting out." Other measures supported by unions—such as immigration laws, apprenticeship requirements, child labor laws, minimum wages, and occupational licensing—restrict trade by raising the relative prices of nonunion suppliers and restricting the ability of others to compete.

Continuous investment of union resources in political lobbying confirms the difficulty of maintaining monopoly gains in a dynamic economy filled with substitutes, ingenuity, and responsiveness to relative prices. Unions, continuously battling the erosion of their privileged positions, urge new political regulations and restrictions, thereby reducing both the free flow of capital and labor and the efficiency of the economy.

Wage and hour regulation by the federal bureaucracy has been an important part of the indirect government support of unions. The Fair Labor Standards Act (FLSA) of 1938, as amended, fixes national minimums, and other laws fix higher standards for wages and employment conditions under government contract or construction work financed wholly or partly by federal money. Examples are the Walsh-Healey Act, the Davis-Bacon Act, the O'Hara-McNamara Service Contract Act, the Work and Safety Act, the Eight Hour Law, the Copeland Act, and the Miller Act. The most important of these laws are FLSA and Davis-Bacon, but Walsh-Healey is discussed as an example of a regulation that has had little impact.

The Davis-Bacon Act

A once-obscure labor law, the Davis-Bacon Act, has been quietly administered to protect the wages and employment of the building-trades unions for half a century. In 1979 the General Accounting Office (GAO) put the act on the front pages by issuing a report based on two decades of monitoring the administration of the law by the Department of Labor.[1] The GAO urged that Davis-Bacon be repealed. The AFL-CIO responded by accusing the GAO, known for its thoroughness and investigative independence, of "lining up with the antiunion contractors in a new attack on the Davis-Bacon Act." And the Labor Department jumped into the act by issuing a fifty-six-page report defending its administration of the law.[2] Political support for repeal continues to grow. The number of House voters for repeal or major amendment rose from 35 in 1976 to 173 in 1978, and more bills for repeal were introduced between 1979 and 1981, although none succeeded. Florida became the first state to repeal its version of Davis-Bacon in 1979, and three more states—Alabama, Arizona, and Utah—had followed by 1981. By contrast, a rally by 4,000 unionists in March 1981 helped the Arkansas legislature find the public interest, and a repeal bill was killed. Nearly forty states have laws patterned after Davis-Bacon, and repeal legislation was pending in eight state legislatures during 1981, under the increasing pressure of federal budget restraint and rapidly rising construction costs.[3]

Davis-Bacon was passed in 1931 after a sharp decline in construction activity at the beginning of the Great Depression. Construction expenditures went from $11 billion annually to $3 billion, with more than half of the reduced activity financed by government. Competition for contracts and jobs was fierce. Mobile contractors, using migrant labor, entered the market to underbid some local contractors. Many contractors, as well as labor unions, welcomed the law to protect themselves from what a congressman called "carpetbagging sharpie contractors."

The law requires that workers on federally financed construction be paid wages at "local prevailing rates" for comparable construction work. The clearly stated intent was to protect local workers and contractors from the competition of outside contractors and migrant workers. The act orders that, for every federal construction project exceeding $2,000, the secretary of labor establish as a minimum construction wage the "prevailing wage for a corresponding class of laborer in the city, town, village, or civil subdivision in which the work is to be performed."

The ambiguity of prevailing wages has given the U.S. Department of Labor the latitude to set minimum wages at union wage rates in about half of its wage determinations. As shown below, this has cost the federal taxpayers at least a billion dollars a year in higher construction and administrative costs.

Since 1931 Congress has extended the prevailing wage provision to include most federally assisted construction, whether state, local, or national government is the direct purchaser. Additional amendments added fringe benefits to prevailing wage calculations in 1964. The prevailing wage is administratively determined by the Wage and Hour Division of the Department of Labor, and minimum wages are set primarily on a project basis. In 1980, for example, 13,115 of the 14,501 wage determinations were issued on a project basis; the remainder were set geographically.

The GAO found that, in a sample of 73 wage determinations, half were union-negotiated rates. Of 530 area determinations, 302, or 57%, were simply union rates rather than rates determined from wage surveys. The GAO found that the Labor Department bureaucrats could not compile timely information on a voluntary basis from a multitude of relevant sources. The Wage and Hour Division does not use a consistent methodology in its surveys, adds and deletes wage data on an ad hoc basis, includes previous Davis-Bacon projects in the data, adopts arbitrary job classifications, and imports urban wage rates into rural-area projects in order to benefit unions. At the very least, the Department of Labor sets the *average construction* wage in an area as the *minimum wage,* and more often sets the union wage as the minimum wage.

When surveys are conducted to fix wages, the Labor Department first investigates to determine if a majority of workers receive an exact wage rate, to the penny. If not, the Labor Department will set any exact wage paid to 30% of the designated group of employees. If the 30% rule is not met, the average rate is set as the minimum. Obviously, this procedure makes union rates likely to be set as minimums because nonunion wages typically vary according to experience and productivity, with no large number receiving exactly the same wage.

To illustrate, a wage survey in Carson City County, Nevada, showed that two painters were employed at $6.25 per hour, two at $8.74 per hour, one at $9.00 per hour, and three at $12.40 an hour.[5] On another project in Fairfax County, Virginia, to pave 1.6 miles of Interstate 66, the department fixed higher minimum wages for work on the median strip of the highway than for work on the highway itself because the strip might be used for a Metrorail system in the future. The minimum for unskilled labor was $4.50 per hour on the highway but $9.68 per hour for work on the median strip. The minimum for operating engineers on the highway was $5.00 per hour but $11.49 per hour on the median.[6]

The classification of labor by type is another source of mischief. For example, in some southwestern states adobe is widely considered the cheapest and most effective building material available. Davis-Bacon does not cover *adoberos* (adobe workers), so the Labor Department classifies them as masons or bricklayers, while in private construction adobe workers receive approximately half the wage of a mason because being an *adobero* requires more muscle and less skill than being a mason or a bricklayer. Result? The administrators of Davis-Bacon inflate the cost of adobe relative to other materials, and the more labor-intensive, appropriate, nonunion material is not often used on federal housing projects in the Southwest.[7]

The effect of the Labor Department's administration of the law is not to protect local contractors but to protect unions. Contractors would use prevailing wage rates in their bids, just as they do in bidding for private contracts, and most contracts would go to local construction firms because they would be low bidders. But under Davis-Bacon, local contractors are reluctant to bid on projects with Davis-Bacon wages because of morale problems. Employees fortunate enough to work on federal projects receive more than their counterparts on other jobs, and when the project ends, a return to previous wages can reduce productivity or increase agitation for unionization or union wage rates. High minimum wages also discourage contractors from hiring young and minority workers. Apprentice rates are fixed so high that employers prefer to hire skilled journeymen. Fixing union rates as minimum rates also discourages minority contractors, most of whom are non-union, from bidding on federal contracts. This decreases minority employment in construction and contradicts federal procurement policy aimed at favoring minority enterprises.

The net effect of Davis-Bacon is to protect unions and to diminish the amount of construction that a federal dollar can buy. Taxpayers are denied some of the benefits of greater productivity and lower costs stimulated by greater competition. A dramatic example is housing for the elderly. The original bid on a project of forty-four units for the elderly at Keyser, West Virginia, was $740,000, or $16,800 per apartment, without Davis-Bacon. When Davis-Bacon was imposed, the bid jumped to $1.2 million, $27,300 per apartment—or we could say that $740,000 would buy only twenty-seven units instead of forty-four units, all else being equal. Sentiment is building to exempt some federal projects from Davis-Bacon requirements. In June 1979 an amendment to exempt American Indian housing and neighborhood self-help programs from Davis-Bacon was defeated, while the Armed Services Committee voted to exempt military construction.

Davis-Bacon triggered an interesting bit of follow-up legislation in 1934, when Congress passed the Copeland Act, which imposed a fine of $5,000 or five years imprisonment on recipients of kickbacks. Government investigators found that laborers in the building trades were paid the government-mandated wage but kicked back a percentage of their pay in order to keep their jobs. This behavior occurs because of the natural tendency of competition to establish prices and wages that clear the market. The Copeland Act's prohibition of kickbacks is like the Interstate Commerce Commission's prohibition of rebates. The ICC fixes freight rates above competitive levels, and then competition among the carriers for shipments leads carriers to offer rebates (kickbacks) in order to get work.

Construction is one of the largest industries in the U.S. economy, with almost $250 billion in annual revenue, or 8% of GNP. About 20% of all construction is regulated by Davis-Bacon. The GAO estimated the cost of Davis-Bacon in 1977 at more than $500 million in extra labor cost plus $189 million in administrative costs borne by contractors and $12 million incurred by federal agencies, including the Department of Labor, for a total cost of $700 million. The United States Chamber of Commerce, on the other hand, published an estimated total cost of Davis-Bacon of $2.8 billion a year, including direct costs of $1 billion and indirect costs of $1.8 billion. It estimated that repeal would reduce the price of a new home by $740 and expand construction employment by up to 150,000 jobs.

Although these estimates may appear far apart, they are not dramatically different. The GAO estimate of $700 million is a conservative figure for the immediate cost of Davis-Bacon to the taxpayer, comparable to the $1 billion estimate by the Chamber of Commerce. Labor costs constitute about 30% of total costs on a typical construction project, and union wage rates are at least 20% higher than prices for comparable nonunion labor services, so we can say that Davis-Bacon drives up the cost of projects by about 6% (.3 x .2). Since federally financed construction in 1980 was about $40 billion, an upper limit on the direct cost to federal taxpayers in that year would be $2.4 billion, and a lower limit $1.2 billion, on the assumption that costs increase on only about half of federally financed projects (union wage rates are decreed as "prevailing" in about half of Davis-Bacon determinations). If record-keeping adds another 10% to costs, it would correspond to the GAO estimate of $200 million per year in administrative cost.

Sentiment against the Davis-Bacon Act is not confined to building contractors and heartless economists. In December 1979 an editorial in *The New York Times* said that "the best possible reform would be to erase it [Davis-Bacon] from the books. That, unfortunately, would be extraordinarily difficult; not surprisingly, organized labor bitterly opposes repeal since the law reduces the incentive of contractors to hire nonunion workers."

Construction workers are among the highest paid in America, earning twice the hourly rate of workers in retail trade. Yet only 20% of all construction work is regulated by the Davis-Bacon Act. If Davis-Bacon is repealed, high wages in construction will not change, but Americans in general will benefit. Building-trades unions would lose one of their shelters from competition, and they would have to compete by offering buyers more for their money. The Davis-Bacon Act is a typical example of the gross errors in economic policy, all of which stem from government intervention on behalf of the interests of people as producers rather than as consumers. Everyone knows that services are rewarded in proportion to their scarcity in the marketplace. The fewer the competitors, the better. So producer groups try to restrict supply by seeking legislation to hobble potential competitors. Isolated instances of monopoly enrich the protected beneficiaries, but the system becomes a bad joke on everyone as more interest groups gain protection. Industry after industry gains protections to boost price and reduce supply, and the abundance of competitively supplied goods disappears. In a word, poverty.

The Walsh-Healey Act

Davis-Bacon has proven its value to building-trades unions, but Walsh-Healey, passed in 1936, turned out to be ineffective for unions. The intent of the Walsh-Healey Public Contracts Act was to establish government administration of employment conditions for all government contracts over $10,000, much as Davis-Bacon did in construction alone. The law allowed the secretary of labor to fix minimum wage scales among nearly all government contractors.

The first wage determination under Walsh-Healey became effective on 9 February 1937 and called for an hourly minimum of 37.5 cents for suppliers of men's work garments. Appropriately enough, this happened to be the union rate. In the next wage determination, an hourly minimum of 67.5 cents was fixed in the hat and cap industry—the union rate again. The Labor Department evolved more and more legalistic procedures to determine wages, but an interesting aspect is that the department began by gathering together people from the industry to discuss the "need" for standards. "Responsible" employers—that is, unionized employers—generally urged that standards be imposed in order to discipline "unscrupulous," low-cost competitors.

Government contracts subject to Walsh-Healey were estimated at 3,000, valued at $177 million in 1937; these figures had risen to 93,000 and $20 billion by 1966. The potential scope for the act was still huge in the early 1960s, but the Department of Labor never settled on a consistent method to determine the "prevailing wage" and generated persistent controversy and resistance in the business community. Only sixty-one original wage determinations were made between 1937 and 1964, and many of these minimums were ineffective because they were based on wage surveys two and three years old, and hence were below the actual market wage rates being paid at the time. Herbert C. Morton calculated that fewer than 10,000 workers per year had their wages increased by as much as 10% during the period 1961 to 1964.[8]

The wage-fixing mechanism of Walsh-Healey was rendered inoperative in 1964 by a District Court decision, *Wirtz* v. *Baldor Electric* (337 F.2d 518 [1964]). The secretary of labor used data collected by the Bureau of Labor Statistics to determine prevailing wages, but the data were gathered for other purposes on the promise to cooperating employers that no individual company would be identified. The legal problem was that outsiders could not check sources; the court said that this denied due process.

Evidence that Walsh-Healey is dead for wage- and hour-fixing purposes can be seen in the fact that the act no longer excites controversy in the business community, whereas Davis-Bacon still does. The annual report of the Labor Department stopped issuing wage determinations under Walsh-Healey in 1966 when it said, "Currently, there are 23 effective determinations in excess of $1.25 an hour—the generally applicable minimum wage under the FLSA....Because of adverse court decisions, and administrative problems emanating therefrom, no new wage determinations were made under the Public Contracts Act during the past year."[9]

The wage-fixing aspect of Walsh-Healey has disappeared, but the act remains on the books for other forms of regulation. In 1968–69 the Labor Department used the safety provisions of the law to fix radiation exposure levels in uranium mines. The department proudly pointed out that it had "the immediate effect of closing the mines in which this problem was most serious." The act also was used to set standards for noise, dusts, mists, and gases and was the forerunner for OSHA regulation.

The demise of Walsh-Healey, compared with the long, potent life of Davis-Bacon, has not been explained clearly by any observer. The intent of the two pieces of legislation was similar, yet the two acts experienced very different administrative histories. A facile explanation would attribute the different administrative histories to differences in bureaucratic ambition or guile, but this approach offers no insight at all. We are better served by assuming that the desire to extend federal control is uniform throughout the federal bureaucracy, at least in the absence of solid evidence to the contrary, because then we are forced to look for differences in objective circumstances. The comparative success of Davis-Bacon as a vehicle for union and bureaucratic wage-fixing seems to rest on four circumstances: application to a single industry, the concentrated political clout of the old-line building-trades unions, the historically diffuse opposition, and the relative ease of administration. Gradual change in the technology of large-scale construction and reasonably well-defined occupations in the building trades made it administratively easier to impose sensible-sounding minimum wage rates by craft on building contractors, and the Department of Labor simultaneously was serving a unified constituency. These characteristics have sharply eroded over time, however, and therefore Davis-Bacon stands in danger of repeal.

By contrast, these favorable wage-fixing circumstances never existed for Walsh-Healey. It was in trouble right from the start. The first version of the bill failed in the House in 1935 in the face of potent opposition, despite perfunctory passage in the Senate, and then a revised bill passed in 1936 over substantial opposition in the business community. Although the business community lost the legislative battle, it did not lose the subsequent administrative war. Walsh-Healey was an administrative nightmare because of huge diversity among the suppliers of batteries, rainwear, envelopes, soap, surgical instruments, paint and varnish, and thousands of other manufactured products purchased by the federal government every year. Firms differ sharply in size, technology, region, local labor market conditions, wage systems (e.g., hourly versus piece rates), occupational definitions, and so on. Moreover, union political pressure on the bureaucracy was far from single-minded as a result of the many new industrial unions of the 1930s and 1940s, their rivalries to organize workers, and their conflicts with the craft unions. Opposition to Walsh-Healey decisions continued throughout the life of the act's wage-fixing period, and time-consuming adversary hearings, appeals, and court battles were common. For example, when the secretary of labor set a nationwide minimum wage rate of $1.00 an hour in the textile industry in 1955, southern textile firms unsuccessfully carried their opposition up to the court of appeals and then failed to carry it to the Supreme Court. The secretary of labor, of course, was supported by both the AFL-CIO and New England textile companies who feared the competitive disadvantage of a geographic wage differential.[10] The administrative costs of imposing sensible-sounding minimums in such fluid, diverse circumstances, across so many industries, were simply unmanageable, and the business community kept up the drum roll of opposition to these arbitrary political prices until active wage determination died of its own overweening ambition.

The Fair Labor Standards Act

When Congress passed the Fair Labor Standards Act in 1938, it set a national minimum wage rate of 25 cents an hour. This wage applied to an estimated 43% of employees in private nonagricultural work. On 1 January 1981 the minimum reached $3.35 an hour and covered an estimated 84% of private nonagricultural employment. Over the forty-odd years of its life, the minimum wage has fluctuated at just under half of the average hourly wage in manufacturing.

The primary beneficiaries of the law are federal bureaucrats who enjoy the powers of enforcement, labor unions, some unionized employers (who enjoy some protection from competition), and the reduced number of unskilled workers who can obtain employment in the covered sector. Bureaucrats benefit directly, and the unions benefit by the indirect effects of the law. When the cost of low-wage, low-productivity labor is raised, employers adjust by using fewer workers and by using them more efficiently. They substitute in a variety of ways. Managers of gasoline stations, for example, install self-service pumps and hire fewer attendants, and restaurants use individually packaged sugar and catsup so that they can get along with fewer waitresses. Despite ingenious substitutions in production, the prices of goods and services that use low-wage labor, especially retail trade and services, rise relative to the prices of other goods. Consumers purchase fewer of these goods, buying other purchases instead. These ripple effects in production and consumption increase *relative demand* for high-wage (union) labor, although the demand-depressing effects of operating in a less productive economy harm union members as well as unemployed and nonunion people.

The support of minimum-wage legislation by organized labor is widely advertised as evidence of unions' concern for the welfare of all workers, but the actual effect is to deny inexperienced workers the very opportunities that would allow them to increase their skills and productivity. Most new entrants into the work force can improve their skills most effectively by receiving experience and training on the job. This experience and training will qualify them for higher-paying jobs in the future. Many young people, members of minority groups, women, and older people find it much more difficult to find beginners' jobs because minimum-wage laws and union-imposed wage rates price them out of the market. Yet accepting a low-paying job for its on-the-job training is no different, in principle, from paying to go to school. One sophisticated economic study has estimated that more than half of the training in the United States occurs on the job rather than in school.[11] The restrictions on employment opportunities imposed by the minimum-wage law have caused unmeasured waste and ruined uncounted working careers, most visibly in the ongoing tragedy of our inner cities.

The impact of higher minimum-wage rates has been moderated by the rising price level and rising real wages, but the increase in coverage has multiplied the perverse effects of the law. Minimum wages were originally applied to mostly high-wage industries (mining, manufacturing, transportation) and then extended to industries with lower wages (services and retail trade). Today we think of industries like retail trade and services as teenage-intensive, but before the minimum-wage law went into effect this was not true. In 1930, for example, teenagers generally worked where adults worked, and the age distribution of workers across industries was amazingly uniform because minimum-wage laws did not price beginners out of any economic sector.[12]

A minimum-wage law restricts employment opportunities for low-productivity workers in covered sectors and forces them into uncovered sectors, where they can price themselves back into work, or else it pushes them out of the market work force entirely.[13] Since the U.S. minimum-wage law is approaching complete market coverage, eventually there will be no place for these workers to run. Employment effects have been especially devastating for black youth. From 1954 to 1956, for example, almost 60% of black males age sixteen to nineteen had civilian employment as opposed to 54% of white males the same age. As minimum-wage coverage expanded, employment of black youth fell, until only 30% of black male youths were employed from 1975 to 1977, while the employment ratio for white youth stayed constant at over 50%. A recent econometric study claims that all of the decline in black teenage employment during the 1950s and 1960s occurred in agriculture in the South and that the federal minimum wage acted as a barrier to employment opportunities outside agriculture.[14]

Rigorous empirical work on the effects of the minimum-wage law has generally, though not universally, supported the predictions of economic reasoning. But it is important to understand why any discrepancies exist. The minimum is kept "within reason"—that is, less than most people earn—so the employment effects are limited to subgroups and special pockets of the economy. They are more difficult to detect convincingly. If the law fixed the minimum above the wages of a large number of people, say \$20 per hour, the destruction of employment would become obvious. For example, the U.S. minimum-wage law initially applied the 25-cents-an-hour minimum to Puerto Rico, when the average wage in Puerto Rico was below 25 cents an hour. Within two years employment declined by half, and the Puerto Rican government pleaded for exemption. The AFL vigorously opposed the exemptions, but they were gradually granted on a piecemeal basis to alleviate some of the suffering.[15]

The minimum-wage law contains a number of exemptions and specifies some groups that are subject to lower minimum wages, despite objections from the AFL-CIO. Even the Labor Department implicitly recognizes that the minimum-wage law destroys employment: its 1978 annual report said, "The lower minimum wages, allowed under the Fair Labor Standards Act, were designed to prevent the curtailment of employment opportunities for handicapped workers, students and learners, and others." The "others" category does not include black youths, the elderly, and part-time workers who cannot work unless they can find employment at \$3.35 per hour or more.

Expanded coverage helps unions organize sectors of the economy such as the retail trade, hospitals, janitorial services, and state and local government, which were previously not covered by the federal law. Federal regulation diminishes the efficiency advantage of non-union enterprises, thereby easing the way for unions to add workers, further raise wages for their well-paid minorities, and exert more control over the work place and the industry. The competitive expansion of new enterprises and the corresponding opportunities for untrained labor are thwarted by wage laws, while unionized enterprises and industries are protected by these barriers. Government subsidies to finance small businesses are supposed to offset these government-imposed costs on small enterprise. And one intervention leads to another.

7
Economic Effects of Unionism

*Unions have been very effective at promulgating the view that the labor
movement has played an essential role in improving the economic
well-being of all workers. In fact, there is no evidence,
theoretical or empirical, to support this view.
—Dwight R. Lee, 1980*

Unions have an announced objective of pushing up wages and fringe
benefits for labor, and they have a coercive grant from government to
pursue this goal. So two questions arise: How successful have they
been? And what are the effects of unions on the level of national income, labor's share of income, unemployment, and inflation?

I know of no professional economist who contends that the economic actions of labor unions raise the standard of living for *all
laborers*. This would be impossible unless unions raised labor's share
of income without reducing national income, or increased national income without reducing labor's share. Not even the Harvard-NBER
group headed by Freeman and Medoff claims that unions have these
effects; they say only that unions increase productivity in some instances and reduce it in others. Economists have spent their time inves-
tigating what I would call less frivolous questions, such as these: How
much do unions raise the relative wage rates of their members? How
much do unions reduce national income? Who bears the costs of union
gains?

Unionists proudly claim that they have done more than any other institution to raise the standards of living of all working people in the
United States. This claim is hopelessly wrong but so widely believed
that its falseness cannot be emphasized often enough. The claim should
automatically arouse suspicion based on Adam Smith's dictum, "I

have never known much good done by those who affected to trade for the public good." A high-wage economy occurs because large amounts of capital invested per employee multiply the output from human effort. More capital, managed with greater efficiency, is the only route to a higher standard of living for the average worker. Rational analysis shows that union wage pressure forces other workers into lower-paid, less-productive jobs, and hence reduces the real income of workers as a group below what it would otherwise be. To put it mildly, the interests of the leaders of organized labor are not synonymous with the interests of *all labor.*

Union Pay

Unions can raise the pay of some members relative to other workers, even though, overall, unions reduce the flow of real wages in the economy. In recent years economists have devoted a great deal of effort to estimating the magnitude of union effects on relative earnings. Answers have varied considerably, depending on the method of estimation, the data, time period, and other factors. The result is that few are willing to give a single number that summarizes the effect of unionization on relative wages, although this is not the same as saying that nothing is known.

From a theoretical standpoint, the lack of a single answer is not surprising. To assess the independent effect of unions on the pay of members we must figure out what their pay would have been *without* a union. We must know what would have happened but didn't. In the language of economic historians, we must select a counterfactual. The best we can do is compare the earnings of union workers with the earnings of comparable nonunion workers.

This procedure obviously sets the stage for controversy, often quite technical, over whether a particular method adequately controls for other differences between union and nonunion workers that might affect earnings. Indeed, there is controversy over whether unionization can be treated as a wholly independent variable in statistical regression models. Good economists can have different judgments about whether or not the true effect of unionization on earnings has been isolated in a particular study.

The difficulties are highlighted by viewing the problem from an employer's point of view. Suppose your plant is unionized and, following threats, strikes, and disruption, you agree to raise pay by 20%. Now you face the problem of getting your unit labor costs back down and remaining competitive in the product market. A number of adjustments become necessary that were not economical at lower rates of pay. First, you employ less labor, using normal attrition, layoffs, or other devices to reduce employment. You substitute labor-saving machinery, use more capital-intensive production techniques, and contract out more work to economize on expensive labor. Second, you demand more effort per hour from your workers because they are now being paid more than they can earn in the open market and are more eager to retain their jobs. The union, of course, fights management for control of such speedups and other changes in working conditions, but ordinarily some additional productivity can be realized. Third, because money wages are only part of the compensation package, you can reduce the nonmonetary rewards of the workers. Employees are effectively paid in wages, bonuses, fringe benefits such as employer-paid insurance, air conditioning, low noise levels, music, locational convenience, free parking, safety measures, courteous management, company parties, sports programs, on-the-job training, and schooling subsidies. In the absence of unions, employers try to adjust these forms of compensation to minimize unit labor costs, and at the margin, an additional dollar spent on each form of compensation yields the same gain in productivity or reduction in other labor expenses. Union wages prevent this free-market adjustment, but the wage increase can be partly or fully offset by reducing nonpecuniary forms of payment. Fourth, since overall compensation generally is more attractive as a result of union pressure, higher-quality laborers are hired from the queue of qualified applicants. More productive people end up in unionized jobs because of "cream skimming" by employers. These employees also have lower rates of turnover, further reducing the labor costs associated with hiring, firing, and quitting. The net effect of the initial wage boost of 20% might be controlled to something like a 5% real premium after all adjustments by an enterprise. And outside observers, therefore, might come to widely varying conclusions about the effects of the union, especially since some enterprises would pay a 5% premium in the absence of a union.

Now consider the nonunion employees whose earnings might be used for comparison. In general, the relative wage advantage of union members has two causes: (1) unions raise wages above competitive levels, and (2) nonunion wages are restrained (depressed) by the increased supply of people seeking work in the nonunion sector. However, in specific instances it might pay a nonunion employer to grant union wage rates in order to reduce the chances that his employees will unionize. Perhaps only a handful of similarly situated employers would find it profitable to concede part of their cost advantage this way, because it is like throwing in the towel without a fight. But this tactic might avoid some of the nonwage costs of unionization like rigid work rules, strikes, and walkouts in enterprises that are at serious risk of unionization. The scientific problem is that the "threat effect" of unionism can raise the wages of similarly situated nonunion workers (although threats also diminish social wages by discouraging investment) and, therefore, statistical estimates of the wage-increasing effects of unions would be understated. The solution is to make wider comparisons, but this means greater correction for differences among employees in other wage determinants like schooling, sex, race, industry, occupation, experience, geography, cost of living, fringe benefits, and marital status.

To muddy the waters further, a two-way dependence can develop between high wages and unionism. The common view is that unions get high wages for their members, but high-wage workers also are more likely to unionize. Members of the Airline Pilots Association, to use a dramatic example, averaged $60,000 a year in 1976 for their three-day week. This two-way dependence makes the independent effect of unionism on wages more difficult to untangle. High-wage workers can more easily afford to unionize because they face relatively inelastic demand for their services, have low turnover rates, make large investments in their training and skills, perhaps including training that is relatively specific to a particular enterprise, and also work in concentrated industries with few firms or with geographically concentrated firms. Union officials also direct their efforts toward compact, cohesive groups that promise to be easy to organize. From an econometric point of view, these considerations imply models with two or more equations and two-stage-least-squares estimation, or more exotic techniques.

Some of these theoretical considerations suggest that empirical estimates will underestimate the union effect on relative wages and that other estimates will bias it upward. The best available evidence on this issue has produced estimates of the relative wage advantage of union workers over nonunion workers with similar characteristics of 0% to 100%, depending on the union and time period. The premier empirical work in the field is still the book by H. G. Lewis.[1] In summarizing, refining, and extending all the known work up to that time, much of it done at the University of Chicago, Lewis observed that most of the studies looked at situations where a measurable union advantage was likely to exist. Nonetheless, a wage advantage of more than 25% was relatively rare. Among unions with comparatively large effects in certain periods were the mine workers, building trades, printing, entertainment, airline pilots, and seamen. Unions with negligible wage effects in the past, according to Lewis's estimates, were garment workers, textile workers, shoe workers, and white-collar government workers.

Unions tend to raise wage rates and also make them more rigid over time. The typical bargaining agreement is negotiated every three years and, although many agreements have cost-of-living adjustments or wage "reopeners," prices are relatively fixed for definite intervals. This means that the union advantage is likely to fluctuate relative to nonunion employments, where adjustments are more flexible. Lewis estimated that the general wage advantage of union members was 45% in the early 1930s. It slipped to 22% in the late 1930s, then to 6% in the early 1940s, and down to zero in the late 1940s. Then it rose to 12% in the early 1950s and 16% in the late 1950s. There is a plausible interpretation of these seemingly wild fluctuations. The figures for the early 1930s reflect the rigidity of union contracts relative to nonunion wages during the Great Depression. Of course, union membership was shrinking, very few members could secure full-time employment at union rates, and informal wage-cutting was common. The late 1930s was the period of aggressive peacetime expansion of unionism; the 1940s reflected wage-price controls and a failure to ancitipate fully the wartime and postwar inflations; and the 1950s emphasized survey data gathered from households; in principle, these data are better because of more detailed information about individual characteristics. The tendency in the studies using single-equation models is to find results similar to Lewis's. Leonard Weiss found a 6% to 8% gain for operatives and craftsmen; Frank Stafford in later data found a 16% advantage for all occupations; Paul Ryscavage, a 12% advantage; and Orley Ashenfelter, a 15% advantage.[2] Construction unions appeared to raise wages the most: laborers and operatives enjoyed the largest advantage, as much as 50%, while craftsmen got smaller gains of 25% or less. A small advantage for the highly skilled is consistent with a leveling or egalitarian policy by union negotiators. Parsley could cite only five studies on the union-nonunion differential in the United Kingdom, and the numerical magnitudes ranged up to a 60% relative wage advantage, though the overall pattern appeared similar to that in the United States.[3]

Two- and three-equation models tend to reduce the estimated potency of the union wage effect. Some investigators find that a significant positive effect of unionism on earnings disappears or becomes insignificant when the model takes into account the positive effect that high wages may have on the probability of union membership. Others contend that a significant effect of unions on wage rates remains in simultaneous-equation models, although it is smaller than single-equation models suggest.[4]

In summary, technical economists have not reached a consensus on the exact magnitude of the relative wage effect of unionism. Albert Rees, a distinguished labor economist, once ventured the guess that about one-third of unions had virtually no effect on wages, one-third had moderate effects of 10% to 15%, and one-third had a large effect of 25%. More recently, though, he has written: "My own best guess of the average effects of all American unions on the wages of their members in recent years would lie somewhere between 15 and 20 percent. This is a somewhat higher range than I would have guessed a decade ago. The difference is more the result of the availability of new data than a belief that union power has been increasing."[5] H. G. Lewis and Milton Friedman seem to cling to their earlier estimates of average gains of 10% to 15%. The safest statement appears to be that few economists would quarrel with 10% or 15% as a lower limit of the average boost that unions give to relative wages, but the issue remains empirically alive.

Union Pricing, Sick Industries, and Revitalization

Industries rise and fall, expand and contract, come and go. The reasons are diverse but, ordinarily, change is benign and in accord with evolving consumer preferences, income, and technical advance. To prohibit change would be to condemn ourselves to stagnation and regression. However, the role that unions and labor costs play in the process of industrial decline has been largely ignored.

There appears to be a striking association between unionism and sick industries. Great Britain is a case unto itself (economist Pierre Rinfret calls Britain an "industrial museum"), but in the United States naming a sick industry usually amounts to naming an industry with above-average unionization, while the reverse is true for a healthy industry. Railroads, coal mining, and the movie industry are obvious examples of the deleterious effects of union pricing and work rules in the past, while postal service, unionized construction, autos, rubber, and steel come readily to mind as examples today.

Industries like electronics, finance, agriculture, professional services, and retail trade are dynamic, productive, and nonunion. Leading firms like Texas Instruments, Xerox, McDonald's, IBM, Michelin, and Sears are nonunion. Despite all the somber talk about the decline of American industrial competitiveness and managerial vigor, the bulk of the U.S. manufacturing industry fared very well in the late 1970s. From fashion goods to airplanes, computers, and even textiles, American industry enjoyed a tremendous export boom. Indeed, a merchandise export surplus of more than $20 billion each year with the Common Market is a problem in international economic policy. Surprisingly, much of the world is always begging for protection from U.S. mass production, pleading, "Protect us from the unfair competition of well-paid, efficient American workers who work with so much machinery that they flood our markets with vast amounts of cheap goods." Most U.S. industry is still highly competitive because hourly labor costs are not significantly higher than those in Japan, West Germany, or most of Northern Europe, yet output per hour of U.S. labor tends to be high. Low labor cost per unit output is a major factor attracting large amounts of foreign investment, including Japanese investment, into the United States. Political stability, of course, is another major reason for the attraction of the United States to foreign investors. Fortunately, this inflow has augmented a low rate of domestic capital formation in recent years.

Despite all the publicity, autos and steel are the exception, not the rule. Their contraction basically was the product of dramatic increases in the obstacles placed in their way by unions, government, and energy costs. Both autos and steel are saddled with union monopolies, with virtually no nonunion plants. Their labor costs skyrocketed in the 1970s, and the United Auto Workers and United Steelworkers also monopolized labor costs for many other suppliers to these two industries. The second factor is that the companies were forced by regulations to spend millions in precious capital to comply with the gusher of safety, energy, and environmental regulations spouted by Washington.

No matter how measured, labor costs in both auto and steel had risen to between 50% and 100% above the average in all manufacturing by 1980. Japanese and German auto and steel firms, though, had labor costs in the neighborhood of average U.S. manufacturing labor costs, or about $8.50 in hourly wages and $3 in fringes. U.S. auto companies now pay more than $21 an hour in wages and fringes (Chrysler has a cost advantage of about $1 an hour), or nearly double the U.S. manufacturing average of $11. Peter F. Drucker even claims that the Ford Motor Company pays $27 an hour, compared with other high-paying industries like chemicals, at only $15 an hour.[6] Table 7-1 shows official data on labor costs in motor vehicles, as well as monthly quit rates, compared with data from all manufacturing. The hourly premium in motor vehicles rose from 15% in the 1950s to 85% in 1981, while the quit rate remains below half that in manufacturing.

Yale Brozen has assembled detailed evidence to document the role of the United Steel Workers (USW) in the steel industry's malaise. Steel companies signed the Extended Negotiating Agreement (ENA) in 1973 because they found that resisting the USW negotiators gained them nothing. Each time the union was about to lose a strike, government officials would pressure industry to give union leaders what they wanted, in order to end the strike, and it made no economic sense to suffer through strikes that industry (consumers) could not win.

ENA effectively ended the use of strikes in steel in 1973, and steel labor costs then skyrocketed. In 1973 steel workers earned 46% more than the average in all manufacturing, as shown in Table 7-2. By 1980 the premium was 88%. In dollar terms, the premium over average labor costs in all manufacturing went from $2.40 to nearly $10.00 per hour. As Brozen wrote, "Modernization and trigger price mechanisms cannot cure the sickness of the steel industry. Labor costs must be brought under control."[7] The quit rate in steel is only one-third that in automobile manufacturing, and one-sixth that in all manufacturing.

Unions are clearly implicated in the demise of these once-great industries, although unions cannot assume "full credit" for their collapse. Regulatory costs also played a role, and this is common knowledge. Consider the chain of events when the government imposed airbrake standards on heavy-duty truck manufacturers. These businesses spent millions of dollars trying to comply, but their new products met a chilly reception with truck buyers: Chrysler discontinued Dodge heavy-duty trucks; Diamond Reo went bankrupt; Mack killed its husky Brockway division; White Motor went into bankruptcy; and AMC, builder of U.S. Army trucks, was taken over by Renault. More generally, in transportation equipment, Chrysler has been in the intensive care ward for some time, losing $3.4 billion from 1979 to 1981;

Table 7-1

Relationship Between Motor Vehicle and All-Manufacturing Employee Compensation for Wage Earners

	Average Hourly Earnings						Hourly Employment Costs[2]		
	Motor Vehicle		All Manufac- turing		Percent Premium[1]		Motor Vehicle	All Manufac- turing	Percent Premium[1]
Year	(BLS)		(BLS)						
	Hrs. paid	Hrs. wkd.	Hrs. paid	Hrs. wkd.	Hrs. paid	Hrs. wkd.	(GM)	(BLS)	
1952		$2.11	$1.65				$2.26	$1.96 (2.8)	15
1957		2.64	2.04				2.90	2.53 (1.6)	15
1958	$2.64		2.10		26		(0.5)	2.64 (1.1)	
1962	3.10	3.26	2.39	$2.55	30	28	3.71 (0.6)	2.85 (1.4)	30
1967	3.66	4.11	2.82	3.04	30	35	4.87 (1.3)	3.43 (2.3)	42
1972	5.35	6.00	3.82	4.14	40	45	7.58 (0.8)	4.84 (2.3)	57
1973	5.70	6.47	4.09	4.45	39	45	8.10 (1.0)	5.26 (2.8)	54
1974	6.23	7.20	4.42	4.83	41	49	9.52 (1.0)	5.75 (2.4)	66
1975	6.82	7.96	4.83	5.29	41	50	10.59 (0.6)	6.35 (1.4)	67
1976	7.45	8.72	5.22	5.72	43	52	11.23 (0.7)	6.92 (1.7)	62
1977	8.22	9.64	5.68	6.24	45	54	12.56 (0.3)	7.59 (1.6)	65
1978	8.98	10.56	6.17	6.79	46	56	13.76 (0.3)	8.31 (2.1)	66
1979	9.74	11.54	6.69	7.37	46	57	15.13 (0.7)	9.08 (2.0)	67
1980	10.66	13.34	7.20	8.02	48	66	18.44 (0.5)	9.92 (1.5)	86
1981	12.28	—	7.98	—	53	—	19.80 (0.6)	10.72 (1.3)	85
5/82 (p)	12.90	—	8.45	—	53	—	—	—	—

(p) Preliminary.

1. Percentage by which motor vehicle hourly earnings or compensation exceed the corresponding figures for all manufacturing.

2. Quit rate shown in parentheses (monthly quits per 100 employees in the motor vehicle industry and in all manufacturing).

Source: Yale Brozen, see Note 7, Chapter 7; based on U.S. Bureau of Labor Statistics, *Bulletin* 1312-11; *Employment and Earnings* (March 1982, June 1982). BLS stands for Bureau of Labor Statistics. Hourly employment costs are for General Motors production workers, *General Motors Annual Report.*

Table 7-2

Relationship Between Steel and All-Manufacturing Employee Compensation for Wage Earners

| | Average Hourly Earnings[1] | | | | Hourly Employment Costs[2] | | |
Year	Steel (BLS) (AISI)		All Manufac- turing (BLS)	Percent Premium[3] (BLS)	Steel (AISI)	All Manufac- turing (BLS)	Percent Premium[3]
1947	$1.44	$1.46	$1.22	18	$1.56		
1952	2.02	2.04	1.64	23	2.32	$1.96 (2.8)	18
1957	2.73	2.73	2.04	34	3.22	2.53 (1.6)	27
1962	3.29	3.33	2.39	38	4.16 (0.3)	2.85 (1.4)	46
1967	3.62	3.66	2.83	28	4.76 (0.8)	3.43 (2.3)	39
1972	5.15	5.22	3.81	35	7.08 (0.6)	4.84 (2.3)	46
1973	5.56	5.69	4.07	37	7.68 (0.9)	5.26 (2.8)	46
1974	6.38	6.55	4.40	45	9.08 (0.7)	5.75 (2.4)	58
1975	7.11	7.23	4.81	48	10.59 (0.2)	6.35 (1.4)	67
1976	7.87	8.00	5.19	51	11.74 (0.3)	6.92 (1.7)	70
1977	8.67	8.91	5.63	54	13.04 (0.4)	7.59 (1.8)	72
1978	9.70	9.98	6.17	57	14.30 (0.4)	8.31 (2.1)	72
1979	10.77	11.02	6.69	61	15.92 (0.4)	9.08 (2.0)	75
1980	11.84	12.11	7.27	63	18.45 (0.2)	9.92 (1.5)	86
1981	13.11	—	7.98	64	20.16 (0.2)	10.72 (1.3)	88
1982 (May)	13.75	—	8.45	63	23.40[4]	—	—

1. Does not include pay for holidays not worked or vacation pay.

2. Quit rate shown in parentheses (monthly quits per 100 employees). Employment cost includes holiday and vacation pay plus other employee benefits.

3. Percent by which steel hourly earnings or compensation exceed the corresponding figures for all manufacturing.

4. *Wall Street Journal,* October 6, 1982, p. 29.

Source: Yale Brozen, see Note 7, Chapter 7; based on U.S. Bureau of Laboar Statistics, *Bulletin* 1312-11; *Employment and Earnings* (March 1981, June 1982); U.S. Council on Wage and Price Stability, *Prices and Costs in the United States Steel Industry* (October 1977).

BLS data include all steel manufacturers in SIC 3312.

AISI data include only wage employees engaged in steel-producing operations.

Ford has been on the verge of outpatient status, and General Motors remains subject to contagion.

The steel industry, defined as the fifteen big steelmakers, has not been in much better shape than autos, but the market is proving its resilience once again in the form of so-called mini-mills. About sixty firms use cheap and abundant scrap steel, produce relatively simple products for predominantly local markets, and avoid the high labor and energy costs that plague the giant firms. Smaller firms don't need the enormous blast furnaces to melt iron ore or the complex pollution-control equipment required today. Most mini-mills, which tripled their output over the last decade and now produce about 15% of domestic steel shipments, pay wages below those stipulated in the basic steel agreement. Unionization efforts have been unsuccessful because the USW cannot match the prevailing combination of wages and job security. Nucor Corporation, based in Charlotte, North Carolina, for example, paid its average production worker $22,000 in 1979, not far below the average of $24,000 paid to those unionized steelworkers who had jobs that year, but Nucor has never laid off a worker. Compensation at Nucor depends on productivity: "We pay our workers to work," says Nucor president Kenneth Iverson, "and that's what they do."[8] Nucor is not burdened with the host of restrictive work rules in the USW basic steel contract, either.

Fringe Benefits

According to National Income Accounts, supplements to wages and salaries rose from 1% of all employee compensation in 1929 to 16% in 1981. Supplements include employer taxes for compulsory social insurance as well as payments for private health, welfare, pension, and insurance plans. When benefits like paid leave, vacations, holidays, sick leave, meals, and recreation facilities are added, fringe benefits generally total 30% or more of wages and salaries. A poll of 922 firms by the U.S. Chamber of Commerce for the year 1980, for instance, showed that companies spent an average of $5,500 per employee on benefits, nearly 37% of payroll.[9]

The trend toward payment in fringes means that more and more of each worker's pay comes in forms that restrict the ability of people to spend their wages, or save, invest, or provide for risks as they individually see fit. A private welfare system has emerged, primarily by political intent. Opinion-makers, politicians, and bureaucrats feel that since people do not pay and are not paid in the "proper way" in unrestricted labor markets, they must be encouraged into "responsible" patterns of expenditure. In a word, government is practicing paternalism. Skeptics, however, might like some evidence that government itself can spend wisely before it assumes the burden of directing citizens in their own spending.

The progressive income tax, rather than labor unions, plays the largest role in the growth of fringe benefits. When a business enterprise pays a dollar in cash wages, the worker pays income taxes on it; for example, a 25% marginal-tax bracket means that the dollar is worth only 75 cents to the employee. On the other hand, fringe benefits, at least those approved by the Internal Revenue Service, are nontaxable. If the employer purchases a dollar's worth of medical insurance for the worker, who values it at 80 cents, the employer is no worse off and the employee is better off. Fringe benefits expand, compared with cash wages, as a partial escape from the income tax, and the trend has accelerated as inflation has swept people into higher tax brackets. If this reasoning is correct, indexing the tax system against inflation, as promised in 1985, should restrain growth of fringe benefits, although no one has done a careful empirical study of this issue. Other factors promoting insurance as a fringe benefit, compared with individual purchase of insurance, are economies in administrative costs and avoidance of the so-called adverse selection problem—the phenomenon that insurance tends to attract buyers who expect to be heavy users of the insured services. Group purchases can permit an employer to cater to special groups and lower the cost of recruiting and holding workers as well. Building a racquetball court, for instance, could conceivably attract more workers than adding an equivalent sum to wages.

What role do unions play? Nobody really knows, and there is little empirical work on the question.[10] Three considerations can be mentioned. First, if unions raise wages, enterprises try to offset the raise by reducing nonwage payments. Union officials, therefore, contest management on all forms of working conditions and bargain for both wages *and* fringes. Second, if union officials are better judges of what workers want than are the personnel managers who simply talk with and observe workers, follow trends elsewhere, and cope with turnover, then labor representatives *might* reflect membership sentiment in demanding more amenities and financial insurance rather than higher wages. Third, and most important, negotiated fringes confer more power on union officials than do gains in wages. Higher paychecks seem routine, are paid directly by businesses to employees, and disappear from member consciousness as the product of "struggle" by union leaders. A union leader who thinks up a novel fringe benefit, however, and successfully negotiates it is very likely to earn plaudits, even public acclaim, as a benefactor of the worker. Less innocently, union leaders are likely to have far more financial control over benefit funds accumulated on behalf of workers (see Chapter 10). Even if most union leaders avoid the temptation to plunder the funds, members are in a subordinate position to union leaders, relative to direct cash payments. As the cliché goes, unionized employees have two bosses instead of one.

Impact on National Income

Unions reduce the real value of national income for the same reason that other cartels and monopolies do: they restrict supply, distort the structure of relative prices, and produce a misallocation of resources that reduces the level of national income. Employment, investment, and output are too small in the union sector and too large in the non-union sector because of union wages and fringes (that is, monopoly prices). In other words, if our economy behaves in a predominantly competitive way, unions cannot improve allocations by fortuitously offsetting monopsony power or other unspecified imperfections of markets. An efficient level of monopoly unionism is zero under free-market conditions.

The loss in national output due to distortions in resource allocation caused by union-nonunion wage differentials has been estimated at 0.33%,[11] or about $11 billion in a $3,200-billion economy. This traditional method of measuring welfare loss underestimates the social cost of union monopoly for three reasons: (1) it assumes that labor that is disemployed in the union sector due to high wages is completely re-employed in the nonunion sector without raising the average number of unemployed; (2) no account is taken of welfare losses due to union work restrictions; and (3) union transfers of purchasing power ("union rents") are not costless to extract from the rest of the economy. The last point is an especially serious source of underestimation because resources are consumed daily in order to achieve and maintain unionization of labor inputs. In the long run, the costs of competing for the additional earnings received by union members and union leaders would equal the value of the additional earnings due to unions; in other words, the result would be a complete waste of resources. The private rewards of unionism would be dissipated in the social costs of competition over the income.[12] A lower-bound estimate is that union rents from additional earnings and benefits exceed $30 billion per year. This assumes that the 26.8 million employees represented by all unions and employee associations have average annual earnings of only $12,500 and that the average union wage differential is only 10% (26.8 million × $12,500 × .10 = $33.5 billion). Actual figures are likely to be higher, so the estimate is conservative. If something like one-half of union rents are social costs, the loss in national income due to unions is about three times greater than $11 billion, and amounts to 1% of national income.

Unions indirectly destroy $30 billion of goods each year, as calculated above, through their economic effects, and if this entire amount were turned into useful goods and services, the income per person in the United States would rise by $110 per year, or roughly $440 per family of four. More realistically, we might hope to eliminate half of the annual waste of income caused by unionism.

The destruction of 1% of national income each year might seem small, but the estimate rests on lower-bound assumptions about the cost of unionism. The real cost of the promotion and imposition of unionism on the U.S. economy by the national government is probably considerably higher, although difficult to measure. My own unsubstantiated hunch is that real income would rise by 10% if the economic power of unions disappeared. Unionism discourages investment, innovation, and entrepreneurial risk-taking. The prospects for extraordinary returns are reduced, and the effects on the dynamics of the economy are substantial, although hard to estimate. The constant threat and fear of union strikes, disruption, and instability have untold potency in decreasing investment and productivity. The fear is more important than actual strikes because it is always there. People figure out various ways to get around unions, but no one can accurately predict how much human ingenuity would be released to reshape and multiply the national wealth if these obstacles to trade were reduced or eliminated.[13]

Labor's Share

Interest in labor's share of national income has a long and passionate history. Reputable economists have been interested in scientific explanations for the distribution of income by factor type ("functional shares") from the inception of economics as a separate discipline.

Classical economists like David Ricardo and Karl Marx believed income distribution, by factors, was the preeminent economic problem. They are succeeded by today's post-Keynesians who are especially abundant in Great Britain and enjoy small-minority status in the United States. The second impetus for concern over labor's share comes from assorted socialists, Marxists, labor economists, and unionists who have always believed that labor's share was too low, although most did not specify the "correct" percentage. Unionists, of course, have long insisted that they can raise labor's share at the expense of capital, that is, at the expense of people like the legendary widows, orphans, and fat cats who receive investment returns from rent, interest, and profits.

In an era of rising concern over whether private returns are too low to induce enough capital formation, much of the historical emphasis on raising labor's share is beginning to seem antiquated. The old emphasis on labor's share was largely a product of a mistaken mind set, in my judgment. A rise in labor's share necessarily reduces capital's share, and vice versa, because "shares" must add up to 100%. This kind of arithmetical approach to economic analysis commonly leads to serious errors in thought because it quickly slips into the assumption that output is an independent variable and that the economic problem is merely how to slice it up "fairly." In other words, the question is quickly transformed into: How can we raise labor's share closer to 100% in a zero-sum game? This approach emphasizes conflict rather than the sort of cooperation among labor and capital suppliers that actually generates output, and it falsely separates rewards from what happens in the production process. Its popularity on the political left is explained by the fact that such models lend themselves to political-power interpretations of the distribution of income. These theories usually have severe problems with the facts, though. For example, in 1933, at the depths of the Great Depression, the national income of $40 billion had a labor share of 74%, a proprietor's share of 14.5% (including farms); rent was 5.5%, interest 10.3%, and corporate profit was *minus* 4.3%. The power of labor, by such a theory, apparently was at an all-time high relative to that of corporations, whose owners lost $1.7 billion that year while labor received $29.5 billion.

Belief in political models of factor shares stems from a period when it was slightly more credible to divide people into separate classes labeled "capitalists," "proletarians," and "landowners," who were rich, poor, and rich respectively, and who depended exclusively on profits, wages, and rental incomes respectively. These class views still permeate the culture and politics of poor countries around the world, where miserably low levels of national income ordinarily have labor shares of 50% or less, relatively high land shares, and relatively high interest rates and high returns to other forms of very scarce capital.[14] In high-income countries like the United States, labor's share is 80%, employee pension funds constitute 30% of corporate ownership, and the relevance of Marxist models of distribution is zero.

Moreover, once factor incomes by type are no longer directly linked to "the poor" or "the rich," percentages tell us little. Suppose labor received 1% of national income and owners of various forms of capital got the remaining 99%. Would it matter? It might be a very agreeable and egalitarian society, by accepted norms, if everybody owned capital and ownership shares happened to be relatively evenly distributed. In blunter language, when people complain about shares, they usually mean they want more income. Somebody with 50% of $100 is not happier with 60% of $10 instead. As the old saw has it, you can't eat percentages.

National income is *net* income from production, or GNP minus an allowance for capital depreciation. Effectively, national income is the maximum a society can consume without diminishing its stock of productive goods. Historically, labor's share of this income has risen about 10 percentage points in the United States since the beginning of the century.[15] Although it is not logically impossible that unions played a role in the rise, a number of economic studies conducted up to the early 1960s could find no significant effect of unionism. As Rees has said, "no union effect can be discovered with any consistency."[16] The main reason for the rise in labor's share was the shift from unincorporated enterprise, especially farming, into government and corporate employment where labor is paid by wages and salaries. A host of other complex developments were involved, though, including changes in the relative quantities, qualities, and prices of human and physical capital. Overall, labor and capital shares in any period are the outcome of an immense number of market transactions under gradually changing circumstances, and no single explanation can account for such a complex aggregate result.

Can unionists raise the relative wages of their members and yet fail to raise labor's share of national income? Yes. Unions do not necessarily raise labor's share in unionized industries, much less in the entire economy. When unions impose higher wage rates, managements use more labor-saving equipment and fewer labor hours per unit of output, so the wage bill rises less than proportionately. Outlays on wages may actually decline if substitutions for union labor are extensive—that is, if the elasticity of demand for union labor exceeds one. If wage rates rise by 10% and employment falls 12%, then wage outlays shrink. Moreover, greater use of capital per unit of output means larger outlays on equipment, so there is no guarantee that higher union wages increase labor's share of income in unionized industries. Systematic studies on pre-1960 data found no association between the degree of unionization and labor's share of industry income.[17]

We have now reached a point in economic thought where few people are concerned about labor's share being too low. On the contrary, some business analysts, economists, and even politicians are concerned that the ratio of labor income to total income may have risen so high that it threatens productivity and capital formation. Inflation and rapid growth in federal taxation, spending, deficits, and regulations have cut the rates of saving and capital formation, and wasted much investment, but labor pricing and costs have played an important role in our productivity difficulties, too. No one can currently assess, with any degree of conviction, the role that unions might play in driving up labor's share in specific cases, but the attempt should be made. We can safely call for more research on the question.

Peter F. Drucker argues that, once labor receives between 80% and 85% of income (value added) in a company, industry, or national economy, productivity falls and makes capital formation difficult, while an 85% or 90% labor–income ratio makes it impossible.[18] His ratios are not implied by a strict economic model; they are only plausible empirical generalizations. Perhaps more impressively, Drucker points to countries where labor income accounts for more than 85% of income—Britain, the Netherlands, Belgium, and Scandinavia—and they are in deep trouble. The Germans and Japanese by contrast have labor–income ratios of 70% to 75%. Labor–income ratios seem more important than the proportion of income redistributed through government transfers, because in Germany the transfer ratio is high and in Japan it is low. The U.S. is not really high among high income countries in transfer ratio or in labor–income ratio, but Drucker argues that some of our key industries, especially autos and steel, have high labor–income ratios.

Whether he is right about the importance of labor–income ratios for recent situations in the U.S. or elsewhere remains to be seen. The argument is impeccable in the limit: if labor received 100%, no one, including workers, would invest. But it is an empirical question if some industries or countries currently exceed some realistic threshold to labor's share and if unions play a crucial role in this stagnation process. This is an important issue and more systematic studies are needed to identify the role of unions and the role of labor income in the factors causing stagnation. Only then can we reliably judge their relative importance. In the meantime, wouldn't it be ironic if socialists in the U.S., Britain, and Scandinavia admitted that a decrease in labor's share, conceivably, could be necessary to raise the standard of living for the common man? Not a very likely admission, I suppose.

Distributing the Burden

The question of who bears the burden of union wage gains and productivity restriction is difficult—nay, impossible—to answer with precision. My own guess is that the reduction in national income, like taxes, is borne by all citizens, roughly in accord with the degree to which they participate in the market economy as consumers and factor suppliers. The problem of precise determination is analytically equivalent to finding out who pays for the corporate income tax: Do investors, employees, managers, or customers suffer the loss of income due to the tax? The difference between union compensation and competitively determined pay can be thought of as a tax, a private tax disguised as a payment for the real market services of union members. In principle, investors can suffer some of the loss through a lower rate of return, nonunion employees through lower relative wages, and consumers through higher relative prices for union-produced goods and services, but the exact effects are difficult to trace. Most economists emphasize nonunion workers as the primary victims of union wages. Surprisingly, however, economists do not agree as to who shoulders the burden of the corporate income tax, and this question has received far more attention than the effect of union pricing has. On theoretical grounds, *corporate* investors are not especially exploitable by unionists because investment is always diverted to where returns are the highest, over the long run, whether here or abroad, whether in corporate or noncorporate investment. Under certain assumptions, however, capital owners in general bear the burden through a lower private return on all capital throughout the economy, including returns on home ownership. The crucial assumption is that the aggregate stock of national investment is independent of the private rate of return, in the relevant range, rather than being depressed by the lower returns caused by unionism.

In terms of the effect of union gains on the personal distribution of earnings among households, unions, if anything, have caused slightly more inequality. Although unions tend to compress the range of earnings among their own memberships, unions raise wages for workers who would be better-paid anyway, at the expense of the worker in the nonunion sector and at the expense of the general consumer, both of whom have lower average incomes than union workers (see Chapter 4). The poor, the disadvantaged, and the unemployed who are beaten by organized workers in picket lines are proof enough of what friends the poor have in unions.

The difference between union wage rates and free market wages need not go to union members either. Although most increases in labor costs go to members, union officials can capture shares of the union monopoly position in three ways. First, union members can receive the union wage, but leaders can impose dues, fees, and assessments that reduce the net wage to competitive levels. Second, union officials can extract illegal kickbacks from employed members, a practice that amounts to auctioning off scarce union jobs. The third method is to negotiate competitive wage rates and collect money directly from employers (kickbacks, shakedowns). Techniques include so-called sweetheart contracts and tampering with union-administered pension and welfare funds. The three methods are used in varying degrees, depending on the costs of using each method, the probability of detection, the probability of internal union opposition, and the chances of prosecution. The temptation for union officials to exploit these opportunities is great and always present. Union leaders are properly praised for honesty and integrity on retirement because there are so few built-in incentives for responsibility in union leadership, relative to incentives in other occupations. Honest union leaders are honest in the face of strong temptation.

The Teamsters provide a good example of a union whose leaders have succumbed to temptation. The National Master Freight Agreement, which is supposed to cover all trucking and related freight operations in most parts of the country, seems to have been designed to tempt people to make sweetheart deals. Wages and benefits specified in the agreement are so high and work rules so restrictive that it fosters the hope—and correctly gives the impression—that individual employers can be let off the hook. Eugene R. Boffa, Sr., a convicted bank swindler from New Jersey who has connections with Teamsters leaders, runs two labor-leasing companies that supply truck drivers who receive wages, benefits, and working conditions far below the master freight agreement. Teamster officials apparently remain unconcerned about undercutting wages. Mr. Boffa gets a fee of 8% to 10% of wage and benefit payments, a fee that can easily amount to hundreds of thousands of dollars a year for a single firm. Boffa's clients have included J. C. Penney, International Paper, Avon, Monsanto, and Inland Container. Companies that deal with Boffa are free from grievances, picket lines, and visits from Teamsters business agents. Mr. Boffa provided *The Wall Street Journal* with a copy of the contract his firm signed with Iowa Beef Processors in 1972. Average earnings were 9 cents per mile when the National Master wage for the area was 14.4 cents per mile; fringe benefits also were much lower than those specified in the National Master Agreement.[19] In August 1981 a federal judge sentenced Boffa to 20 years in prison and fined him $47,000 for two counts of violating the Racketeer Influenced and Corrupt Organization Act through his labor-leasing enterprises.[20] Boffa's son, Robert, was sentenced to twelve years in prison and fined $24,000. Meanwhile, members of PROD, a dissident group in the Teamsters, hope to reform the union, a dim prospect at best.

Unemployment

No two statistics receive more attention in Washington each month that the unemployment rate and the consumer price index (CPI). The general perception of whether a government's economic policies are succeeding or failing often rides on decimal-point changes, up or down, in the unemployment rate and the CPI, or rate of inflation, as it is called.

Many people appear to believe that unions are responsible for inflation and that government is to blame for unemployment. The truth is probably closer to the reverse: government is responsible for inflation and unions are responsible for unemployment. Unionists constantly advertise their deep concern for the suffering of the unemployed, and they lobby for more government programs to support the unemployed, yet unions and union-supported measures are major obstacles to expanding employment opportunities and diminishing unemployment. Unions add to measured unemployment in four ways: (1) union pricing, (2) work rules, (3) disruptions directly reducing employment opportunities and efficiency in our economy, and (4) politically pressuring government to expand its income-support mechanisms, which indirectly increases unemployment. Rises in unemployment also intensify political pressures to inflate the money supply, government spending, and job programs, thereby creating the classic inflation-unemployment dilemma.

The obvious way that unions create unemployment is by pricing labor out of work. Hourly wage costs of $20 add up quickly. A medium-sized building contractor with a crew of one hundred has labor costs of $16,000 per day at these prices. No wonder he employs labor sparingly and wants a high rate of output from the labor he uses. High union wages do not *necessarily* increase official unemployment permanently, because labor excluded from unionized employment can drop out of the labor force or seek employment in the nonunion sector. Dropping out means returning to housework, going to school or enrolling in a training program, enlisting in the military, retiring, going on welfare, or resorting to stealing and other forms of crime. The primary alternative to limited employment opportunities in the unionized sector, however, is employment in the nonunion sector, where relative wages are probably 6% lower due to the distorted allocation of labor and capital.[21]

Union pricing tends to increase the average level of unemployment among nonunion workers, although the size of the effect is unknown. The average level of unemployment among union members also is higher because of inflexibility in union pricing, especially when demand slackens in unionized industries and downward adjustment of wages is forestalled by contractual inflexibility. When unemployment among union members reaches 50%, even union officials seem to be willing to soften it by making wage concessions. These cases are not well publicized by unions, which pretend that they protect members against wage cuts, but cuts do occur. UAW delays in scheduled wage increases at Chrysler are well known, but *Monthly Labor Review* has also cited numerous examples of wage cuts by, for instance, meat cutters and retail clerks in southern Ohio and northern Kentucky (May 1979, p. 57), bricklayers in New York City (January 1979, p. 44), plumbers in the state of Washington (November 1977, p. 56), and plumbers in Florida (July 1977, p. 53). Naturally, unemployment rises to disastrous levels before union officials admit their error in gauging market demand for their members' services or admit that unionism cannot create the desired level of wealth for its members. Wage-cutting and concessions by unions during the 1981–82 recession became so widespread that they acquired the name "givebacks." Yet labor remains vastly overpriced in many sectors. In the state of Michigan, for example, well over half a million people (approximately 640,000 officially) were unemployed on a typical day in 1982, yet unions imposed labor costs of $21 an hour on many manufacturers. Although large numbers of qualified production people are available at lower prices, U.S. auto manufacturers suffer a $1,500 labor cost disadvantage per car relative to Japanese producers.

The nonprice effects of unionism also decrease employment in unionized industries and raise general unemployment. Work rules, restrictions, and featherbedding described in Chapter 4 create unreported unemployment of union workers on the job because they have more "down time" and are less effectively deployed at the work place. Strikes and boycotts also disrupt production, not only among direct disputants but indirectly in other firms, thus raising the average level of unemployment and decreasing efficiency in our economy. Union price and nonprice actions in the marketplace raise reported and actual unemployment in our economy, although the total effect may add little more than one percentage point to the reported unemployment rate. However, given the fact that one percentage point is over 1 million people and that various welfare programs are tied to the unemployment rate, sometimes by explicit "triggering" mechanisms, one percentage point may account for untold billions in additional government expenditure. For example, if each additional unemployed person cost the taxpayers only $400 per month, government expenditures would rise by $400 million per month, or $4.8 billion per year.

Recessions and depressions before the 1930s in the United States were short-lived because sellers, including labor unions and workers, had to accommodate themselves to new demand conditions if they wanted to continue working, producing, selling, and eating. Prices and wages adjusted themselves to market-clearing levels because there was not much choice. This flexibility allowed full employment production to revive more quickly. Today we have elaborate income-support mechanisms supplied by the modern welfare state, which bears a large part of the blame for slow adjustment in prices and wage rates whenever a spending slowdown occurs. Government offers a variety of cash and noncash benefits to the jobless; therefore, people are not so pressured by economic conditions to accept lower wages or less prestigious employment in order to get and keep work. Finding work is not so urgent in a welfare state. Enterprises also have an incentive to lay off employees rather than reduce their hours when labor demand temporarily declines. Supplementary unemployment benefits for some union members provide a whopping 90% of regular take-home pay, and workers sometimes use their seniority in order to be laid off for an "unemployment holiday." Harvard economist Martin Feldstein, now chairman of the President's Council of Economic Advisers, contends that half of all temporary layoffs are the direct result of the incentives of unemployment insurance.[22]

The U.S. Department of Labor proudly says that unemployment insurance tends to prevent the "breakdown of labor standards." "Labor standards" is the bureaucracy's phrase for wage and working conditions, so an accurate translation into economic terms is that paying people to be unemployed keeps excess labor off the market and makes wages of those who are working higher than they otherwise would be. This is another example of the common confusion between wage rates and labor earnings. Unfortunately, postponing wage adjustments is no way to revive employment or production or to cure unemployment and inflation. John Maynard Keynes recognized this point when he declared, "There is no positive means of curing unemployment except by restoring to employers a proper margin of profit."[23]

A recent study by Professors Benjamin and Kochin analyzed unemployment in Britain from 1921 to 1938 when it averaged 14% and never fell below 9.5%.[24] Keynes found that hard to explain, and it led him to a new theory of aggregate demand deficiency that still rules the economic policies of Western governments. Benjamin and Kochin, however, found that the reserve army of the unemployed was made up largely of volunteers, attracted into unemployment by the highest benefits relative to wages in British history. German unemployment compensation followed a similar path. Instituted in 1927 to replace a national relief program, compensation during the late twenties and early thirties was about as generous as Britain's and a 45% unemployment rate in Germany was more related to the dole than to a world depression. The Scandinavian countries and Belgium had the same experiences. Grubel and Walker confirm the relationship between jobless pay and unemployment in contemporary studies of nine countries.[25] The moral is that if the cost of any activity (including unemployment) is reduced, we get more of it.

Outlays on unemployment programs have risen sharply in recent years, with spending of over $20 billion per year, and federal unemployment programs have proliferated to include Unemployment Compensation for Federal Employees, Veterans Readjustment Assistance Act, Unemployment Compensation for Ex-Servicemen, Federal Supplemental Benefits, Supplemental Unemployment Assistance, Extended Benefits, and special programs for unemployment attributed to imports (Trade Adjustment Assistance Act), or deregulation. The political question is this: What groups, aside from the federal bureaucracy administering these programs, are pressuring to expand them? We know it is not the general public because surveys of public attitudes show that the public is very skeptical about the wisdom of cash payments to the jobless. The public believes that unemployment compensation is a program to subsidize loafers, and a majority of every population group consistently favors making unemployment insurance laws stricter.[26] In a rare popular referendum, the CIO, after failing to gain the liberalization which it wanted from the Ohio legislature, took its cause to the voters in 1955 and lost by a two-to-one vote.[27]

The interest group pressuring legislators to liberalize coverage, benefits, and duration is made up basically of unionists. They favor more federal control of the state-administered systems, higher benefits, national uniformity in standards, and extended duration of benefits, and they oppose experience-rated taxes that allow enterprises with fewer layoffs to pay less in unemployment taxes. We need not look far for the reasons. Union membership is concentrated in sectors of the economy where demand is relatively cyclical, which essentially means industries that produce durable goods or directly depend on them for their sales; 54% of union membership is in manufacturing and construction, which only have 30% of all nonagricultural employment. Furthermore, high benefits and a distorted allocation of unemployment taxes reward unions and penalize nonunion enterprises. Unemployed union members receiving unemployment benefits also have the right to reject employment that pays less than union scale on the grounds that it is "unsuitable."

Unionists would like the incomes of organized workers secured from interruptions by strikes and other labor disputes. Strikers are not generally eligible for unemployment compensation, although there are subterfuges that allow unionists partially to circumvent the administrative restrictions. In New York State and Rhode Island, however, strikers may receive unemployment compensation after a strike is eight weeks old. Bell Telephone lost its suit against these laws in the U.S.

Supreme Court—*New York Tel. Co.* v. *New York St. Dept. Labor* (98 S. Ct. 1328 [1979]) after arguing that the company would effectively be paying its own employees to strike because the company was liable for higher unemployment taxes after the $49 million in claims paid to its strikers during a 7-month strike in 1971. Strikers also became eligible for benefits under the federal railroad program 1 January 1953, and the railroad companies were forced to pay out more than $53 million to help finance strikes against themselves between 1953 and 1972.[28]

Strikers have access to welfare payments, food stamps, and private charities like the United Fund, although no one has published a recent estimate of the full extent of these payments. In 1972 Thieblot and Cowin estimated the public welfare support of strikers at $329 million yearly, excluding unemployment compensation, and the authors concluded that "public welfare support is widely available to strikers, that its use is already substantial, and that its use is growing rapidly."[29] To cite specific instances, the General Motors strike of 1970 involved 330,000 workers who received an estimated $30 million in public aid. In 1960 approximately half a million steel workers held out for 116 days because they received about $45 million in welfare and unemployment benefits from government sources. I.W. Abel, then secretary-treasurer of the Steelworkers Union, said that the money "made the strike endurable. The sum exceeded by far the amount that the union poured into the districts and the locals."[30]

The AFL-CIO produces a steady stream of literature supporting welfare payments to strikers, arguing, for example, that taxpayers' dollars are used to feed criminals in prison and to provide food, shelter, and clothing for enemy prisoners of war. Are fellow Americans engaged in industrial warfare entitled to less? they ask, adding that it has never been the American tradition to starve those with whom we disagree.[31] Ironically, one judge recently used exactly this kind of language to describe the control of Laborers' Union officials over the livelihoods of its members.[32] In another example of union support for welfare payments to strikers, unionist James Compton described the union victory at General Electric this way: "one of the key contributions to the strike's success was that of the AFL-CIO Department of Community Services and its hundreds of local strike committees, which...showed the way in drawing upon the resources of federal, state and local welfare agencies...in producing food and financial aid for the strikers and their families."[33] The payment of food stamps to strikers has been discussed extensively in Congress, but no one knows how widespread it is because the U.S. Department of Agriculture has not published its studies.

England has gone farther in providing strikers with routine state benefits, although the incidence of reported strikes is lower in Britain than in the U.S.[34] The rationale offered by John Gennard to justify government financing of strikers is interesting, if conventional. Gennard claims that strikers are an economically weak party in labor disputes, that governments have a public duty to support weak groups against the strong, and therefore, that a "policy of State *neutrality* in strikes would involve *active intervention* to ensure the employer and the employed could bring equal power to bear in their bargaining." A book reviewer aptly called this argument "a bit of sophistry," but unfortunately such sentimentality and woolly sympathy form the intellectual foundation of labor policy.[35] Public financing of strikers means that the general public pays twice for industrial disputes, once in the form of additional taxes and again in higher relative prices and lower output of union-made goods. Welfare recipients who are not strikers also tend to suffer from fewer welfare funds after consumption by strikers, unless the political process completely makes up the difference at taxpayer expense.

The overall percentage point or so rise in the unemployment rate caused by unionism can be put into perspective by comparing the situation in the labor market to that in agriculture. Governmental action raises the prices of some farm products, creating a surplus or glut. Government then steps in to act as a buyer of last resort through various devices such as storage programs, crop loans, overseas sales and gifts ("dumping"). In labor markets, government intervenes to raise the price of labor through support of labor unions and direct wage-fixing, which causes higher unemployment (labor surplus or glut). Then there is political pressure for government to act as employer of last resort, to subsidize the jobless, and so on. Some of the government spending alleviates the human suffering caused by union pricing and wage-fixing, but ultimately it is the formula for stagflation. It is a nice illustration of Brozen's law: If you perceive a problem for which government regulation seems needed, further examination will reveal that some existing government regulation is responsible for the problem.

Although unions are implicated in the unemployment problem, any discussion of unemployment is not complete without recognition that the bulk of unemployment reflects ordinary turnover. Although nobody knows exactly how much unemployment is "normal," most unemployment in the range of 4% to 7% represents individual mobility, free choice, and routine adjustment to new circumstances. Labor services are resources, just like capital goods, apartments, and other services whose owners adjust to new circumstances and have unemployment rates of 4% to 7%. When the U.S. unemployment rate is 6%, more than 6 million people are unemployed, but this hardly means that 6 million families experience long periods without a paycheck, a picture often painted by unionists and other collectivists to indict the failures of capitalism. They attribute all failures to free-market capitalism, of course, despite the fact that we have a mixed or interventionist system in which there are many potential sources of failure, especially in the form of government and unions. Must government create more jobs in the private and/or public sector so that the 6 million unemployed may find work?

The truth is that for the majority of people unemployment represents a brief period between jobs, or between school or housework and a job. Although it is unfashionable to say so, it is not hard to find work. The inflow of millions of people from Mexico, Latin America, and Asia totally falsifies the contention that there are not enough jobs here. There is an infinite amount of work to do. To say there are not enough jobs is misleading; speakers really mean that there are not enough attractive, well-paid, "decent American" jobs. These attractive jobs are not so easy to find, and people, therefore, pass up opportunities to mow lawns and do "stoop-labor" because they expect to locate more attractive alternatives. Much unemployment can be described as unpaid employment in production of information about available work, or else paid leisure from unemployment benefits.

Of the 8 million unemployed in a typical month, 4 million accept job offers within 4 weeks, but the level of reported unemployment does not decline a bit because a new stream of 4 million people simultaneously begins the searches for employment. The bulk of this unemployment is by choice, reflecting the confidence people have that they will shortly find acceptable jobs. About 60% of the unemployed are between jobs, and the remaining 40% are entering the labor force for the first time or reentering after a long absence. The unemployment process can be compared to a bathtub with an open faucet and an open drain. The water level represents the unemployed in any month. It remains at the same level, but it is a constantly changing group of people. New job seekers flow in, and, after a time, most flow out to new jobs. Ironically, although 7 to 8 million are unemployed in any month, over 30 million experience some unemployment during an entire year. Most unemployment does not involve long-term hardship, however, because only 5% of the jobless, about 400,000 people, remain unemployed as long as 6 months. Some people casually look for a job now and then, others seek part-time work. People under age 25 make up half of the reported unemployed. Others refuse job offers in the belief that they will find a better position, and others receive generous unemployment checks. In sum, unions contribute to measured unemployment, though perhaps they are not the main cause; but unions are also culpable for producing more discouraged workers, dropouts from the labor force, and welfare dependents missed by the conventional unemployment statistic.

8

New Unionism in the Public Sector

Striking firemen in Anderson, Indiana, the state's eighth largest city, refused to respond to a fire which raced through a downtown city block, causing damage estimated in the hundreds of thousands of dollars. Volunteers rushing to the scene were delayed by picket lines.
—Associated Press, August 1978

Settlement of an 8-week teacher strike in St. Louis came after Missouri Governor Joseph Teasdale made $1.4 million available for teacher salaries from State funds, and city businesses pledged up to $600,000 to help cover any deficit.
—Monthly Labor Review, May 1979

Although private-sector unionism has been the nearly exclusive object of attention in the preceding chapters, public-employee unionism is a central source of controversy in the 1980s, and we now turn to an analysis of unions and collective bargaining in government.

Unions and employee associations in the public sector have virtually exploded from 1 million members in 1960 to about 6 million in 1980. Back in 1960 total civilian employment was 2.4 million in the federal government and 6.4 million in state and local government, and only 11% of all government employees were unionized. More than half of them were in postal unions. By 1980, however, the unionized percentage jumped to nearly 45% in a considerably larger work force of 2.8 million federal and 12.6 million state and local employees.[1] The fourfold gain in the proportion of public employees in unions is as dramatic as the gain in the private-sector unions between 1933 and 1945. The new explosion has not been digested yet because it was so recent, rapid, and nonviolent compared with the experience of the thirties and forties.

Although work stoppages increased in the public sector from thirty-six in 1960 to an average of four hundred per year during the 1970s, strike incidence still is below that in the private sector. (See Table 8-4.)

There is little doubt about the new size of public employee unionism. Government employees represent nearly one of every three organized workers today. The National Education Association is the second largest national union, with membership estimated at more than 1.6 million members of the nation's 2.2 million teachers. The NEA has one of every four public employee union members. The American Federation of Teachers claims another 450,000 members. The American Federation of State, County, and Municipal Employees' 750,000 members merged with the New York Civil Service Employees Association's 260,000 members to form the fifth largest national union in 1978. The AFL-CIO belatedly formed a Public Employees Department in November 1974. Unionization has spread among such traditionally nonunion and professional workers as police officers and college faculty members. By 1978 one of every four of the nation's 540,000 faculty members was represented by a union, and various estimates placed union membership among the nation's 680,000 police officers at 50%. Overall, private-sector union membership declined from 24% to below 17% of the total work force from 1958 to 1976 while government union membership grew from 1.3% to nearly 6% of the total work force.[2] It is the new unionism.

Explaining the Growth

We do not have to look far to find an explanation for the burst of unionism in government employment. As described in Chapter 5, the Wagner Act of 1935 specifically excluded government employees from its coverage, no doubt with the view that only private employers abused their helpless employees, but President John F. Kennedy signed Executive Order 10988 in January 1962 to promote unionism in the federal bureaucracy. Kennedy had received considerable campaign support from unions. Based on the National Labor Relations Act (NLRA), his order declared that "the efficient administration of the government and the well-being of employees require that orderly and constructive relationships be maintained between employee organizations and management." Note that the language did not say "orderly relationship between employees and managers" but "between *employee organizations* and management." The order set up procedures for determination of bargaining units and recognition for unions, compelled agency heads to bargain in good faith, and specified unfair labor practices for unions and management. The order was less generous than the NLRA in that it prohibited strikes, union shops, and other forms of compulsory unionism, established no separate NLRB-type agency, required that agreements conform to civil service regulations, and required a statement of management rights in every contract. But it was a beginning.

The state of Wisconsin had enacted bargaining legislation in 1959 to cover all employees of local governments, but Kennedy's executive order triggered a series of bargaining laws in states like Michigan, New York, Washington, and Pennsylvania, which have substantial unionism in the private sector. At last count, only a dozen states, mostly in the South and West, did not have some kind of mandatory bargaining law to promote public employee unions.

The General Issue

The use of union power in government is still a subject of intense controversy, and is likely to remain so during the foreseeable future. Union lobbyists continue to push for more favorable legislation because the laws vary across states and none, including the federal orders, is as favorable to unions as the Wagner Act. Legislation urged by the NEA and the Municipal Employees such as the Clay Bill, goes beyond the Wagner Act by ordering every governmental unit to obey an NLRB-like national board, which would enforce a national labor law authorizing a long list of privileges, including monopoly status for a union without secret ballot elections, authorizing strikes of public employees, and so forth. Currently, the Federal Labor Relations Authority (FLRA) acts as a mini-NLRB to decide disputes between union officials and their government counterparts. Stanley McFarland, director of government relations for the NEA, has said that the NEA "is looking for something like a National Labor Relations Board at the federal level to handle state and local government–management labor disputes."[3] Under such a system, according to McFarland, collective bargaining would be the same everywhere in the country. Given the success of NEA in gaining a U.S. Department of Education with a $14-billion annual budget in 1979, the odds of a national labor law for state and local governments are certainly greater than zero. Constitutionality would be a question, but it was for the Wagner Act, too.

Unionists base their arguments on two contentions: (1) government is just another industry whose employees deserve union protection, and (2) public employees have been denied equal protection of the law. Ralph Flynn, for example, refers to "the plight of 14 million American workers who are *not* protected by the Wagner Act: the employees of our federal, state, and local governments."[4] The late George Meany referred to second-class citizenship and claimed that public employee unions should not be denied the "right" to bargain collectively because there is no significant difference between private and public employment.

Opponents of unions in the public sector argue that public employees should be excluded from Wagner-type bargaining laws because government is *not* just another industry. Differences can be grouped into six categories, with three differences in kind—sovereignty, taxation, and the "necessity" of certain governmental services—and three differences in degree from the private sector—fixity of location, civil service privileges, and managerial incentives.[5]

Sovereignty

The issue of sovereignty is nicely posed by a pair of quotations, the first by Franklin D. Roosevelt (1937) and the second by George Meany (1974):

> A strike of public employees manifests nothing less than an intention on their part to obstruct the operations of government until their demands are satisfied. Such action looking toward the paralysis of government by those who have sworn to support it is unthinkable and intolerable.

> Certainly, it's against the law to strike the civil service, but it's AFL-CIO policy to ignore those laws...You stop the job. You shut it down. You take the consequences, and you fight. And if the guy happens to be the mayor of a city or the governor of a state, it doesn't make a damn bit of difference.

Sovereignty means the supreme and unchallengeable power of compulsion. A genuine sovereign cannot be *forced* to do something by a private person or agency and still remain sovereign. Whoever can force government authorities to submit to his will *is government,* so the contradiction between governmental sovereignty and collective bargaining is clear and simple: Who's in charge? Government cannot claim to exercise supreme authority within a limited sphere and yet allow private groups to forcibly shut its operations down.

Many instances of this contradiction have been played out in conflicts between government and unions during strikes, but my favorite example also illustrates Lenin's concept of the strategic minority. During the spring of 1979, a well-organized group of 1,300 computer operators and clerks in selected offices went on strike, representing more than 350,000 members of two civil service unions in Great Britain. With so few on strike, the union's strike funds of $2.6 million guaranteed their full salaries for four months while other members continued working and replenishing the fund.

Strike targets were selected with great thoughtfulness. About 150 computer operators in Customs and Excise halted collection of hundreds of millions of dollars per week in the value-added tax (the national sales tax), thereby cutting off a major source of income to the government. Cipher operators in the Foreign Office, who code and decode messages to and from embassies, crippled London's ability to communicate with its foreign embassies. Clerical workers shut down the courts of sessions and the sheriff's courts in Scotland, all but halting the wheels of justice in Scotland. Computer operators shut down "Ernie," the computer at the Department for National Savings that pays prizes to winners in a government lottery and pays people who want to cash in their government savings bonds. Strikers delayed payments of $90 per pig to farmers whose pigs were killed by disease, but avoided hitting computers that processed checks to the elderly, poor, or sick—which might have provoked an antiunion backlash. The response of Margaret Thatcher, then Conservative party leader, was to suggest negotiating no-strike agreements with groups of important workers in exchange for special wage arrangements.

There is a certain irony in the unionization of public employees. After all, government originally sanctioned union threats and force against enterprises and nonunion workers in the private sector, and now unions are prepared to do the same against government itself. What is good for the goose may not be good for the gander (no doubt because it is good for neither). Governments that submit to coercive strikes necessarily govern with the forbearance of labor officials, an unhappy arrangement that cannot be viable in the long run.

Taxation

The second difference between government and the private sector is that most government services are paid for by general taxes. Taxpayers are forced to pay, whether they want the services or not. In the private sector, buyers have the option of not buying the good or service, or else buying it from someone else. No private enterprise (except unions) can extract revenues by force; enterprises must cater to buyers by means of voluntary exchange. Union power in the private sector is also constrained by management's incentive to hold down costs and stay competitive. Enterprises whose labor costs balloon out of line cannot survive in the marketplace.

Governments do not face the same market pressure for efficiency. In principle, they can cover the costs of generous union settlements by raising taxes or by reducing government services. Yet state and local governments do not have the bottomless purse of the federal government because taxpayers can move out of a city, county, or state more easily than they can move out of the nation. The economic base erodes if taxes become oppressive, as it did in New York City. The next political step is to resort to federal guarantees and subsidies in order to gain access to the federal printing press. New York City is an example, and Britain and Italy are major instances of this kind of governmental spending pressure that was partly due to generous wage settlements with unions. Local responsibility for spending has gradually eroded in the United States, too, because intergovernmental transfers from the federal to state and local governments now exceed $80 billion per year, though the Reagan administration has restrained growth in these outlays.

The union issue might be termed taxation without representation. Unionists effectively say that the government (ultimately the taxpayers) is not paying them enough and that they intend to force government to pay them more. If there is not enough money, raise taxes, they say. If the government tries to hire replacements to perform services, organized workers physically try to prevent it. Even if some replacements work, they sometimes must be fired after the strike because retaining them constitutes an "unfair labor practice." Strikers quit and yet do not quit because they have a permanent grip on their jobs, and hence on the taxpayers. The tax problem is especially visible when compulsory arbitration is used to settle labor disputes in the public sector. Compulsory arbitration involves calling a third party in to dictate a settlement to the disputing parties, a procedure often linked with a no-strike clause. These settlements sometimes are thrown out by the courts because they allow a private party, not accountable to the public, to dictate a major determinant of taxes, namely, the pay of government employees. The wage bill approaches 50% of state and local government spending and as much as 80% of some agency budgets. Consider, for the sake of illustration, that if taxes equal expenditures (balanced budget) and are spent exclusively for employee compensation, and if compensation per employee is decided by an arbitrator, then government could control its spending only by changing the number of employees. Even this avenue of adjustment is closed in many instances because layoffs, force reductions, and employment levels are also subject to binding arbitration. At least nineteen states have compulsory arbitration as a final step in public bargaining disputes. Most of these arbitration laws have been upheld in the courts, but courts in California, Utah, South Dakota, Connecticut, and Colorado have declared them unconstitutional delegations of legislative authority to private individuals.

Necessity of Certain Government Services

Government at all levels spends 40% of national income, and governmental activity on such a scale cannot be entirely "necessary." We got along with 10% or less up through the 1920s. A great deal of activity involves regulatory, bookkeeping, and administrative functions within the civil service, activities that have little direct value to citizens. In fact, if unions struck in these areas, there would be a net benefit to society because private wealth-producing activity would be released from burdensome regulation. Political pressure would mount for abolition of these functions, endangering bureaucrats' jobs. Unions, therefore, do not concentrate their efforts here.

Unions force gains by disrupting or threatening to disrupt essential services where public demand is positive—for example, police and fire protection, garbage removal, hospital care, prison security, water supply, toll bridges, mass transit, air traffic control, postal service, and education. Most of these services have been coopted by government, crowding out private suppliers. The public has been compliant because these services were widely thought to be too vital to be left to the uncertainties of the marketplace. The sad fact is that there never were convincing arguments why most of these services should be government monopolies in the first place.

There are many substitutes for goods and services produced by private firms, a situation that protects consumers from the disruption of service by any single firm or even by an entire industry. But the marketplace cannot protect the public very well when there are no good (legal) alternatives to certain government services. The nature of the services (arguably) might limit competing suppliers, in accord with the notion of "natural monopoly" or pure public goods (for example, protective services rendered by police and judiciary), but usually government either prohibits or severely handicaps private competitors. Examples are fire protection, garbage removal, schooling, hospitals, public utilities, and even prison security. Private contractors can supply these services, and are allowed to do so in some instances. Naturally, they are more efficient than govenment bureaucracies and generally perform the same service at 60% of the cost. Contract bidding and other forms of competition are entirely possible, but they have been little used by local government to give taxpayers more for their money.[6] Multiple producers vastly reduce the vulnerability of citizens to extortion, to put it bluntly, by public employee unions in a centralized system of government monopolies. As Thomas R. Haggard says,

> If government were reduced to its proper size and if government did not try to perform so many services (often on a monopoly basis) that could be better left to private industry, the problem of public employee unionism would diminish considerably, if not disappear altogether. . . . That is perhaps not a very realistic solution, but I cannot resist venturing it nonetheless.[7]

Most observers argue that protective services by police and courts, however, are unique services that can be provided only by government; in fact, law and order is the basic reason for the existence of government. Only anarchists argue otherwise. If we can get along without public protection from aggression, we have no need for government in the first place. Coercive strikes by suppliers of fire and police protection, therefore, are applauded by very few observers.

The result of a police strike is analogous to the looting that follows a natural disaster. Owners are not around to protect their property, and even some normally law-abiding citizens find the temptation to take something irresistible. Looting and stealing rise sharply because, with no policemen on duty, the probability of apprehension or punishment is close to zero. In such situations citizens form vigilante committees, or more often, the National Guard is called up. No mayor or governor can stand idly by during a police strike while society reverts to lawlessness, and either the National Guard or the army ("scabs") usually is called in temporarily to secure law and order. Collective bargaining for public employees and strike threats by those employees are two sides of the same coin, as any realistic person must admit.

Special Position of Civil Servants

Remaining differences between public and private employment are matters of degree. Civil servants already enjoyed a privileged situation before they acquired the ability to cut off the government's supply of labor. Their income is derived from the involuntary payments of fellow citizens, and bureaucrats exercise the coercive power of government. The traditional argument for restricting civil servants' activity in politics was that those with income derived from taxes should not have more influence over taxes than other citizens.

Even without a collective contract civil servants often have more security and protection from management discipline and dismissal than private-sector employees who work under union contracts. In 1978, for instance, only 300 of the 2.8 million federal employees reportedly were dismissed or terminated for incompetence. Civil service rules sometimes prohibit management from replacing strikers with new permanent employees, eliminating an option enjoyed by private enterprises in labor disputes.

Inability to Move

Public enterprises cannot physically move or go out of business in response to high labor costs. The closest private-sector analogue is the construction project, which is produced on the site under a tight schedule, a primary source of economic power for building trades unions. In technical terms, public demand for labor is potentially inelastic with respect to wages; that is, a given percentage rise in wages reduces employment by a smaller percentage. Alfred Marshall's four conditions for inelastic demand for labor were:

1. low elasticity of substitution of labor for other inputs
2. low elasticity of demand for final product
3. low ratio of labor costs to total costs
4. low elasticity of supply of other inputs

The public sector is likely to have a low elasticity of demand for the final product, with no a priori distinction with respect to Marshall's other conditions, except perhaps a high ratio of the cost of labor to total costs. The reasons that final demand is likely to be inelastic are that (1) economies of scale in production imply a large volume of work, (2) consumer fees are zero or nominal because agency income derives from general tax revenues, (3) consumption is often legislatively required, and (4) private suppliers are handicapped. Add the inability to relocate or shut down, and you have a nearly ideal economic situation for unions to exploit.

Very few empirical studies have confirmed the inelastic demand hypothesis, though. Demand elasticity is likely to vary across services. Thornton estimated a wage elasticity of demand for teachers using state data, and found an elasticity between –.56 and –.82, which is inelastic and roughly on a par with estimated elasticities in the private sector.[8] Matters are further complicated by the theoretical proposition that a true monopolist always exploits inelasticities by raising prices until elastic demand is encountered, so if monopoly unions in the public sector successfully exploit their advantage, we should find elasticities greater than one in the observed ranges of prices and employment.[9]

Managerial Incentives

Business firms in the private sector have a strong incentive to pay their employees competitive wages. If they pay less, they cannot maintain the size and quality work force they want. If they pay more, the firm's earnings are dissipated, which reduces the equity value of the company and opens the firm to takeover, merger, proxy battles, and other corporate maneuvering to replace inefficient managers. Residual earnings can be captured by new managers and owners who are more efficient.

Political managers, on the other hand, do not face the same pressure to pay competitive wages. No one can capture the residual earnings from more efficient management because nobody has formal ownership of government profit. Turnover probably is higher among politicians than among private managers, although I know of no systematic evidence on this hypothesis. Public employees can be promised generous retirement benefits, with a tax bill pushed into the future when someone else holds office. Also, the state traditionally prides itself on being a model (read "generous") employer. Managerial salaries can be positively related to the wage levels of public employees and the size of agency spending, which provides an incentive to negotiate higher wages. Also, disharmony and friction in the manager's life due to union pressure may be relieved by high compensation, and although some of these same considerations apply in the private sector, they apply with less force.

Unions are strategically situated to influence the choice of managers, which has no direct parallel in the private sector (yet). The general public naturally hopes to keep its tax bill down, but beyond this hope it has little direct interest in or knowledge about specific wage determinations or their implications for the taxes the public eventually must pay. Public unions, on the other hand, have a strongly focused interest. Politicians are vote-conscious in an era when five and fewer percentage points separate winners from losers in many elections. Unions can supply formidable organization, campaign money, workers, and direct influence over some members' votes. Public employees participate in elections at substantially higher rates than the general citizenry does, thereby forming a more potent voting bloc than their share of the work force might suggest.[10] In some instances, union officials of the National Education Association or the American Federation of Teachers have run in and won elections to school boards. Every group has the right to use the ballot box to advance its interests, but public employees are better situated to succeed than are most private sector employees. Political pressure from interest groups like the Chamber of Commerce or general voter backlash rather than economic competition in the product and factor markets ultimately holds the line on labor costs. Public employee unions naturally try to extract as much money and power as they can without arousing the anger of the general public.

Pay in the Public Sector

Public employee unions theoretically have the potential to raise wages and benefits, but what is the evidence of their effects? Prior to the 1960s the image of government and civil service employment was routine, even boring, work, but it was work that put a relatively low demand on ambition, and it offered secure, if unspectacular, compensation. Now it is widely believed that many government workers are overpaid for what they do.

A number of studies have investigated this question as it applies to specific groups of government workers, but first, let us consider the overall trend of earnings in various sectors of the economy. The U.S. Department of Commerce publishes data on employment, wages and salaries, and nonwage compensation by industry each year in *National Income and Product Accounts*. Table 8–1 shows the trend in wages and salaries for federal employment and for state and local government employment relative to wages and salaries in private nonagricultural

Table 8-1

Ratio of Government Wages and Salaries per Full-Time Employee to Full-Time Wages and Salaries in the Private, Nonagricultural Sector, 1950–81

Year	Civilian Federal Employees	Local and State Government Employees
1950	1.11	.91
1951	1.11	.89
1952	1.14	.89
1953	1.13	.88
1954	1.12	.91
1955	1.16	.91
1956	1.15	.90
1957	1.13	.91
1958	1.21	.93
1959	1.18	.92
1960	1.20	.94
1961	1.23	.96
1962	1.22	.97
1963	1.22	.96
1964	1.25	.96
1965	1.26	.96
1966	1.25	.96
1967	1.22	.99
1968	1.26	1.01
1969	1.27	1.01
1970	1.35	1.03
1971	1.37	1.04
1972	1.37	1.03
1973	1.39	1.03
1974	1.36	1.01
1975	1.35	1.01
1976	1.36	1.00
1977	1.37	.99
1978	1.38	.98
1979	1.38	.96
1980	1.34	.95
1981	1.33	.95

Source: Calculated from the *National Income and Product Accounts*, U.S. Department of Commerce, Office of Business Economics, *Survey of Current Business*, July 1952–82, Tables 6.6B–6.9B.

employment. The data are adjusted for full-time equivalence to control for discrepancies due to part-time employees. The data include all wages and salaries paid, including those for supervisory and management personnel. No adjustment is made for the mixture of occupations or for the difference in quality of labor between the private and public sectors, except for initial differences reflected in the wage differentials of 1950–51.

The relative increase in federal pay over the years is dramatic. In 1950 and 1951 federal salaries were 11% higher than private pay. The advantage averaged 24% during the 1960s and 37% in the 1970s. If this thirty-year trend had continued, the federal advantage would have grown to 52% in ten years and 63% by the year 2000. However, in the first few years of the 1980s the federal advantage slipped back to a 33% premium. George Borjas constructed a table similar to Table 8-1 based on Office of Personnel Management data. He found that the federal pay advantage rose from 24% to 52% between 1955 and 1978.[11] Ironically, federal legislation enacted in 1962 mandates that federal pay be comparable to pay for similar work in the private sector.

The wages of state and local government employees also have increased relative to those of comparable workers in the private sector, but not as dramatically as federal wages. During the 1950s state and local pay averaged 10% less than private pay, presumably reflecting the lower effort, greater security, and more numerous fringe benefits of public employment. During the 1960s state and local earnings converged on private pay, however, and they exceeded private pay by 3% and 4% in the early 1970s. Data for 1977 and 1978 show state and local pay dipping 1% and 2% below private pay, and they were 5% below by 1981. The slight edge of state and local pay over the private sector disappeared, although if state and local pay grew relative to private pay at the same overall pace since 1950, state and local pay would exceed private pay by 10% by the year 2000.

A comparison of wages and salaries alone ignores the potential disparities in other forms of compensation between government and private employment. The National Income Accounts publishes data on "employee compensation," which includes wages, salaries, expenditures on fringe benefits, and employment taxes for social insurance programs. The pattern in these data is nearly identical to that of wages and salaries alone, but the data for employee compensation are not shown here because the National Income Accounts do not separate federal civilian employee compensation from military compensation, which biases downward the rise in federal civilian pay. Also, it is difficult to evaluate fringe benefits among sectors simply on the basis of current outlays. At a minimum, we can say that fringe benefits in public employment exceed the value of fringes in the private sector by reputation, but it cannot be verified directly in the national income accounts.

Can the upward trend of relative pay for government employees be attributed to union pressure and collective bargaining in the public sector? Perhaps, but there are other credible explanations. Government has grown rapidly, and pay for high-growth industries traditionally exceeds general increases because labor must be attracted from other sectors. This argument may be relevant for state and local government, but is improbable for federal employment because direct federal employment growth has lagged behind growth in overall employment. Second, pay in comparable jobs may be identical in private and public employment, but the mix of occupations may have been upgraded in the public sector. This is a favorite argument of union leaders when they demand higher wages, especially since it is difficult to agree on what exactly is comparable. Third, the hazards of some kinds of public employment seem to have increased since the late 1960s, forcing higher pay to attract and retain employees of constant quality. For instance, police duty, fire fighting, and teaching may require higher "combat pay" since the urban riots of the late 1960s and a general decline in law-abiding behavior. Growing cities like Houston find it difficult to recruit police officers and teachers on the basis of compensation recently offered.

In the last twenty years, the number of federal bureaucrats grew only from 2.4 million to 2.8 million while the civilian labor force grew from 69 million to more than 100 million. Defenders of the federal bureaucracy can argue that the number of hardworking public servants increased slowly compared with the labor force to be served, but J. T. Bennett and M. H. Johnson show that these statistics are deceptive.[12] First, federal full-time employment must be inflated by 5% because of the "twenty-five-and-ones," the one employee in twenty classified as full-time for twenty-five of the twenty-six federal pay periods each year, except when the head count is taken, and they are counted as part-time. More important, Bennett and Johnson point out that there has been a massive shift in the proportion of employees in grades GS-13 and higher, which expanded from 6% to 14% of federal civilian employment between 1959 and 1978. The ratio of GS-13s to GS-18s tripled from 62,000 to 196,000, positions where managerial power and policymaking authority are concentrated. The sharp rise in high-salaried executives accounts for some of the federal pay advantage. And 500 new GS-15s can impose far more cost on the productive sector of the economy than 500 new letter carriers.

Growing centralization of power is indicated by the 371,000 federal civilian employees who now work in the District of Columbia and near-by Maryland and Virginia. This is more than the government employed in Washington at the peak of World War II, despite the fact that total federal civilian employment was 3.8 million in 1945. There are more civilian federal employees in Washington now than there were during any U.S. war—Korean, Vietnam, or the War on Poverty (remember the Great Society?). Federal use of private consultants and contractors conceals the swelling in the federal bureaucracy, although it has the vir-tue of flexibility, introduces nonunion competition, and in principle lowers costs of production. An estimated 8 to 10 million consultants, contractors, and their employees now depend on federal grants and contracts and form a hidden army of government employees and voters. Maryland's Montgomery County and Virginia's Fairfax County have the highest incomes in the nation. As one father advised his son, "Get into poverty. That's where the money is."

Federal Wages and Salaries

Detailed studies confirm that federal pay is higher than the wages of similar workers in the private sector. Douglas Adie found that wages in the Postal Service increased by 100% between 1958 and 1972 while wages increased an average of 80% in other industry groups.[13] The tendency for the Postal Service to grant its employees greater than average pay increases is shown in Table 8-2 for 1960 to 1974. Also, gross earnings in 1976 for nonsupervisory postal employees were $7.20 per paid hour compared with $3.72 in banking, $4.58 in insurance, $6.56 in telephone communications, and $6.69 in electric utilities for nonsupervisory employees. Carrier supervisors also consistently re-ported that the average carrier route could be served in six to seven hours instead of the eight hours assigned for pay purposes, and Adie found that fringe benefits were a slightly higher percentage of payroll costs in the Postal Service than in all industries. More attractive com-pensation implies that turnover should be lower in postal employment,

Table 8-2

Percentage Change in Average Hourly Wages, Postal Employees and Manufacturing Employees, 1960–74

Year	Postal Workers	Manufacturing Workers
1960–69	51.0	33.2
1969–70	10.7	5.5
1960–71	11.9	6.4
1971–72	6.2	6.8
1972–73	5.8	6.4
1973–74	12.6	10.0

Source: Douglas K. Adie, *An Evaluation of Postal Service Wage Rates* (Washington, D.C.: American Enterprise Institute for Public Policy Research, 1977), p. 45.

---

a hypothesis confirmed by data in Table 8–3, which show that postal turnover rates are only one-third those in manufacturing.

Postal wage rates generally exceeded comparable private-sector rates by 20%. National uniformity for postal pay means that it was only slightly above competitive levels in markets like Chicago and New York City, but well above competitive levels in most of the country where the cost of living is lower. The 1981 contract, negotiated under a strike threat, called for a 26% increase in wages over three years, assuming that the Consumer Price Index rose at an annual rate of 8%, plus comparable gains in fringe benefits. The largest class of postal workers had a wage base of $21,146 per year in 1981.[14] The Postal Service is one of the highest-paying employers—if not *the* highest-paying employer—in the country.

Other studies confirm Adie's evaluation of postal wages. Sharon Smith used data for 1973 and 1975 and found that, after differences in employee characteristics were accounted for, postal workers of both sexes "receive wages which are superior to the wages of nonunionized private sector workers of similar socioeconomic characteristics and at least comparable to unionized private sector workers."[15] Quinn used data for 1969, the year before the postal strike of 1970, and found a basic wage differential of 11% in favor of postal employment in a sample of white males age fifty-eight to sixty-three. The differential could not be explained by any differences in measured productivity characteristics.[16]

Table 8-3
Annual Turnover Rates in Postal, Federal, and Manufacturing Employment

Year	Postal	Federal	All Manufacturing
1970	20%	22%	58%
1971	15	19	50
1972	15	20	50
Quit Rates			
in 1972	7	8	27

Source: Adie, p. 64.

In the most recent study available, sponsored by the U.S. Postal Service, University of Pennsylvania economist Michael Wachter compared postal salaries with those of a cross-section of U.S. workers whose jobs require similar levels of education, skill, and experience and found that postal workers were paid more than comparable employees in any private industry except mining.[17] In 1960 postal salaries were 20% higher than the average wage paid in the private sector, and in 1980 they were 29% higher. Perhaps the clinching evidence is that the quit rate in the Postal Service was only one-quarter that in manufacturing: in 1980 just 2.8 postal workers per 1,000 resigned, compared with 12 employees per 1,000 in manufacturing.

Sharon Smith has done a number of studies on public–private pay differentials and finds a consistent premium for federal employees after controlling for individual characteristics. In a 1976 study she compared federal and private employees in an area including the District of Columbia, Maryland, Delaware, and Virginia, using Census data on wages and salaries (excluding fringe benefits) in 1960 and 1970. In 1960, federal pay was 64% greater than private earnings, and regression analysis showed that the premium was reduced only to 41% after accounting for differences in such variables as schooling, experience, family status, and race. By 1970 the federal pay advantage had risen to 69%, a premium that was reduced only to 42% after controlling for measured variables.[18] In a more recent paper, she used data from 1977 and 1978 for twenty-nine large cities. Regression analysis controlled for education, experience, marital status, ethnic differences, sex, veteran status, region, occupational group, part-time, dual job holders, union membership, and level of government. Compared with statistically similar individuals in the private sector, there was a net advantage of 11% for men and 21% for women in federal employment, no significant advantage in state employment for either sex, and a 9% advantage for men and zero for women in local government. Although the federal advantage was not as large as in earlier studies, she argued that federal employees had lost little of their advantage since 1973 because the data were for large cities only, where the federal advantage is narrowest.[19]

Joseph Quinn used data gathered in 1969 for white males between the ages of fifty-eight and sixty-three and found a wage differential of 40% for federal workers compared with private employees, and only half of this differential could be explained by differences in personal characteristics.[20] State workers enjoyed a 28% premium and 17 of the 28 percentage points could be explained by regression analysis, leaving an 11% advantage unaccounted for. Local employees received wages 9% lower than private-sector workers, but the difference was not significantly different from zero by standard tests.

The existence of superior federal pay is confirmed by calculations from the national income accounts and specific, detailed studies. But how much of it can be attributed to union push? It is difficult to tell. Sharon Smith believes the increase had little to do with public employee unions. Much of the advantage might have occurred anyway. The Federal Salary Reform Act of 1962 required that "federal pay rates be comparable with private enterprise pay for the same level of work," a policy reaffirmed by the Federal Salary Act of 1967 and the Federal Pay Comparability Act of 1970, delegating authority to grant federal pay increases to the president. Pay comparisons for white-collar civil service and postal workers are based on an annual wage survey conducted by the Bureau of Labor Statistics, but there are operational problems, just as there are in administering Davis-Bacon. There is always a range of wage rates for any job description. Which rates are appropriate? Should fringe benefits count? What about jobs where direct private-sector analogues do not exist? Can BLS employees be trusted to make unbiased and competent judgments?

The survey canvasses only establishments with more than 250 employees in manfacturing and retail trade and more than 100 in other industries, and it excludes nonprofit organizations and industries like agriculture. The General Accounting Office estimates that three-fourths of all nonfederal white-collar wage and salary workers are excluded, producing an upward-biased sample of wage rates. A tremendous excess of qualified federal job applicants cannot affect raises in government service pay scale under this procedure. Also, government employment policies deliberately discount productivity traits to a greater extent than the private sector does. Civil service exam points, for example, are awarded to veterans, minorities, women, and those who live in certain locations, a selection procedure that must lower productivity in any occupation.

The belief that federal employees are overpaid has become so widespread that even government studies are beginning to find it. A recent report by the Congressional Budget Office said that the average blue-collar government employee gets about 6% more pay than a private-sector employee does for comparable work in his own area of the country, and about 15% more in fringe benefits.[21]

State and Local Wages and Salaries

A number of studies of state and local government have been triggered by the worry that unions might drive up public expenditures and taxes. The evidence is mixed, but most of the studies find relatively modest wage effects for state and local employee unions. Some studies find no wage effect due to public employee unions, many find modest effects of 5% to 10%, and a few find increases as large as 15% to 20%. In general, wage effects appear to be smaller than they are in the private sector, where a majority of unions seem to raise their members' wage rates more than 10%. Such variety is not surprising in view of the varied political relationships across time and space, and differences in data, models, and estimation procedures in public-sector studies.

James Freund found no union effect in a sample of fifty-five cities using data on all city employees during 1965 to 1971.[22] David Shapiro in a study of older males found no evidence of a union wage effect for the earnings of either white or black men in white-collar jobs, but he found positive union wage effects of 20% for whites in blue-collar jobs and 10% for blacks in blue-collar work.[23] However, teachers, police, and fire fighters have received the most attention. David Lipsky and John Drotning reviewed the empirical literature on teacher unions and found between 0% and 29% wage gains due to unionization but a mean effect of only 2% to 4%.[24] Richard P. Victor reviewed the literature and concluded that teacher salaries increased from 5% to 20%.[25] Alan G. Balfour found no evidence that collective bargaining made any difference in teacher salaries, other compensation, or promotions.[26] The Public Service Research Council, using data from the U.S. Department of Labor, calculated that from 1969-70 to 1975-76 teachers in nineteen states without mandatory bargaining laws averaged 40.5% salary increases while those in thirty states with mandatory bargaining averaged 36.6% increases.[27] Teacher unions apparently had modest wage effects during the 1970s.

More recently, however, W. H. Baugh and J. A. Stone provided evidence, using national samples of teacher data, that teacher unionism produced relatively small gains in the early 1970s, *but* also that union gains increased substantially in the late 1970s, reaching 12% to 22%.[28] The real wages of unionized teachers increased from 1974 to 1978, according to their analysis, while those of nonunionized teachers declined.

W. W. Brown and C. C. Stone found that faculty unions in higher education were ineffective in raising wages, benefits, or promotions.[29] They also found a modest increase in student-faculty ratios after unionization, which implies a slight deterioration in working conditions. Other studies essentially agree with the Brown-Stone findings.[30] On theoretical grounds, college faculty unions are ineffective because interruption of classes and research is not a potent economic weapon. By contrast, a strike by primary and secondary teachers turns loose a horde of children who must be supervised. From the point of view of colleges, collective bargaining still is expensive because additional staff are required to negotiate and administer contracts and grievances. Rutgers University, for example, processed seventy cases between 1970 and 1975. The estimated cost per case ranged from $20,000 to $50,000 depending on whether negotiating time was included.[31] J. T. Bennett and M. H. Johnson cite a survey that asked college presidents to respond to the statement, "Where it occurs, faculty collective bargaining will help improve the quality of educational services on campus." Nearly all presidents, 96% at nonunion campuses and 93% at unionized campuses, disagreed with the statement.[32]

Police and firefighters also have received a lot of attention, and the results are not dramatically different. Roger Schmenner found that unionization is associated with 15% higher salaries for police and firefighters in a time-series analysis of 11 large cities; Richard B. Victor found that police union contracts raised wages from 8% to 12% in a sample of 190 cities, and firefighter unions had no independent effect unless a police union contract was in effect; Orley Ashenfelter found union effects of 6% to 16% for a national sample of 225 small and medium-size cities in the early 1960s; Ronald Ehrenberg found effects of 7% to 10% in 270 municipalities in 1969 for firefighters; Casey Ichniowski found a 15% wage increase for firefighters; Ronald Ehrenberg and Gerald Goldstein found a 6% wage increase for police services in a sample of 478 cities over 25,000 population; Ann Bartel and David Lewin in a sample of 215 municipalities for 1973 found a 5% and 7% increase for a police union contract in a single equation model and a 16% effect in a two-stage analysis when unionism was endogenous; finally, a study by the Minnesota State Finance Department reported that lower- and middle-level state workers earn more than comparable private-sector workers.[33]

Other Benefits

There is evidence that fringe benefits for public employees exceed fringes in the private sector. There also is a growing fear that many government units are accumulating tremendous unfunded pension liabilities, although no one has issued a well-documented estimate.

The tradition of superior public-sector fringes is old. As early as 1868 the U.S. Congress adopted a law that set a day's work at eight hours in all government employment. The federal civil service retirement system was established in 1920, as was the New York City Employees' Retirement System, long before private pensions were common. Current evidence, although incomplete, suggests that government fringes and job stability continue to be superior. In a 1976 publication, the Bureau of Labor Statistics reported that federal fringe supplements were 36% of pay, compared with 34% for state government workers and 24% for employees in the private sector.[34] A study of U.S. municipalities found that municipalities outspend private industry for fringes by 1% to 6.5% of wages per hour.

Anthony Pascal of the Rand Corporation surveyed empirical studies of government fringe benefits and found that benefits for municipal workers in Los Angeles averaged 40% of salaries, pension benefits rose 50% faster than negotiated wage rates in state and local governments between 1962 and 1972, and that fringe benefits were 46% of pay for municipal police and fire personnel in the national data.[35] A regression analysis by Ann Bartel and David Lewin found retirement pay 38% higher as a percentage of annual salary for police in cities with union contracts.[36] This premium fell to 28% if New York City was deleted. The Temporary Commission of New York City Finances in

1976 reported that the hourly payroll cost of a New York City police officer more than doubled to over $21 per hour when the cost of fringe benefits was added to salaries.

What about work demands and working environment in government compared with the private sector? This is more difficult to measure, but Joseph Quinn systematically assessed the differences in terms of five characteristics—repetitive nature of work, physical effort, unpleasant odors, cold, and noise—and found that "federal and state employees have more favorable distributions than private-sector workers in all five dimensions."[37]

Pensions are difficult to compare, and adequate studies do not exist. Robert Tilove studied the data for the late 1960s and 1970s and found that public plans were approximately twice as generous as those prevailing in private industry.[38] He argued, however, that many public employees did not have dual coverage under Social Security, and after that was taken into account, employees of state and local government received combined benefits only one-third higher than those in the private sector. The public advantage also was diminished by an unknown amount because of the prevalence of employee contributions in public pension plans compared with the noncontributory character of some 80% of private plans. Tilove believed that many pension plans were not actuarially sound and that many career bureaucrats would receive more after-tax income from pensions and Social Security after they retired than they received while working.

Both beliefs seem well founded, and confirmation has arrived at the federal level of government. A report issued by President Carter's Commission on Pension Policy claimed that seven of ten government workers wind up with both Civil Service and Social Security pensions, double-dipping, which is relatively easy because minimum Social Security benefits are generous because of redistributive intent. The commission found that federal retirees received substantially larger pensions than did private retirees who had combinations of Social Security and private pension benefits. The Chamber of Commerce said that private enterprise spends an average of 13% of payrolls for pension while government spends 31%, and the commission report concluded that "if the government pension system were subject to the same funding requirements as private plans, the cost in 1980 would be 79.8% of payroll."[39]

The consensus on compensation of public employees was summarized in 1980 by economist Morley Gunderson:

U.S. evidence, based on the estimation of earnings equations for public and private sector workers or on occupational wage survey data, suggests a pure wage advantage associated with public sector employment. The advantage has persisted over time, is greater for females than males, greater in low-level occupations than high-level occupations (there is some evidence that higher level occupations pay less than the competitive wage); is greater at the federal level than the state level, and is greater at the state level than the local level. . . . The monetary value of fringe benefits also appears to be greater in the public sector, which suggests that the pure wage advantage is a conservative estimate of the total compensation advantage. The Canadian evidence generally confirms these patterns.[40]

Work Rules

Unions try to regulate the work environment, which necessarily limits flexibility. For example, police and fire fighter unions have tried to control transfers among precincts through contract provisions. More dramatically, a 1970 strike by the New York City teachers' unions defeated a citizens' plan to decentralize city schools in the Brownsville dispute. In Milwaukee, the city government laid off 250 sanitation employees and contracted with a private supplier for the service. Two months after the service took effect, the courts ruled in favor of the government employees union, and the city had to terminate the contract, rehire the original employees, and reinstitute the governmentally provided sanitation services. It is difficult to cost out the effects of these restrictions, but in the private sector work rules are generally believed to inflate labor costs per unit of output as much as the wage effects of unions. The value of public services per tax dollar is necessarily lower as a result of union work rules. Moreover, all the traditional work rules of, say, the construction trades are carried over to the public sector when plumbers, electricians, and other workers are employed.

Strikes by Public Employees

Pro-union legislation has been associated with an upsurge in strike activity, following the pattern in the private sector. Table 8-4 shows that the number of work stoppages has risen tenfold since 1960 and the number of days idle increased thirtyfold. By comparison with disruption in the private sector, however, the public sector has been peaceful. Some 20% of employees are in the public sector, but fewer than 10% of all strikes and fewer than 5% of days idle occur in government employment. Perhaps the strike is regarded as a weapon to be used with

Table 8-4

Work Stoppages and Days Idle,
All Levels of Government
1950–80

Year	Work Stoppages	Days Idle (in thousands)
1950	28	32.7
1951	36	28.8
1952	49	33.4
1953	30	53.4
1954	10	10.4
1955	17	7.2
1956	27	11.1
1957	12	4.4
1958	15	7.5
1959	25	10.5
1960	36	58.4
1961	28	15.3
1962	28	79.1
1963	29	15.4
1964	41	70.8
1965	42	146.0
1966	142	455.0
1967	181	1,250.0
1968	254	2,550.0
1969	411	745.7
1970	412	2,023.3
1971	329	901.4
1972	375	1,257.3
1973	389	2,303.9
1974	384	1,404.2
1975	478	2,204.4
1976	378	1,690.7
1977	413	1,765.7
1978	481	1,706.7
1979	593	2,982.5
1980	536	2,347.8

Sources: Data for 1950–77 from U.S. Bureau of Labor Statistics, *Analysis of Work Stoppages, 1977,* p. 74; Bulletin 2032 (Washington, D.C.: U.S. Government Printing Office, September 1979); *Analysis of Work Stoppages, 1978,* Bulletin 2066 (June 1980), p. 32; *Analysis of Work Stoppages, 1979,* Bulletin 2092 (April 1981), p. 36; *Analysis of Work Stoppages, 1980,* Bulletin 2120 (March 1982), p. 40.

somewhat more care in the public sector, or perhaps a strike threat is more effective or managements capitulate more quickly.

There is a positive association between mandatory bargaining legislation and strikes across states, as well as over time. The Public Service Research Council reported that teacher strikes occurred one-third as often in states without bargaining laws from 1969–70 to 1975–76.[41] Of the 223 strikes that occurred in states without legislation, 144 took place in Ohio where 472 of 640 school districts bargain without mandatory state legislation. Pennsylvania is one of the few states to legalize public employee strikes and since 1970 more teacher strikes have occurred in Pennsylvania than in any other state.

Voter Backlash

The power and independence of public employee unions are potentially great, but it is ultimately like the independence of the Federal Reserve Board: both are on a short political leash. The experience in San Francisco illustrates it well. San Francisco is a good "union town," just like New York and St. Louis. During the late 1960s and early 1970s, public employee unions helped city employees to achieve greater prosperity.[42] From 1968 to 1976, the city's pension contribution for miscellaneous employees went from 10.4¢ to 18.4¢ per payroll dollar. Over the same period the city's pension contribution for police went from 18.1¢ to 73.9¢ per payroll dollar, and for firefighters it went from 25.6¢ to 67.1¢ per payroll dollar.

Another example was salaries for street sweepers. In 1972 a former aide to Mayor Joseph Alioto was appointed general manager of the Civil Service Commission, and street sweepers were reclassified from miscellaneous to craft pay status. As a result, wages of street sweepers increased by 17.9% in 1973 and later kept pace with the large increases paid to general laborers. The Laborers' Union, which represented city street sweepers, provided active campaign support for Alioto's election.

In the fall of 1975 a backlash developed due to a combination of national and local events. New York City's default crisis had occurred in the spring, triggering concern throughout the nation that public employee pay was largely responsible for the fiscal crisis in central cities. In the fall of 1975 police and fire fighters in San Francisco launched a joint strike, an unprecedented event in the city. Public revulsion was fueled by a series of newspaper stories about a system where street sweepers were paid an annual base salary of $17,300 and city plumbers' base salary was $35,000.

The political winds abruptly shifted, and a series of charter amendments dissipated the power of public employees. Revisions eliminated the improvements for city employees adopted in the early 1970s, although the law limited the new system to new employees only. Other amendments required immediate dismissal of any employee participating in a strike and ordered that future disputes over prevailing pay procedures be decided by public vote. It may not be coincidental that Table 8-1 shows that the relative wage advance for state and local government employees peaked in 1973 and declined to 98% of private pay by 1978. Union leaders read newspapers, too.

Another example of backlash occurred in New Orleans in 1979. Just before a policemen's strike began, public opinion, as reported by a local newspaper, was 67% in favor of the policemen. After the first four days of the strike, the same newspaper poll found that only 17% supported the policemen.[43] The overwhelming popularity of President Reagan's decision to dismiss the striking air traffic controllers in August 1981 is an important example of the increasing unpopularity of the use of threats and strikes by public-sector unions.

9
Inflation and Unionism

Government can print money but not wealth.
—Anonymous

Although unions are not directly to blame for inflation by pushing
up wage-costs, they cannot escape responsibility for wage-push
pressures which create widespread prospective or actual
unemployment of workers and for resisting the steps required to attain
non-inflationary prosperity in those circumstances.
—W. H. Hutt

Inflation is the number one economic issue in the nation and promises to remain so many years into the future. Between 1967 and 1983 the average level of prices tripled, as measured by either the consumer price index or by the producer price index. Double-digit rates of annual price increases became routine, though the rate declined to 6% in 1982. At the 13% annual rates of inflation in 1979 and 1980, today's $80,000 house would cost $920,000 in twenty years and a Big Mac would be $13. Along with virulent inflation have come high levels of unemployment, a rapidly growing welfare state, meager capital formation, and sluggish growth in the production of market goods and services. Variously called the British sickness, Englanditis, the Western disease, and stagflation, the destructive power of inflation, if anything, has been underestimated by most American commentators and by the American public. Inflation is gradually destroying our productive capacity, our spirit, our optimism about the future, and the institutional basis for our prosperity.

For many years the general public has suspected unions to be prime culprits in the inflation drama. Public opinion polls consistently show that the public blames big labor more than big business for inflation, and editorial writers have repeated the argument innumerable times:

(1) unions push up wages and benefits, (2) labor costs per unit of output go up, and therefore (3) prices must rise, Q.E.D. The argument is simple and direct; too simple, in fact, because, although correct as arithmetic, it is seriously incomplete as economic analysis. The problem is that all prices do not necessarily go up. On the contrary, other prices tend to fall, provided that the monetary authorities do not increase the volume of spending in the economy.

Suppose some unionists force employers to raise wage rates. What happens? Fewer people are employed because of the law of demand, output is smaller, and prices rise in that sector of the economy. What happens to the workers and assets temporarily idled by the new exercise of union monopoly power? They eventually must find work somewhere else in the economy, albeit in less productive pursuits. Costs of production tend to be gently bid down or restrained from rising in nonunion enterprises, and the newly available resources raise output and lower prices for consumers, a result guaranteed by competition. The consequence is that the exercise of union power in an economy with a substantial free-market sector and a stable volume of spending cannot cause a sustained rise in the general level of prices. Literally millions of prices change every month, up and down: If unions and governmental edicts force up costs and prices in one sector, the economy adjusts by reallocating men and assets to less productive employments. The free market absorbs the resources idled by price-fixing abuse, just as it does in the Soviet Union to a certain degree, although real income is reduced and real labor income falls proportionately, more or less.

The role of unionism in the inflation process is too subtle for us to be able to say that unions directly push up wages. Unionists contribute to inflation in two general ways: On the supply or production side, they brake the growth of productivity and increase unemployment through their pricing and work rules; on the money-spending or demand side, they are the most important interest group pressuring government policymakers to maintain full employment by spending more and by printing more money to do so. In a 1978 opinion poll, a majority of Americans (57%) correctly named government more than unions (28%) or business (15%) as being primarily responsible for inflation.[1] These are not mutually exclusive alternatives, however, because unionists man the bellows that fan the inflationary pyre.

Inflation: Made in Washington

Prosperity has many fathers, but inflation is an orphan—so goes a new version of an old saying. Surprisingly, though, the mechanism of inflation is one of the best understood phenomena in economics. If economists know anything at all, they know how to create and sustain inflation. There has never been a sustained rise in money prices without sustained increases in the money supply, increases in excess of the growth of output. Nor has a sustained increase in the money supply occurred without price inflation. In fact, an old definition of inflation is "rapid growth in the stock of money and credit resulting in a continuing rise in the general level of prices." In other words, inflation is "too much money chasing too few goods."

Price inflation confirms a fundamental law in economics: if something increases rapidly in supply, all else being equal, its relative value must fall. A rapid increase in the amount of dollars in the hands of the public, compared with increases in the amounts of other goods, necessarily diminishes the exchange value of each dollar. A numerical rule of thumb is that a sustained rise in prices is impossible if expansion in the amount of dollars is kept in line with the growth of real production. Conversely, a sustained rise in prices is unavoidable if the money supply grows more rapidly than output.

To refine the argument slightly, the exchange value of a unit of money (its "price" in terms of goods) will remain constant if the amount of money and the willingness to hold money both grow at the same rate. During inflation, the demand for money does not grow as rapidly as the government prints money, and price inflation is the mechanism that finally brings the dollar demand into equality with dollar supply.

The monetary authorities do not directly determine the value of money, because they influence only its supply, not the demand for it. In a stable environment, the demand for money—that is, the willingness to accept and hold inventories of cash in exchange for real goods and services—tends to be a stable function of a few variables. In particular, demand tends to grow apace with output. This is not an iron law, however, because even on a steady-state growth path the demand for money could grow more or less rapidly than output, depending on changes in consumer preferences, new payment procedures, and so forth. The monetary authorities, however, can easily avoid substantial inflation or deflation in the price level by gradually adjusting the money supply to newly evolving patterns of demand.

In the short run—say, six months or less—the monetary authorities (the board of governors of the Federal Reserve Board) do not directly control the rate of price inflation for two reasons: (1) demand for money can fluctuate, (2) the immediate supply of money in the hands of the public can fluctuate. "The Fed" does not have *direct* control over the amount of money in the hands of the public (M1 or M2).* These quantities are determined by a complex interaction between the public and the banking system. The short of it is that the money stock expands when commercial banks expand their inventory of loans, thereby creating new deposits in the banking system. The key to the creation (and destruction) of money is that the commercial banking system can increase demand deposits (checkbook money) only if it has excess reserves. Currency in commercial bank vaults and deposits at the Federal Reserve constitute reserves, and the Fed directly controls the dollar amount of reserves in the banking system. The Fed increases reserves whenever it buys U.S. government securities from security dealers, because the Fed's payment for securities is deposited in a bank and immediately becomes excess reserves in the banking system. Commercial banks lend out this new money, and banking deposits eventually increase by a multiple of the reserve injection. Where did the Fed get the money to buy interest-bearing Treasury debt? It just wrote a check on itself. It takes paper and ink and creates something that is accepted as money by everyone else. Social convention gives it value, not promise of redemption into gold or other specified commodities at a fixed rate of exchange.

Demand for money can fluctuate sharply from a long-term path if output departs significantly from long-run trends ("bad harvests") or, more important, because of expectations of more inflation once inflation is under way. This defensive behavior by the public is the reason that price inflation tends to outrun the rate of expansion in money supply. Early on, prices tend to rise less rapidly than money increases because the people are caught unaware, but as they learn that prices are rising, they adjust their behavior in expectation of more inflation, and prices begin to accelerate faster than the money supply does. Inflation never has a steady, constant rate, which makes it impossible for the public to anticipate perfectly, but few are fooled about what government has been doing to the currency.

---

*M1 is defined as the sum of currency, demand deposits (conventional bank checking accounts), traveler's checks, and other checkable deposits. M2 is defined as M1 plus savings and small-time deposits, Eurodollars, and miscellaneous items.

The Fed money managers are the immediate cause of inflation. Whenever they increase their portfolio of U.S. securities, they pump in reserves, and thereby inflate the money supply. "Monetizing the debt" is the expression. The money supply explodes when the Fed increases the monetary base (currency plus reserves) on which all deposits rest. The general public anticipates and reacts as best it can. Technically, there is no mystery about how to end price inflation, because the Fed has long had the ability to restrain the money supply. The problem always has been finding the political will to do it.

Fiscal Policy: Made in Washington

The Federal government has had a discretionary monopoly over money production since President Roosevelt in 1933 abolished the government promise to its citizens to convert U.S. dollars into gold at a fixed rate, on demand. Politicians were no longer constrained in domestic monetary policy by this "barbarous relic," and Nixon administered the coup de grace in 1971 when he suspended the U.S. guarantee to convert dollars into gold at fixed rates on demand by foreign central banks. The last vestige of paper currency based on a commodity standard was destroyed, supplanted by government officials deciding how much money to print.

The creation of dollars speeded up after 1960, and the reason is well known: new money pays for part of the enormous growth in federal spending, whose lush profusion was so earnestly desired by so many in Washington, D.C. People in government like to spend money, just like everybody else, and they want to spend it without legislating new taxes. Inflation allows government to spend much more than citizens are willing to surrender through ordinary taxes. Throughout history, as Milton Friedman says, "inflation has been irresistibly attractive to sovereigns, because it is a hidden tax that can be imposed without specific legislation. It is truly taxation without representation."[2] Since 1960 the federal government ran deficits in twenty-two of twenty-three years, and federal spending grew from less than 18% of GNP to 25%. Spending beyond government income (tax receipts) is financed by Treasury borrowing, with the Fed buying part of the new securities, thereby creating new money and producing the consequent price inflation.

Table 9-1 shows how the U.S. government has spent us into stagflation. An examination of the fifteen-year period from 1967 to 1981 will, if anything, result in an underestimation of the growth of government spending, because 1967 was at the height of the Vietnam War,

Table 9-1
Price Level, Federal Spending, Output, and Money Supply, 1967–81

(All dollar figures in billions except GNP per worker)

		1967	1981	Ratio (1981 ÷ 1967)
1.	CPI	100	272	2.7
	GNP Implicit Price Deflator	79	194	2.4
2.	Federal Outlays	$164	657	4.0
	Federal Interest-Bearing Debt	322	1,027	3.2
	Total Federal Liabilities	1,000	9,000	9.0
3.	GNP, current prices	796	2,922	3.7
	Real GNP, 1972 dollars	1,008	1,510	1.5
	Civilian employment (thousands)	74,372	100,397	1.35
	Average weekly hours worked	38.0	35.2	0.93
	Real GNP per Employed Civilian	13,600	15,040	1.1
4.	Money Supply			
	Currency	40	123	3.1
	M-1	185	442	2.4
	M-2	524	1,841	3.5
	Fed. Res. U.S. Gov't. Securities	49	138	2.8
	Fed. Res. Total Assets	51	152	3.0

Sources: *Economic Report of the President, 1982; Federal Reserve Bulletin,* December 1982; U.S. Department of the Treasury, *Statement of Liabilities and Other Financial Commitments of the United States Government,* January 1981; *Survey of Current Business,* July 1982.

---

and inflation was well under way already. The price level had risen by 2.7 by the end of 1981, federal spending rose nearly fourfold (non-defense spending even more), and the interest-bearing national debt tripled. Even more telling was the expansion in total federal liabilities, a comprehensive measure of the overall indebtedness of the federal government, which increased ninefold. Total liabilities include interest-bearing debt, federal loan guarantees ($500 billion), the actuarial deficit in Social Security ($5,000 billion), other retirement accounts, and miscellaneous obligations. This total equals three years of GNP, invested and earning interest. Taxpayers do not yet know the half of it.

GNP in current prices more than tripled during the period from

1967 to 1981, but real output only increased 40%, mostly due to a 32% growth in employment. Output per employed person barely grew at all in fifteen years. Meanwhile, the money stock measured in various ways approximately tripled. Rising prices? No surprise at all with output increasing 40% and money supply 200%.

The real cause of inflation is a government that spends beyond its means, impoverishing the nation. The Fed is the immediate cause of debasing the currency, but the board of the Fed is only human. The federal government borrowed an additional $674 billion to spend beyond its tax receipts during the fifteen years, an average annual deficit of $45 billion. This put tremendous political pressure on the Fed to supply part of the funds the Treasury wanted to borrow. The Fed has been anxious to avoid crowding out businesses and consumers who wanted to borrow to purchase productive equipment, houses, and so on. The Federal Reserve Bank bought $91 billion in new debt (the Fed's portfolio of government securities rose from $47 billion to $138), or average purchases of $6.1 billion per year between 1967 and 1981. The Fed, in other words, supplied $1 of every $7 the Treasury borrowed, perhaps a modest amount in view of the continual political pressure to "let 'er rip." The saddest feature of the entire table is the $674 billion in private savings that the federal government has wantonly wasted since 1967, savings that otherwise would have been invested in productive machinery. That is the real cause of our progressive impoverishment.

Why was government so expansive in this period? There is no easy answer. No doubt a complex political mix went into our inflationary malaise, although the intellectual legacy of J. M. Keynes might be the foremost ingredient in our bitter stew.[3] Rational politicians obviously thought it expedient to resort to inflation because it would lose them fewer votes than noninflation. Some of the explosion came from "pull" factors, that is, political pressures from special interest groups, and some from "push" factors within government. As Frank H. Knight put it: "The probability of the people in power being individuals who would dislike the possession and exercise of power is on a level with the probability that an extremely tender-hearted person would get the job of whipping master on a slave plantation."[4]

Union Innocence

What is the exact role of unions in the process of inflation? There is room for dispute, because unions are only one element in a complicated political economy. Monetarist and nonmonetarist economists alike have come up with some ingenious arguments in support of the view that unions and union members are simply victims of inflation along with everyone else in the private sector. The net effect of these arguments, I believe, is to absolve unions from the naive theory of wage-push inflation, but not to absolve them of the major supporting role in the inflation epic.

The first argument in favor of union innocence is that price inflation has been on a rising roller coaster, yet union strength has been waning for a quarter of a century in the U.S. economy. For instance, the share of the labor force organized by unions in the private sector has declined from 25% to 16%. However, unionism has increased sharply among employees in the expanding public sector, rising from 11% to nearly 45%.

Second, some economists argue that if unions had unused monopoly power to raise wages, why didn't they exercise it before? The notion that unions can cause a sustained inflation by themselves depends on the belief that unions have increasing monopoly power, a contention that would have been difficult to support in the United States over the last two decades, when their share of the work force declined to 20%. More generally, the problem is that unions are political organizations that are not as predictable as businesses. Essentially, businesses have so little market power and pursue profits so consistently that economists can effectively predict their behavior and consequently, the behavior of markets. Union leaders, on the other hand, conceivably leave short-term market power unexercised, especially if the dominant leaders are men who wish to preserve the long-run existence of unionism by causing less than complete disruption of the production process. They can be supplanted at any time by more aggressive unionists, however, who might say, "After us, the deluge," so the behavior of unionism is relatively unpredictable. It depends, much more than does business, on the ideas and ambitions of a handful of individuals who wield more potential power than businessmen do.

A third argument to absolve unionism is that union wage rates usually lag behind inflation in the early stages, so why would unionists start an inflation? Since union wage contracts tend to be more inflexible than nonunion wages, it would not pay to trigger an inflation or accelerate an inflation because union members would lose, relative to others. Also, wage escalator or cost-of-living-adjustments clauses in contracts are not a direct cause of inflation because they merely lag behind movements in the CPI. When inflation moderates, wage gains moderate.

The fourth argument is much the same. With some 200,000 union contracts elapsing on different dates, it would require an uncanny degree of coordination among rival unionists to arrange an inflation. Unionists work in different enterprises, industries, occupations; have different beliefs about the future, different incentives, different degrees of economic power; and simply are not a monolithic presence in the U.S. economy.

Fifth, there is little evidence that the prices of goods and services in the unionized sectors rise more rapidly during inflation than do the prices of nonunion goods. In fact, if anything, the reverse is true. The disaggregated CPI shows that the prices of medical care, housing, energy, agricultural commodities, and services have outrun the general rise in prices, while prices in apparel, automobiles, transportation, printed materials, and durable goods rose less than average. The latter group is more unionized than the former, and the implicit price deflators by GNP, by sector, tend to support the same conclusion.

The sixth argument is by contradiction. If major union contracts or corporate pricing caused inflation, then wage-price controls or guidelines would work. Government need only control wages and prices in the market-power sectors, and inflation is beaten. It has never worked, anywhere in the world or any time in history, so we can safely dismiss the naive theory of wage-push inflation.[5]

Rising money wage rates are basically a consequence of inflationary government policy, not its cause. The true definition of price inflation is rising prices, including such prices as wage rates and interest rates, not just prices of consumer goods. Wage rates do not push prices up; wage rates *are* prices. Put another way, rising prices do not cause price inflation; they *are* inflation.

There is a coherent theory of wage-push inflation by unions, but it depends on government complicity. It can be summarized by the statement of Charles O. Hardy who said shortly after World War II that it is impossible simultaneously to have full employment, stable prices, and strong trade unions; you can have any pair of these but not all three.[6] Restated more precisely, modern governments are committed to continuous full employment as the number one policy goal, and if they really try to achieve that goal, they are telling unions that unionism has a free hand. Unionists cannot price themselves out of jobs, no matter how high their wage rates go. Business managers presumably capitulate to union demands in this environment because they rely on new government-issued money to inflate spending and thereby validate the wage concessions without destroying employment and output. This is the real difficulty with government responsibility for full employment, as enshrined in the Employment Act of 1946 and the Humphrey-Hawkins Act in 1978.

The monetary authorities count on a time lag between rising costs and prices of output to induce businesses to expand their employment and output. The price–cost margin is temporarily widened by surprise surges of spending, and it induces businessmen to increase their investments in labor, plant equipment, and inventories. Unanticipated inflation expands the levels of output where prospective marginal profit equals the rate of interest. This theory of inflation is logical and consistent, but it poses two problems. First, the policy problem is that unanticipated inflation becomes anticipated inflation, even over-anticipated inflation, and then input prices rise as rapidly or more rapidly than output prices through cost-of-living adjustments. Interest rates rise, costs rise, initially profitable investments become losers and are abandoned, and loss-avoiding outputs decrease. People can be fooled only temporarily. The monetary authorities must accelerate inflation beyond expectations in order to prevent workers and machines from being idled more rapidly than money is printed. The logical end of this process is hyperinflation, economic collapse, and abandonment of the currency, a situation that occurred in Germany in 1923, for instance. This raises the question of why representative political authorities would pursue such a policy of artificial stimulation of a unionized economy, unless they are ignorant of the consequences of accelerating inflation or unless political pressures simply make it expedient.

The second major problem with this model of inflation is the difficulty of determining whether it is the primary mechanism driving U.S. policymakers. I rather doubt that it is the central motive. Although the model may be relevant to the United Kingdom, the United States is not a replica of that economy. Unionism is a less important factor here, and policymakers have spent little time blaming unions for inflation, which is a common practice in Great Britain. Further, there is the question of whether American politicians consciously pursued this path of self-destruction. It is hard to falsify the model, but I believe that union pricing failures are a secondary factor in U.S. inflation.

Union Guilt

We can be sure that unions are not the proximate cause of inflation, but they are the key group pressuring politicians to inflate. The pressure takes three forms: (1) union-induced unemployment tempts government to restore "full employment" by inflation, (2) union restrictions on efficiency and production limit aggregate supply (hence real demand), and (3) unions push for more government spending and easy money, thus raising total spending.

The evidence to support these assertions is abundant enough. In fiscal 1981, government spent $21 billion for unemployment benefits for the jobless (the equivalent of $259 for each of the 80 million households in the nation), laid out another $12 billion in employment and training outlays "to fight joblessness," and financed 450,000 public-service jobs.[7] Uncounted portions of spending on other problems like Aid for Dependent Children, food stamps, public housing, Medicaid also go to the unemployed. In 1982, government at all levels—state, local, and national—spent more than $1,000 billion (that's $1 trillion), which amounted to 40% of national income, or $13,000 per household. The Social Security Administration annually calculates social welfare expenditures (private spending apparently adds little to social welfare), which rose to $520 billion in 1981; that is 25% of national income, up from only 9% of national income in 1947. The media commonly attribute high levels of joblessness to too little government spending, insufficient deficits, and stingy monetary policy. Yet the real cause is artificial wage-fixing by unions and government, which destroys productive opportunities, plus welfare doles that are too attractive to refuse. As economist Benjamin M. Anderson said to Henry Hazlitt in 1934, "We can have just as much unemployment as we want to pay for."[8]

A major problem with welfare is that benefits frequently exceed wages for entry-level jobs. Recipients under multiple programs like welfare, rent subsidies, Medicaid, and food stamps can easily lose more than $1 in benefits for every $1 they earn, and this sharply discourages them from working. Charles Hobbs calculated that in 1976 the average welfare family of four received cash and in-kind benefits totaling $14,960, "an amount slightly higher than the median family income in that year."[9] Nathan Glazer cited a case in 1975 in which a family on welfare had cash income and free health and education services amounting to $16,000 without any welfare cheating, and Glazer pointed out that a working family had to earn at least $20,000 to match this standard of living because of taxation. Someone receiving $10,000 a year in benefits is not eager to sacrifice them for a $10,000 job that requires tax payments, needs 2,000 hours of effort, may be inconvenient, might be uncertain in duration, and could be unpleasant.

Massive redistribution of income is doubly destructive because it raises marginal tax rates on both taxpayers and recipients, discouraging both groups to save, work hard, exercise foresight, and prosper. Elaborate experiments with negative income tax plans in Denver and Seattle have confirmed substantial work reductions among the poor, much to the surprise of the investigators.[10] Perhaps more disconcerting is the ruin of families that occurs when welfare makes low-income males irrelevant as breadwinners. The proportion of all black families headed by women rose from 22% in 1960 to 39% in 1977, while white families with female heads rose from 8% to 12%. How many middle-income families would stay together if a woman could draw $40,000 on welfare for her family? How many poor families stay together at $15,000 in welfare benefits? Only immigrant families who are ineligible for these doles will work, advance, and stay together in our economy, free of the destructive temptations of permanent dependency. Naturally, hard work for the poor annoys union officials, who favor the "trickle-down economics" of welfare and state control.

Government and unions are constantly parading as the source of high wages, after arbitrarily forcing them up, and then government is pressured to recognize reality by crudely reducing real wages through inflation in order to permit high levels of employment. If money-wage rates were allowed to seek their market-clearing levels, there would be an immediate outburst of prosperity and curtailment of inflation as capital and labor were freed to seek their highest returns. The total flow of wages would increase roughly in proportion to the gain in real national income, although individual union members might suffer short-term reductions in real hourly wages. Probably more than 90% of the population would experience immediate gains in real wage income, while the remainder would recover from their declines within four years because of a robust expansion in real demand. A richer economy not only means more aggregate supply but also means more real demand for everyone, including former beneficiaries of protectionism. All boats go up (and down) with the tide, in the expression of Jack Kennedy.

Unions not only increase the level of unemployment, as shown in

Chapter 7, but also impose inefficiencies that limit production and heighten inflation. In fact, the most serious economic indictment against unions is that they reduce the level of (real) wages in the economy. Real wage payments per hour of labor depend on overall productivity, and all data, whether over time or across countries, show that the rate of productivity advance is virtually identical to the growth of real wages per hour. Perhaps the best-known examples of union imposed inefficiencies are instances of featherbedding, like union firemen on diesel locomotives or standby orchestras required by union musicians at performances by out-of-town bands. The economy is littered with featherbedding stories ("overmanning" in Britain), some of which are cited in Chapter 4 and all of which reduce the efficiency of the economy. Elsewhere, this book documents the inefficiencies caused by union measures like wage differentials, the Davis-Bacon Act, minimum wages, restrictions on capital mobility, work rules, building codes, licensing, lengthy apprenticeships, closed shops, and so on. If the market process were allowed to circumvent these impediments to trade, nearly everyone would be richer, and unionists would be left with little but social activities to justify their collection of dues from members and nonmembers.

Union political activities promoting federal spending and easy money are a far more important factor in the inflation process than the union drag on productivity growth. Although the elimination of union restrictions would provide an extraordinary outburst of prosperity for a few years, these gains would be rapidly exhausted as we returned to a longer-run growth path, although at 10% higher per capita incomes. Union pressure on federal spending is the main ingredient in double-digit inflation. Dwight Lee has assembled a wide range of evidence to document the legislative agenda of labor, as have Dan Heldman and Deborah Knight.[11] A great deal of union lobbying directly increases demand for the labor services of union members, such as the AFL-CIO's aggressive support for railroad jobs, federal housing construction, urban transit, dams, shipbuilding, merchant marine projects, space programs, bail-outs for New York City, Chrysler, Supersonic Transports, and so on. More generally, union lobbyists support all welfare expenditures, partly to disguise the unemployment effects of union wage rates and work rules.

Nearly one of every three union members is now a government worker: firemen, policemen, civil servants, teachers, electricians, and others. Every increase in public spending, even if intended for the elderly, disadvantaged, poor, halt, and lame stops first at the desk of public employees where generous salaries, benefits, and perquisites are deducted for the "burdens" of administering, implementing, interpreting, and adjudicating programs.

At the Democratic national convention in 1980 over three hundred teacher members of the National Education Association made up the largest single block of delegates. All their expenses were paid by the NEA. As Elliot Abrams wrote, "Think what the press would have said if Exxon had three hundred delegates, for which it paid all expenses!"[12] Nor is it accidental that more than half of all national union headquarters are located in Washington, D.C., compared with not one corporation in *Fortune*'s top 1,000. Perhaps the best summary of the effect of unions on federal spending was offered by the late George Meany when he boasted: "Every piece of social welfare legislation in the last two decades carries a union label."[13]

Not only does organized labor promote every spending bill in Washington but the AFL-CIO also opposes all limitations on federal spending. To quote from the fount of unionism, "The AFL-CIO opposes all spending limitation bills."[14] The position appears to be another one that does not reflect the opinion of the underlying membership because 78% of all union families approved of a constitutional amendment requiring the federal government to balance its budget on an annual basis.

Finally, Lee cites AFL-CIO sources that advertise their adamant pressure on the Federal Reserve Board to supply more money, "ease" credit conditions, "reduce interest rates," and shorten the terms of the board of governors to make them more "responsive to the needs of the people."[15] Easy money, however, raises interest rates because it pours fuel on the fires of inflation. A 10% rate of inflation implies that interest rates must exceed 10% eventually or else lenders are paying borrowers for the privilege of lending money.

In Sum

No one knows the exact quantitative role that unions play in the inflationary process, but it certainly is positive. They may play a larger role in Great Britain where unions have 55% of the labor force and control the Labour party outright, and where incumbent governments rule by the leave of trade union officials who can bring the nation to its knees any time by a coordinated shutdown of the ports, railways, and power facilities. In 1971 the U.K. had a two-week food supply on hand at the beginning of a port strike, and as one politician remarked, the nation stood at the edge of an abyss for a while. When asked by public opinion pollsters in 1976 who was the most powerful and influential man in Britain, 54% said Jack Jones, the general secretary of the Transport and General Workers; only 25% named James Callaghan, the prime minister.[16] A democratic country cannot tolerate this form of minority power forever, and eventually the British unions will be broken. As Arthur Shenfield writes:

> The situation in which Britain finds itself is not new. Centuries ago there were powerful barons who, with their private forces of retainers and liegemen, were able to make or break the weak kings who formally ruled the country. But this did not last. Strong kings arose who broke the power of these unruly barons. The modern baron is the union leader, and his liegemen are the workers who are dragooned into the union system. But this cannot last. It is a prescription for tyranny and poverty.[17]

The reason for the vast number of articles by British economists on behalf of a wage-push theory of inflation is clear. American economists, conversely, have largely ignored or denied the relevance of unions as an inflationary force. Again the reason is obvious. Unions distort the allocation of labor and lower real income but do not necessarily cause sustained rises in prices. Economists here have failed to recognize that unions add to political pressures for inflation by raising the level of unemployment, reducing productivity, and lobbying for more federal spending, bigger deficits, and easier money.

Inflation is like drug addiction, and union pressure probably does more harm in trying to end an inflation than in originating an inflation. Drugs can alter states of body or mind to exhilarating effect initially, but with continued use psychological or physical dependence develops. Tolerance increases, and larger and larger doses are needed to get high. For hard-core cases, the main purpose of each dose is to avoid the agonies of withdrawal and, in drug therapy programs, relapses are the rule and permanent cures the rare exception.

In Washington, union pushers and their ilk say, Hey, let's stimulate the economy. It's sluggish. C'mon, let's get high. Let's kick up production and employment. How? Inject more money. (I've got the drugs right here.) That's it; put it right into the veins of commerce. Ummm, feels good. Gimme more. Hey, not much of a rush that time. More, more...No, man, I can hold a regular job any time I want. I can always give this stuff up....

The objection to fiscal and monetary restraint, especially during a recession (no matter how high the rate of inflation), is that it is "cruel." Production and employment decline; unemployment lines lengthen. The poorest—those who can least afford it—bear the brunt of the burden, say the unionists. The withdrawal pains are too severe; let's go back on smack again. Union political pressure and cries of compassion create the inflation–unemployment dilemma that makes it so hard for politicians to pay the price to end an inflation. Union lobbying is a formula for hyperinflation with a complete economic collapse at the end. Fortunately, however, union lobbyists are not the sole determinants of economic policy in the United States.

10
Contradictions of Unionism

*You need men and I have all the men and they are here
in the palm of my hand; and now I ask, "What am I bid?"*
—*John L. Lewis*

*The AFL-CIO...supports anti-trust action to encourage competitive
pricing throughout the economy. These laws have fallen victim to court
delays and legal shenanigans. This situation must be stopped if the
government is to prevent monopolistic practices, including administered
pricing of goods, cornering of markets, and dividing markets by cartels.*
—*AFL-CIO*, **The National Economy, 1977**

The main problem in any discussion of unionism is to separate the
rhetoric from the reality. A loss of nerve in the intellectual, academic,
and political communities has long exempted unionism from the normal scrutiny directed at interest groups like corporations and
bureaucracies. Organized laborers have effectively portrayed themselves as underdogs who labor against stunning odds to improve the lot
of all working people. Those who venture to question this picture are
vilified as anti-union, right wing, or reactionary, or are labeled as ex-
ponents of Republican trickle-down economics. Dispassionate analysis
is difficult under these circumstances. In the social sciences, where a
reputation for compassion is valuable and where personal courage is
not especially abundant, most scholars are loath to be tainted by the
charge of antiunionism.

This chapter is based on the premise that what unionists say is important and should be treated seriously, not ignored. We can learn
something by critically examining some of the main contentions of
unionism, by asking whether these contentions are supported by the
evidence and whether union actions are consistent with union talk.
Among the issues taken up are the claims that unions support free

enterprise, that they oppose racial discrimination, that corruption is a very minor feature of unionism, and that unionism promotes political stability.

Union Thought

Union statements are composed of more than declarations of sympathy for the downtrodden, and it pays to examine some of them. A chief candidate is unionists' often announced support for a free enterprise system. This claim has been widely accepted, but there is no basis in fact to support the hypothesis. Unionists say they support free enterprise, a mechanism based on voluntary exchange, mutual cooperation, liberty of contract, and open competition, yet they practice disruption, economic warfare, compulsory bargaining, monopoly, and the politics of hate. There are numerous instances of inflammatory statements that no businessman would dare make. For example, Lane Kirkland, the new president of the AFL-CIO, said in 1978: "There is a term for the kind of campaign that American industry has launched to kill the hopes of the most oppressed and deserving workers in this country. It is class warfare. . . .launched by the most privileged and powerful in our society."[1] Or consider remarks by William Winpisinger, president of the machinists' union: "In my lifetime, no group has ever gotten justice in this country without lawlessness. So if we want to see change, then we may have to stop having to have such a high regard for law and order."[2]

Unionists and their apologists adopt a Marxist interpretation of the world when they declaim about public policy, although they never admit that their view is Marxist. The all-purpose rejoinder is that American trade unionists oppose communism overseas and are a bulwark against communism at home. Tiresome repetition of words and phrases like "class," "struggle," "corporate giants," "greed of the rich," "the enemy," "American multinational corporations," "they keep the profits," "docile work force," and "human needs" says quite a bit about the ideology of unionism, despite well-publicized statements about moderation and "working together." The sloganeering in union circles has a superficial plausibility, especially among people who accept the false analogy between war and commerce. The big have an obvious advantage over the small when it comes to fighting a war, but large and small can prosper in commerce if they please their trading counterparts on the other side of the market. Unionists continue harping about corporate giants and underdog workers because this appeals to a natural sympathy for smallness, family farms and small businesses being prime examples, despite the fact that there is virtually no rational substance to these emotional appeals in the case of unions. Moreover, many unions are huge organizations. Perhaps the most obvious deficiency of union reasoning, if we can truly call it reasoning, is that unionists never urge the logical conclusion of their bombast: overthrow of accused oppressors like bankers, corporate executives, rich investors, and big business. Without private enterprise, markets, managers, and investors, of course, unions would expire as independent organizations.

Big Business Day, held on 17 April 1980, illustrates the ideology and direction of unionism. Supporters were an amalgam of trade unionists, consumerists, environmentalists, and clergy. The advisory board included UAW President Douglas Fraser, UFW President Cesar Chavez, Ralph Nader, John Kenneth Galbraith, James Farmer, Julian Bond, Barry Commoner, Michael Harrington, and Robert Lekachman. The board included no representatives from the business world, but organizers said the movement was not antibusiness. It was supposed to begin a decade-long effort to "educate the people," "correct the abuses of big business," "fight crime in the suites," make nominations to the "Corporate Hall of Shame," and "see business better understood... how it sets prices, persuades consumers, influences legislators, and otherwise plans our lives."[3]

Union leaders generally express opposition to socialism in the abstract, much to the bewilderment of European socialists and American radicals. Unionists know that most socialist governments will not tolerate union power, and recent events in Poland offer vivid evidence for this assertion. However, the predominant effect of union action and rhetoric is to undermine capitalism. For instance, many people cannot imagine an unreasonable union demand. Unionism promotes the idea that only selfish businessmen stand between "labor" and abundant wealth, thereby discrediting businessmen and completely misrepresenting the problem of scarcity. The entrepreneurial effort, capital accumulation, and production arranged by businessmen are the main sources of prosperity; they are not obstacles to the prosperity of working people. Even the use of the term "employer" by unions is misleading, because both businessmen and workers are employed by customers, the people who pay for the product.

Taken to extremes, antibusiness propaganda inflames emotions and induces terrorists to bomb corporate property and kidnap or even kill corporate executives. Today, businessmen in many countries, including some in Europe, live in fear for their lives, and the same situation could arise here, too. The result would be a deterioration of morale of managers, greater willingness to tax and regulate business, greater reluctance to save and invest in corporate businesses, and steady impoverishment of the nation. The reduction in economic growth would likely be interpreted as justification for more government intervention.

Union pressure backs every increase in government spending and every government intervention into industry, old or new. Nationalization of the oil industry? Yes. Nationalization of the health care industry? (The accepted label for this is "national health insurance.") Yes. Subsidies to unionized industries? Yes. And on and on. It is virtually impossible to find specific union proposals that promote free markets or a more liberal market order in international or domestic trade. Even on the issue of wage-price controls, where one might expect unionists to support freedom from government control, Lane Kirkland, leader of the AFL-CIO, calls for "controls on the cost of everything and the income of everybody."[4] Union support for free enterprise is simply another instance of the tribute that vice pays to virtue, because there is no substance to the claim. Union policies lead to more concentration of power over economic decisions in the hands of people in the central government. The more government controls, the more those who control government control. If union officials have given this connection any thought, apparently they believe that they will emerge in control of government.

Unionists really have no concept of what an ordered economy would look like. When caught in a contradiction among their clichés, unionists are likely to obfuscate or plead that they are practical men without ultimate answers. For instance, I heard an address by Harry Hubbard, head of the Texas AFL-CIO, before a group of secondary school teachers. Hubbard advocated wage, price, profit, and interest-rate controls, and a teacher asked him how he could control the prices of imported goods too. Hubbard's reply was, "Well...I never said my plan was perfect." Hubbard could think of nothing else to say, and a few moments of deafening silence passed.

The honest truth is that union thought·is unprincipled. Unions, in other words, have no principles, only advocacy of *ad hoc*, coercive interventions against "bad guys." Like other types of collectivism, unionist thought supplies little more than a language for the resentful, an inspiration for protest and ultimately, revolution. Harsh words, perhaps, but harsh words have a place in the description of reality. I take no pleasure in the description; I wish the rhetoric of unionism were otherwise.

The deceptive language of unionism is not confined to unionists. The courts frequently adopt it and its antimarket premises. Consider, for example, *NLRB* v. *Jones & Laughlin* (301 U.S. 1 [1937]), the main Wagner Act case that ushered in the modern era of labor regulations. The Supreme Court's reasoning in favor of the Wagner Act relied upon the erroneous economic arguments in the act's "Declaration of Policy" plus the main legal precedent urged by the government lawyers, namely, *Texas and New Orleans Ry. Co.* v. *Brotherhood* (281 U.S. 548 [1930]), which made the Railway Labor Act constitutional. The court swallowed the entire government line. Asserting that a single employee was helpless in dealing with an employer, that an employee was unable to leave his job to resist arbitrary treatment, and that a union was essential to give laborers an opportunity to deal in an equality with their employers. The majority of the justices, in other words, asserted that business owners are powerful knaves and employees are helpless widows and orphans.

The announced intent of the Wagner Act was to bring "industrial peace," facilitate the stream of interstate commerce, maintain purchasing power. and "equalize bargaining power." High-minded goals, but granting special privileges to unions cannot achieve them. A more accurate translation of the phrase "industrial peace" is "appeasement of the trade unionists," who advertised themselves as preferable to the communists who would lead workers if the Wagner bill was not adopted. Was it prudent to accommodate unionists on these grounds? Certainly it depends on whether American workers really were incipient revolutionaries, ready to follow communists, or whether that was an empty threat. Moreover, those often-asked questions of politics arise: Will they stay bought? Where does appeasement end?

Facilitate commerce? Unions are monopolies designed to interfere with commerce ("weapons of labor") until demands are met. If I were a dues-paying union member, I wouldn't have it any other way. Maintain purchasing power? But unions push up the relative wage of members and the prices of union-produced goods, reduce real national output, and tilt national policies toward erosion of the purchasing power of the dollar.

Equalize bargaining power? What exactly is bargaining power? It is an example of word magic. Typical of the persuasive words in the politics of unionism, it goes undefined and certainly unmeasured. It presents an interesting scientific problem: How do we know if unions have "equalized bargaining power" if that power is unmeasured? No one has measured power on both sides and then checked to see if the indices moved closer together after unionism. The airy economic notions of the courts often are hard to falsify because their economic assertions lack direct empirical content. Presumably, in the case of bargaining power, we would have to find quantitative symptoms of the alleged reduction in unequal power—maybe a rise in labor's share of value added in unionized industries. Serious economic studies, however, can find no union effect with any consistency.

Union leaders constantly stress the monopsony model of the labor market (single buyer), claiming that giant corporations impose wages that must be accepted by helpless unorganized workers unless their individual strengths are pooled to achieve equitable wages and working conditions. Of course, the definition of "equitable" depends on whether one is paying the price or receiving it, but the union description of a buyer's monopoly on labor services has succeeded so well that it is the pillar of labor policy in every Western country. It has produced a public policy based on the idea that the labor problem is how to arrange an "equal fight" between management and labor, how to establish so-called equal bargaining power. The courts, to put it as gently as possible, are not sophisticated in economic reasoning and are imbued with the union model of labor markets.

Discrimination

Nowhere are the elevated sympathies of organized labor more at variance with the record than in the matter of racial, ethnic, and sex discrimination. National union spokesmen urge support of civil rights and equal job opportunities for minorities, the disadvantaged, and women. Union practices at the work place, however, are quite different. Unions have a history of racist and sexist practices unparalleled in other private institutions in this country. Only government restrictions can hope to overcome the obstacles that unions place in the path of economic advance for minorities.

The historical evidence for these assertions is overwhelming. Labor unions sought immigration laws like the Chinese Exclusion Act of 1882 and the Immigration Act of 1924, which was directed at the Japanese. Ironically, the union-label campaign waged on TV today started in the 1880s as a means of telling customers that a product was made by white laborers rather than by Chinese. The history of the exclusion of blacks from trade unions and of union violence against blacks throughout

U.S. trade union history is too sordid and well known to require retelling.[5] Savage attacks on Negros hired as strikebreakers and replacements in labor disputes from the 1880s to World War II were tragic but symptomatic of the broad suppression of economic opportunity for blacks by white unionists. Although discrimination by unionists is less visible today, it continues. The paucity of black workers in craft unions and their overrepresentation in industrial unions shows what happens when unionists rather than employers make hiring and employment decisions. Industrial unions never had the tight control over employment, and hence over union membership, that craft unions have. Unionists continue to resist quota plans that government tries to impose in order to boost black employment on the federally financed construction contracts so tightly controlled by the building-trades union. Unionists continue to pressure government to shut down and harass enterprises employing Mexican nationals, Cubans, and other immigrants. White vigilantes conduct raids on Filipinos who displace them in the asparagus and lettuce fields in California. And the Equal Employment Opportunity Commission receives more than five thousand complaints each year of alleged discrimination by unions, whose inflexible seniority, pay, and promotion structures restrict opportunity for minority workers in unionized work places.

The hostility of unions toward women is perhaps not as well known, but an 1897 statement by Edward O'Donnell, a Boston union leader, is quite explicit:

> The invasion of the crafts by women has been developing for years amid irritation and injury to the workman. . . . The rapid displacement of men by women in the factory and workshop has to be met sooner or later, and the question is forcing itself upon the leaders and thinkers among the labor organizations of the land. . . . Is it a pleasing indication of progress to see the father, the brother, and the son displaced as the bread winner by the mother, sister, and daughter?[6]

In today's social environment, it is more difficult to find public statements of union hostility toward women, but there is an example from Great Britain. Trade unionists there constantly and unequivocally denounce agencies for temporary clerical workers because the "use of agency staff who are temporary and lack job security undermines trade union organization," according to a document by NALGO, a major British union.[7] The annual meeting of unionists at the convention of Britain's TUC, equivalent to the AFL-CIO, has demanded the abolition of the temporary workers agencies or restrictions on the number of temporaries hired in sectors of industry, decrying "temps as self-interested enemies of the working class."[8] The unions have expressed confidence that government would step in and provide alternatives to the private services after their abolition.

The increasing number of females in the U.S. labor force spells considerable difficulty for unionists. Women are traditionally more difficult to organize because they have temporary careers more often than men do; they cluster in poorly unionized service, professional, and clerical sectors, and they have never been as attracted to the collective message of militance put out by unionists as men have. Nevertheless, there are over five million women in unions and employee associations today, or one of every five union members. But only 12% of working women are organized, compared with 24% of men. Women fare very poorly within the bureaucracy of union organizations, despite the fact that they make up at least half of the membership in twenty-one national unions.[9]

None of this is surprising. It is perfectly consistent with the announced objective of groups of highly paid white male workers to take wages out of competition, to handicap competitors who are less fortunate nonwhites, immigrants, and women. Only the effective propaganda about their unions' "progressive" posture makes their actions surprising to anyone. Analysts on the left have difficulty with this well-observed, sustained behavior on the part of unionists and nonunion people. Union defenders say that blacks and others who accept jobs abandoned by well-paid white strikers are simply "confused" or "ignorant" about the struggles between labor and capital. Such blacks, they claim, have fallen prey to the deceptions and the divide-and-conquer strategy of evil but clever capitalists. And the sometimes violent response of white unionists to blacks was simply an understandable blemish on the benign countenance of unionism. It is not a very flattering portrait of blacks' ability to recognize their own self-interest during a century of labor disputes. Invoking ignorance is no explanation at all. Unionists and their apologists must cover up in order to salvage their barren analysis, which is often in contradiction with the facts. They keep pushing their false belief that workers must be disadvantaged by markets where every individual is free to accept any offer he or she feels is best.

To reestablish their superior moral credentials, unionists often point to their political support of income subsidies and handouts for the less fortunate. But what was called "the dole," or "relief," and now is termed "transfers" and "entitlements" does little more than disguise the suffering caused by unions and their allies in government. Relief is a palliative.

Women's activists generally are clear-headed about the obstacles that unions present to the economic progress they seek, but the same cannot be said for black politicians and leaders. The mayor of Gary, Indiana, is much more likely to travel to Washington and plead for funds for his black constituents than he is to visit the local headquarters of the United Steelworkers to pressure them for a reduction in their barriers to black workers. The public utterances of black leaders were very different in the past. W. E. B. DuBois often commented on trade unions, calling them "the greatest enemy of the black working man." Booker T. Washington was a lifelong foe of trade unions, and most other Negro leaders of the time had the same sentiments. Perhaps Walter E. Williams, a young black economist, sums it up best: "Blacks *do* pose a competitive threat to plumbers, electricians, and carpenters as well as to their unions. Unfortunately, for blacks, particularly those most disadvantaged, black leadership today has formed an association with, and does the bidding of, the very people who are most responsible for narrowing the job opportunities of those whom this black leadership claims to represent."[10]

Plant Closings

Although unions claim to be the main source of higher real wages, they support legislation that imposes severe costs on firms that cease operation for any reason. A bill introduced by Representative William Ford (D-Mich.) requires that firms with as little as $250,000 in annual sales must give notice of intended plant closings for up to two years in advance, pay all employees fifty-two weeks severance pay, and pay local government 85% of one year's taxes; the bill also would force taxpayers to provide a variety of governmental aid to affected workers, communities, and so on.[11] If unions are the source of economic progress, why do they support restrictions on capital mobility? Political support for these additional taxes and restrictions on capital mobility implicitly acknowledges that economic improvements are based on productive plant and equipment, technical advance, and managerial efficiency, not union strikes.

The free market directs capital and labor to those places where they can earn their highest returns. If allowed to operate, resources tend to be reallocated continually to their most productive uses. Efficiency and growth are the results. Unions have impeded this process by restricting the mobility of labor, but they have been relatively unsuccessful in directly restricting capital investment in the past. If Ford's bill passes and the central government takes a greater hand in the allocation of capital, the purchasing power of workers' wages necessarily will fall. Apparently, bills like this one have passed in a few state legislatures.

Proponents of penalizing capital mobility concentrate on the employment losses due to plant shutdowns. TV and newspapers find newly idled resources easy to understand, but this myopia is on a par with an assessment of banking that looks only at withdrawals. Naturally, such an analysis would conclude that banking is doomed. The crucial point is that restrictions on closing plants is equivalent to restrictions on plant openings, because if a firm is forced to continue operating an outmoded plant, it cannot invest in a new facility. Labor and capital remain tied up in inefficient activities because they cannot freely seek their highest payoff. The political appeal of restrictions is that the new victims would be invisible and do not know that their economic opportunities have diminished due to union-backed legislation.

Communities with eroding industrial bases have an alternative to the use of federal coercion if they wish to retain and expand their industries: they can compete with successful communities. They could reduce oppressive taxation, regulation, support for high wage costs and trade unions, and efficiently provide some real public services in return for tax dollars. Unionists, however, are not interested in this answer because they are not interested in competition. Two proponents of legislation to restrict capital mobility, Barry Bluestone and Bennett Harrison, state the issue with reasonable clarity: "Trade unionists are especially concerned with how firms use capital mobility to keep labor off guard, to play off workers in one region against those in another, and how the threat of capital relocation is used to weaken labor's [sic] ability to resist corporate attacks on the social wage itself."[12] Some unionists even declare that shutting down a plant is a criminal action and should be treated as such.

Advocates of restrictions really want protection from the competition of other communities, competition with their production facilities and their workers, while unionists want protection from pricing themselves out of the market. Economist Richard McKenzie says consumers and taxpayers should be particularly concerned about restrictions on plant closings because "As the bill is now written, it hands over to unions the power to price labor out of the market—to turn a profitable concern into a losing proposition—and then gives them access to the coffers of the federal government for a 'bailout' or 'buyout.' "[13] McKenzie also says that in a truly free society people should have the right to decide what they should do, how they should live, and where they should invest their labor and financial capital. Private rights to move, to invest, to buy, and to sell seem to play only a small role in discussions of federal policy in the modern era. A conspicuous illustration of the reach of federal intervention is *Wickard* v. *Filburn* (317 U.S. 111), decided unanimously by the Supreme Court in 1942. Filburn was an Ohio farmer who refused to pay a fine levied on him by USDA Secretary Wickard for growing more wheat than was allowed under quotas established under authority of the 1937 Agricultural Adjustment Act. Filburn used his small amount of wheat over the quota exclusively for feeding his livestock, making flour, and seeding his own farm. The Supreme Court upheld the federal fine, ruling that crops grown on a farm for use on the same farm were part of interstate commerce, despite the fact that the goods were never bought or sold in any market. This ruling raises the more general question of whether "private" resources exist in the U.S. economy for their nominal owners to allocate as they might deem profitable.

In 1981 the Supreme Court ruled that companies need not bargain with unions over plant closings. The case involved a New York company that supplied housekeeping, maintenance services, and workers to nursing homes, versus the National Union of Hospital and Health Care Employees.[14] The NLRB had ruled that the company should bargain with the union over the decision to end a money-losing operation in Brooklyn. A federal appeals court upheld the NLRB order when the company appealed. Over objections of the NLRB, the Supreme Court agreed to hear the case. The NLRB argued that closure is a mandatory subject for bargaining when the decision to close a plant, or part of an operation, does not involve investment or disinvestment of large amounts of capital that will affect the "scope and ultimate direction" of the business. The ruling may prove decisive. It appears to reverse a history of growing restrictions on mobility of capital, although the breadth of the ruling is unclear yet. The general counsel of the NLRB has interpreted the ruling narrowly. And the plant-closing battle recently has shifted from Washington, D.C. to the states, where restrictive legislation was introduced in at least twenty-one legislatures in 1981–82.

Pension Funds

Employee pension funds are another instance in which unions silently admit the power of capital as the instrument of economic advance. A large literature on "pension-fund socialism" has arisen in the last decade. Exact figures differ, but most say that American workers own at least one-third of corporate assets in the nation. At end of 1979 private pension funds had assets of more than $350 billion, and state and local funds had another $150 billion. The most controversial book on this subject, *The North Will Rise Again* by Jeremy Rifkin and Randy Barber, drew considerable attention when it appeared in 1978.[15] The argument concentrated on the pension funds of union members and employees of state and local governments in northern states, arguing that a coalition among unions and northern state governments should jointly manage "their" capital funds to restrain the ongoing reallocation of investment toward the South and West. Unions could seize control of pension plans and invest the funds in northern pro-union enterprises, the argument went. Delegates to the 1979 AFL-CIO convention passed a series of resolutions that urged unions to avoid investing in companies that engage in antiunion activity and to direct funds into "socially worthwhile" channels to aid the unemployed, the underprivileged, and the poor. In 1980 the AFL-CIO's Industrial Union Department issued a report that reviewed the pension-fund investment practices of ten large companies and found that funds "were often heavily invested in nonunion firms and firms with high overseas employment...in ways that take away jobs of employees in this country."[16]

Pension funds, of course, are the savings of workers. Each worker wishes to maximize the return on his or her pension investments in order to enjoy a more comfortable retirement. Employees may want to spend money on "the poor" on an individual basis, but they can do more good if they receive maximum returns on their savings. More important, employees are trying to avoid being poor after their own retirement by setting aside earnings in well-managed pension programs today. Control of pensions by union leaders and politicians guided by "social goals" does not augur well for the well-being of workers. Examples of shady investments by the Central States Teamsters' pension fund (over $2 billion strong and reputedly a "bank for the mob") and the purchase of $3 billion of otherwise unsalable New York City municipal bonds by the New York City and New York State pension funds in 1975 are strong reminders.

Currently, pension assets are turned over to professional managers who are legally required to invest and maximize the return for employees. Private pension plans are regulated by four main provisions in the Employee Retirement Income Security Act (ERISA), which are intended to promote prudent management and high returns:

1. Professional management of corporate pensions, with the obligation to seek the highest return consistent with safety.
2. Minimal or no investment of funds in any company for which plan participants work.
3. No investment in a company in excess of 5% of that company's total capital.
4. No investment of more than 10% of the pension fund's total assets in one company.

These federal regulations do not cover state and local government employees, and their funds are a potentially fertile field for public employee union officials. Other union members are covered by ERISA but are poorly protected because the U.S. Labor Department generally adopts a hands-off policy toward union-dominated pension funds, estimated to exceed $90 billion.

In most craft unions, funds are administered by a board of trustees with equal representation by union and management while industrial union funds are generally administered by management alone. The latter fact is the subject of bitter complaint by industrial union leaders and an extended topic for collective bargaining pressure. Some small unions operate their own plans. A Senate subcommittee found in most instances that a trustee from the union dominated the proceedings at joint boards, including selection of an insurance carrier or fund manager, and trustees from company management usually just went along. The subcommittee report said, "This raised the question of whether or not the fact that the management trustees would have to face the labor trustees across the bargaining table at some future date may have affected their actions as trustees."[17] The subcommittee recommended that the Taft-Hartley Act be amended to require neutral trustees on joint union-management boards.

The future depends on how intensively union leaders pursue these opportunities, the degree to which government enforces contractual law, and the enactment of new legislation. The quality of federal enforcement will prove inferior to state enforcement of state laws on pension management, although the lines of enforcement currently are very confused. It is not even settled as to who legally owns or controls these funds. Centralized bureaucrats, friendly with their union clients and insulated from competition, cannot outperform a decentralized system, despite the reputation for impartiality and efficiency enjoyed by federal bureaucrats. The full extent of union corruption is unknown because indictments and convictions are only a sample, but about 450 union officials and employees have been convicted of serious union-related crimes in the past seven years. Twenty-two civil suits were filed by the government during this period to recover stolen union pension funds, with known financial losses totaling over $170 million. "If the present rate of imprudent investments or outright looting continues," says Robert C. Steward, who heads the Justice Department's organized crime units in New York and New Jersey, "this nation will face a benefit-fund default of catastrophic proportions."[18]

Union Corruption

Prevailing academic opinion is that union corruption and racketeering are unpleasant though minor features of unionism, similar to imperfections in human behavior elsewhere. Clark Kerr, for example says:

> Corruption exists, and it is bad; but right and wrong are quite evident and hardly open to debate. Few unions are involved, and other institutions in society have known and do know it also. . . Violence also is to be condemned. It has decreased greatly as a union tactic. . . These are issues, and they will be for a long time; they deserve attention, but they are peripheral to the main contemporary controversy.[19]

Harvard professors Derek Bok and John T. Dunlop write that "legal safeguards now go far to curb dishonesty and encourage democratic behavior. Probably only a tiny fraction of all union officials in America would stoop to serious abuse."[20]

The general counsel of the McClellan Committee in the late 1950s, Robert F. Kennedy, found abuse wherever he looked:

> In the course of my studies it became plain to me that mistakes had indeed been made. For instance, in the early days of the [Kohler-UAW] strike, the union had formed mass pickets at the plant and with human blockades had kept workers out. And it had erred in other ways: the record shows some eight hundred instances of violence, threats, telephone calls, 75% of which had been directed against non-strikers. . .beatings. . .ten or twelve organizers to come in and lend a hand. . .two or three of these (organizers) were big hulking men, and the testimony revealed they were under no direct instructions and were permitted by the UAW to do exactly what they wished. . . . We have mentioned a few who betrayed their trust—Hoffa (Teamsters), Cross (Bakers), Joey Fay (Operating En-

gineers), Maloney (Operating Engineers), Johnson (Carpenters)....
We uncovered corruption in the Hotel and Restaurant Workers
Union, in the Mail Deliverers Union in New York. Max and Louis
Block, who ran the Amalgamated Meat Cutters and Butchers
Workmen's Union in the New York area were prime examples of
labor officials who misuse their position for personal enrichment
and power....Lloyd Klenert, secretary-treasurer of the relatively
small United Textile Workers of America, and Anthony Valente,
the union's president, used the UTWA's comparatively small treasury to buy luxurious homes for themselves.[21]

Despite this sorry record, Kennedy further said, "The labor movement
in America is a huge, living, human machine....It is subject to human
error. But with a few exceptions, the men who run our great labor
unions in this country are honest, dedicated men."[22]

The academic writers and most other observers, like Kennedy, cannot see any pattern because they firmly believe that unionists are public
servants who countervail "management power," rather than self-
interested, organized minorities with a special privilege to coerce. Each
use of violence is a "mistake," every shakedown an "exception." The
prevailing view of union activity is so strong that the premises of this
theory are never reexamined.

The incentives of coercive-monopoly unionism and the enduring
pursuit of self-interest account for the extraordinary corruption in the
labor-representation industry. Special legal immunities are an open in-
vitation to criminals and racketeers to enter. Successful unions fundamentally depend on force and, naturally, specialists in the application of force generally rise to the top. Racketeers set up labor organizations or take over what once were legitimate unions. Ultimately, it is
difficult to tell racketeer-controlled unions from other unions because
both types depend on violence and the threat of violence. Unionists
counter that they contribute to community service agencies, blood
banks, and scholarship funds. True, but irrelevant. Most people love
their mothers and donate to charities, but these are basically consumption activities; they do not generate income, which is the focus of
economic analysis. The plain truth is that our labor laws have arranged
incentives so that honest, noncoercive union officials find it difficult to
survive in competition with the muscleman types.

"Racketeering" is an interesting word to try to define. Murray
Gurfein offered this version: "Racketeering, a term loosely applied to
a variety of criminal schemes, has not yet received exact legal definition. It usually designates, however, the activity for profit (in connec-

tion with sale of goods and services) of an organized group which relies upon physical violence or an illegal use of group pressure to accomplish its end."[23] Gurfein also called it "organized extortion and levying of periodic tribute." To illustrate a racket, he said: "The simplest type is that in which a monopoly is set up by the racketeers with no other aid than protection by politicians. Illustration is found in rackets in some perishable foodstuffs, where the technique is to coerce retailers through suggestion or ready example of violence to cease buying from the wholesalers and to buy from a new and unnecessary middleman—the racketeer himself."[24] This description is striking in that it comes very close to describing otherwise legitimate trade unionism. Certainly the economic technique is the same; the difference is only in degree of lawfulness. Legal campaign contributions sometimes buy better protection and politicians than illegal bribes do.

If picketing and sabotage can force enterprises to recognize union officials as bargaining representatives and force them to pay higher wages, they can serve other lucrative purposes as well. According to a study by the U.S. Bureau of Alcohol, Tobacco, and Firearms, incidents of union bombings caused $3.8 million in property damage between 1977 and 1979.[25] Many, though not all, union leaders view nonunion workers as renegades and union members as their vassals or, at best, their foot soldiers. This is a natural analogy, since the philosophy of unionism says that individual workers are helpless creatures who lack dignity, pride, and the capacity for independent thought.

Two essential conditions are required for the existence of sustained corruption: (1) a bureaucratically created scarcity and (2) separation of the negative effects of corruption from the bureaucrat's own wealth. In other words, an individual with power to distribute artificially scarce goods can extract bribes from eager suppliants, whether that individual is a building supervisor who accepts "key money" from new tenants to whom he has "granted" a rent-controlled apartment, or a union official who has provided a firm with a worker or has given a union member an employment opportunity. Craft unions fulfill the conditions for corruption best because they have local markets, low public visibility, and frequently a life-and-death grip over employment. Most racketeering, therefore, occurs in the building trades, trucking, longshoring, cleaning and dyeing, restaurant work, garment trades, furriers, theaters, produce, and live poultry. Perishability, tight time schedules, and small businesses make these companies easy marks.

Relatively little racketeering occurs in the large industrial unions, because they are in highly visible national markets (employers), goods are nonperishable, time schedules are flexible, and unions lack a tight grip over employment through closed shops and referral hiring halls. CIO union leaders have been more noted for their "progressive" social philosophy than for racketeering. As C. Wright Mills wrote in 1948, "It is said there are racketeers in the AFL and that the CIO has communists. Both statements are true."[26]

There are some ten thousand building-trades business agents in the country, and a story about Frank Sonsini, business agent for Local 32 of the Bricklayers' Union in Newton, Massachusetts, says a lot about their power:

> Members approach him only when summoned, and when he talks they listen carefully.... Almost singlehandedly and without a by-your-leave to international headquarters, Frank Sonsini can negotiate a contract or call a strike. When there are jobs to be had, he decides which members can get them. No one joins Local 32 without his approval. He runs the pension and health-care plans. "Frank operates like a king," says an admiring colleague.[27]

Some academics spend a great deal of effort studying the internal operations of labor unions, and they lament the lack of union democracy and the low caliber of leadership. The Labor-Management Reporting and Disclosure Act (Landrum-Griffin) was passed in 1959 in order to correct the situation after the McClellan hearings exposed widespread graft and corruption among union officials. The act defined a bill of rights for members (strongly opposed by unionists), required unions to adopt written constitutions and bylaws, regulated the use of trusteeship, set election standards, and permitted members to sue officials for misuse of union funds. If unions were nothing more than private associations, this law would have constituted an extraordinary intervention by the central government into the private affairs of association members and their elected leaders. But unions, of course, exercise coercive power over many job opportunities, and the resulting abuses of power by union leaders must then be regulated.

The net effect of these regulations has been virtually nil, except for a blizzard of paperwork filed at the Labor Department. An investigation on the scale of the McClellan hearings would uncover as much or more corruption in unions today, and the Organized Crime Strike Force of the Justice Department is slowly establishing it. An experienced Justice Department prosecutor said, "Organized crime in labor is probably the most serious problem in the criminal field. It overrides everything else. It is frightening to the economy. I can name four national unions now in the hands of hoodlums."[28] The four unions are commonly believed to be the Teamsters (nearly 2 million members), Laborers (475,000), Hotel and Restaurant Employees and Bartenders (430,000) and International Longshoremen's Association (60,000). These four unions accounted for about one-third of the 450 union convictions over the last seven years; the remainder were spread over unions like the UAW.

If things are so miserable, why don't union members throw the rascals out? First, most union locals do not really have serious corruption. There are 71,000 locals in the country and approximately 500,000 elected unionists, but most have little significant power over a union-created scarcity and, therefore, few temptations to abuse power. They are stewards, grievance committeemen, and the like who debate where the water cooler should go rather than what wages will be and who decide which members will get work, which firms will get workers, when to strike, and how to handle union funds. The Justice Department estimates that less than one-half of 1% of union locals in the United States are plagued with systematic corruption, many of them in Chicago, Miami, and northern New Jersey. Second, apathy is widespread. There is not much incentive for one person to buck the system. Most people want to work and then be left alone with their families. Opposing the system means bearing heavy personal costs without gaining much personal profit, unless one plans to run for a union office. Furthermore, if leaders are displaced, the same corrupting incentives remain for their successors. Third, very tangible restraints discourage troublemakers, especially in the craft unions. Economic pressure is foremost, with brass knuckles held in reserve. A dissident gets no union job opportunities, and that's usually sufficient to discourage everyone under unionized systems of rigid seniority, wage structures, and promotion opportunities. Formal union complaint proceedings are controlled by the union leaders, who can impose fines and suspend workers. One union reportedly disciplined over four thousand members and fined them $300,000 in a single year.[29]

Employees can petition to have the union decertified as a bargaining agent, or they can campaign for new leadership or protest election results, but the drawbacks of both actions are formidable. For example, union officials are allowed to expel members who file a decertification petition without fear of nullifying the election results. If a member suspects election fraud, the member must exhaust the remedies under the union constitution and bylaws before a complaint can be filed with the secretary of labor. If the secretary finds probable cause he or she brings a suit in federal court. In addition to tangible obstacles, union ideology denounces "dual unionism," "raiding," "factionalism," or any other form of individualism or competition against entrenched leadership.

Most union constitutions provide that a member may be disciplined for "conduct unbecoming a union member," or "conduct detrimental to the best interests of the union," or "slandering an officer," or "undermining the constitution." Yes, they specify member rights too, but it is reminiscent of the Soviet constitution, initially widely praised in the West as the most perfect document in history, despite the fact that it was based on the one-party (monopoly) principle, thereby completely negating human liberties. The trappings of democratic rule are a very light camouflage for the feudal conditions under which people in the Laborers' or the Operating Engineers' union work. Union power holders have the same view of "deviationists" as Soviet rulers do. Valery Chalidze, editor of *Kronika Press,* a periodical of Soviet dissidents, says that Soviet propaganda maintains that "the individual has no need for freedom of speech, it stresses instead expression of the collective will."[30]

Multiple salaries and expense accounts totaling six figures are common among the statesmen of the labor movement. These incomes entice people with modest schooling and modest alternative employment options to put considerable effort into keeping their jobs. Thirteen of the top fifty-four national union officials in the country received over $100,000 in 1979, according to financial reports filed with the Department of Labor. The late Teamsters' president Frank Fitzsimmons topped the list with $296,000, including $124,000 in legal expenses to defend himself against a challenge from dissidents who charged him with union improprieties.[31] Less visible are the unknown hundreds of officials in craft unions who draw three and four salaries from various union organizations and have three or four severance-pay and retirement accounts.[32]

Since 1967 the chief compliance officer within the U.S. Department of Labor, who is responsible for monitoring the handling of union funds, has come from the ranks of unions: Thomas R. Donahue from the Service Employees; W. J. Usery, Jr., from the Machinists; Paul J. Fasser, Jr., from the Steelworkers; Bernard E. DeLury of the Lathers' and Teamsters' unions, and Francis X. Burkhardt of the Painters. Arthur L. Fox, an attorney for PROD, a reform-minded organization of Teamsters, says that putting "a union guy in there to decide whether to prosecute unions is an outrage—like letting the wolf into the chicken coop."[33] There are numerous instances of Labor Department foot-dragging. For example, attorneys from the Justice Department in 1975 asked the Labor Department to take over as court-appointed monitor of the assets of a laborers' union fund after its president was convicted of embezzling union and pension funds. The secretary of labor refused on two occasions, saying that there wasn't any statutory precedent and it would take too much manpower. The embezzler got $2 million more.[34] There is little reason to wonder why the Department of Labor is some-times irreverently referred to as the Department of Organized Labor.

Union officials are elected, yes; votes are cast, yes; and they are counted by whoever has control of the electoral machinery. Most na-tional officers are elected at a national convention by delegates who are beholden to the national officers. Contested elections are rare. The key problem is that it is almost impossible to mount a significant challenge to an incumbent president in a national union without the help of ac-tive members of the union's executive board. Participation in turn depends on whether insurgents are confident that if their challenge fails, they still will be reelected to the board because of their secure power base in the union. In effect, this requires board election by geographic district rather than at-large election. Most unions have at-large elections for board members, the exceptions being some of the old CIO industrial unions like the USW and UAW. Sara Gamm studied all unions of more than 25,000 members that were ever affiliated with the AFL-CIO and found that only twenty-six of the eighty-one unions had executive boards elected by geographic district, and only thirteen had district boundaries fixed by constitution rather than by executive board or president.[35]

Even with direct membership balloting and contested elections, there are many examples of suspicious results. A classic example was the defeat of President David J. McDonald of the United Steelworkers in 1965, an election that he actually may have won, but challenger I. W. Abel had more control over the poorly supervised electoral machinery. There were only five election defeats of an incumbent union president in fifty-one major U.S. unions between 1949 and 1966, including McDonald's defeat.[36] In that period there were over three hundred elections. All five defeats occurred in industrial unions formed after 1930. In the old-line AFL unions, displacement of national union officers is truly a rare event: Dan Tobin was president of the Teamsters for forty-five years; William Mahon led the Transit Union for fifty-three years; John L. Lewis headed the UMW for forty-one years; Joseph Moreschi ran the Laborers for forty-two years; J. A. Franklin led the Boilermakers for thirty-six years, and so on. As a George Bernard Shaw character proclaimed in *The Apple Cart*: "No king is as safe in office as a trade union official."

In high union office you are almost more likely to lose your life than an election. The unsolved disappearance of Jimmy Hoffa in the summer of 1975, and the murder of UMW presidential candidate Joseph (Jock) Yablonski, his wife, and daughter in December 1969 by killers hired by UMW president Tony Boyle are well-known incidents, but there are more. The government has tried many of the key suspects in the Hoffa case in an unsuccessful attempt to get a cooperative witness, and one who appeared ready to talk, Salvatore "Sally Bugs" Briguglio, was gunned down in 1978. Anthony "Tony Pro" Provenzano murdered a union boss, Anthony "Three Fingers Brown" Castellito, in order to take over his 12,000-member Teamsters' local. Tony Pro was convicted in 1978 of the murder plus extortion. He then appointed his daughter to run Local 560, thus retaining control while serving his term in prison. Four officials in the Laborers' union alone have been killed by hitmen. This is the tenth largest union in the nation; it did not hold a convention for thirty years; its leadership is Italian and its membership mostly black.[37]

Union leaders have little to fear from the law, despite increasing enforcement effort. LaVern J. Duffy, former McClellan committee investigator and current general counsel for the Senate Permanent Subcommittee on Investigation, said, "Only a small percent of these crimes are being detected."[38] Punishment of union-related crimes is seldom severe; for example, most embezzlers never go to jail. Of the 450 union officials convicted over the last seven years, only 168 were formally barred from holding union office as required by the Landrum-Griffin Act. Whether Dave Beck, Jimmy Hoffa, Frank Fitzsimmons, or Roy Williams heads the Teamsters, the government has no hope of cleaning up this union or any union that meets the necessary conditions for corruption, conditions largely created by government legislation.

What about the businessmen who cooperate with union corruption? Aren't they as guilty as the unionists who take bribes? By and large, businessmen are as much victims of union muscle as union members are. Businessmen do not seek out additional expenses such as illegal payments to unionists. They pay only because unionists are in a position to extort money by coercive threats, cutting off labor services, or the use of violence. "Extortion" is often a more accurate term than "business bribes to union officials," although sometimes union officials and employers jointly extort funds from employees or from other enterprises. Confronted wtih union monopoly and violence, businessmen are naturally tempted to use the "grease" so forcefully demanded by unionists. It is similar to doing business overseas, where government officials frequently demand payoffs as a routine matter before they will allow American businessmen to do business. Is it bribery or extortion?

Right-to-Work Laws

Contradictions in labor policy are vividly illustrated by the long-standing controversy over union security measures. The private use of force to compel unwilling workers to join a union or to pay union dues makes even the sympathizers of unions mildly uncomfortable, not to mention some union members and nonmembers who are forced to pay, and the issue remains as lively and unsettled as ever in the courts. For instance, the state supreme court in Maine ruled against the agency shop in a school board agreement, while the state supreme court in Washington upheld the legality of the agency shop for state employees that same year (1978).

In public debates the basic defense for compulsory union dues is the "free rider" argument. Union officials argue that, unlike other private associations, they cannot legally exclude nonmembers in a bargaining unit from the benefits of union-negotiated wages, hours, working conditions, and grievance procedures. Therefore, they claim that unions must have the right to negotiate a union or agency shop in order to compel free riders to pay their fair share of the costs of collective bargaining. Correction of the problem, by this view, requires that all persons represented by a union, whether they want representation or not, be compelled to pay dues to the union.

Wide acceptance of the argument is indicated by the U.S. Supreme Court's endorsement in *Employees' Department* v. *Hanson* (351 U.S. 225 [1956]):

> We only hold that the requirement for financial support of the collective bargaining agency by all who receive the benefits of its work

is within the powers of Congress under the Commerce Clause and does not violate either the First or the Fifth Amendment.

Another version of the court's approval is in *Radio Officers* v. *NLRB* (347 U.S. 17 [1954]):

> Congress recognized the validity of unions' concern about "free riders," i.e., employees who receive the benefits of union representation but are unwilling to contribute their fair share of financial support to such union, and gave the unions the power to contract to meet that problem.

The same view generally has been supported in the academic literature.[39]

Samples of collective agreements covering over a thousand employees in the private sector show that more than 80% have union security clauses that compel all employees represented by the union to pay dues. Sample estimates also show that over 20% of public employees covered under union agreements are required to pay union dues. At least 19 million employees are compelled to pay union dues; that amounts to more than $2.5 billion per year.[40]

Empirically, the interesting question is how much of this union income would disappear if union security clauses disappeared? Specifically, how many workers would stop paying dues if compulsion were prohibited, all else being equal? Without empirical evidence the number apparently could range from zero up to 19 million. One way to narrow the range is to look at economic studies that estimate the effects, if any, of right-to-work laws. Such laws exist in twenty states, entirely in the South and West as shown in Table 10–1, and prohibit contracts requiring union membership or payment of union dues as a condition of continuing employment. James W. Kuhn in 1961 estimated that union membership and dues revenue would drop 6% to 15% if the union shop were prohibited. If this estimate were correct today, unions would lose between 1.3 million and 3.3 million members, or between $210 million and $525 million in dues per year. Subsequent econometric studies, however, have found no significant independent effects of right-to-work laws on union membership, strike activity, wage levels, or union organizing activity.[41] If recent estimates are correct, prohibition of compulsory dues would have little effect on union membership or income. However, I have estimated that a minimum of 1 million and perhaps as many as 4 million nonmembers pay compulsory union dues.[42] Unions would almost certainly lose the dues income from these workers because nonmembership indicates an aversion to unions; after the monetary price is paid, the predominant incen-

Table 10-1
States with Right-to-Work Laws

State	Year of Adoption
Alabama	1953
Arizona	1946
Arkansas	1944
Florida	1944
Georgia	1947
Indiana	1957*
Iowa	1947
Kansas	1958
Louisiana	1976
Mississippi	1954
Nebraska	1946
Nevada	1951
North Carolina	1947
North Dakota	1947
South Carolina	1954
South Dakota	1946
Tennessee	1947
Texas	1947
Utah	1955
Virginia	1947
Wyoming	1963

* Repealed in 1965.

tive is to join to receive better grievance service and avoid harassment by union members.

Kuhn estimated that in 1958 groups on both sides of the right-to-work issue spent over $12 million on political battles; considerably more has been spent since then. For instance, unions spent $2.5 million to defeat the right-to-work amendment in Missouri in 1978, and proponents of the amendment spent nearly $1 million.[43] A sizable amount of wealth must be at stake. I suspect that the answer lies in turnover, which exceeds 50% a year in manufacturing employment. Individuals, not job slots, are union members, a fact ignored in statistical analyses of the right-to-work issue thus far. Even in enterprises with constant employment levels, typically one-half are new employees each year. To maintain membership, a union must continuously recruit a new member for each departed member and unionists are anxious to escape

from this market constraint on their behavior. In fact, it is so important to continuing viability in most circumstances that unions must
find a way around right-to-work laws where they exist. Lax enforcement of the laws, unquestioning employees, and compliant employers
who provide substitute arrangements probably account for much of
the failure to find dramatic effects of right-to-work laws. Much unionization in the South, for example, is in national and multinational companies that are anxious to avoid difficulty with unions they deal with in
the North. The empirical effects of right-to-work laws no doubt will
continue to attract empirical research.

Secondary arguments offered by union spokesmen to justify compulsory union dues have been less popular.[44] They argue that federal
labor law can be relied on to prevent union abuses of security provisions, that 91% of the organized workers who cast ballots approved of
the union shop in NLRB elections between 1947 and 1951, and that
security clauses reduce strife by encouraging more "responsible"
union behavior. Consider the following remarks on the union shop
from a prominent textbook in labor economics:

> This argument that the union shop coerces workers into unionism
> against their will appears to have been overdone. Few workers
> seem to have a conscientious objection to unionism. . . . There
> seems little doubt that a union is better able to function in a
> peaceful and constructive way if it embraces most or all of the
> labor force. It is unreasonable to demand that unions be "respon-
> sible" while at the same time denying union officers the control
> over their membership that would make group responsibility
> effective.[45]

It is also claimed that experienced employers favor the union shop
because it "stabilizes" labor relations. The most interesting secondary
argument used by unions attacks right-to-work laws per se instead of
directly propounding the merits of compulsory union dues. The argument opposes right-to-work laws on the grounds that such laws restrict
liberty of contract, that is, the freedom of private parties to agree to
union security clauses if they wish. Ironically, this is the basis for
Milton Friedman's opposition to right-to-work laws also.[46] Legal versions of the argument are based upon the cases of *Adair* v. *U.S.* (208
U.S. 161 [1908]) and *Coppage* v. *Kansas* (236 U.S. 1 [1915]) in which
the Supreme Court invalidated federal and state laws prohibiting
yellow-dog contracts because such laws denied freedom of contract.
Perhaps, needless to say, the doctrine of individual contractual liberty
is a rather unconvincing expedient for advocates of collective bargain-

ing to use. Haggard makes a libertarian argument for right-to-work laws on the grounds that collective-bargaining agreements are not true contracts in which enforceable promises of something of value are voluntarily exchanged between parties. According to this view, right-to-work laws properly prevent the state from enforcing employer promises for which nothing is given in return.[47] Of course, this raises the more general question of what union representatives offer in a contract, other than perhaps a promise to avoid some forms of coercion during the life of the contract (a no-strike pledge).

Under the National Labor Relations Act, union spokesmen use the free rider problem to justify coercive dues. Although the argument rarely includes much detail, an implicit premise is that securing employer payment of union wages for everyone in a bargaining unit, including employees who are nonmembers, is a costly burden to the union and its membership. We are led to believe that unions would not bear the expense to ensure that all workers in bargaining units get union-negotiated conditions of employment unless they had a legal obligation to do so.

This invites an obvious objection. If nonmembers in the unit agree to work for something less than union wages, employers have an incentive to substitute nonmembers for union members. A union's monopoly power would rapidly erode if individual nonunion employees and employers were free to reach agreements that departed from union-negotiated terms. Traditional recognition of this phenomenon is shown in a 1901 statement of the U.S. Industrial Commission:

> if nonunion brick layers are permitted to be introduced at the will of the employers, side by side with the members of the union, there can be no possible guarantee that they do receive the union rate. The union has no jurisdiction over them and no means of knowing what they get. There is a constant probability, therefore, that the employer will introduce as many nonunion men as possible, will hire them below the union rate, and will, as opportunity offers, discharge the members of the organization. Those who are in the union will be tempted to get out of it and work for lower wages in order to retain their employment.[48]

Government enforcement of union conditions on all employees in a so-called bargaining unit relieves unions of this danger to their survival by creating "forced riders." Premium union wages cannot be extracted if employers can hire any consenting adult and if people generally are free to make voluntary exchanges that depart from union terms. The purpose of unions is to restrict freedom of exchange in labor markets.

The ironic conclusion is that "sale" of individual union memberships would generally lead to nothing to sell, that is, zero monopoly rent. A union can extract wage premiums only if it can enforce exclusive hiring of union members or else enforce payment of union wages for everyone hired.

While a free rider problem may be a necessary condition for rationalizing the use of coercion by unions, it certainly is not a sufficient condition. Voluntary mechanisms are always being sold short as devices for resolving problems, including collective consumption problems. The free rider argument is a transparent ruse for imposing compulsory dues. The imposition of union taxation on all employees within the unit enables a redistribution of union costs and an increase in union income. Unions are inconsistent in failing to advocate the benefit principle of taxation for all the governmental welfare programs they favor, though union leaders must be admired for their guile. On the other hand, the arguments of some union opponents are no more correct and no less exaggerated than those made of the unions. Right-to-work advocates basically claim that compulsory union dues is a civil liberties issue. It supposedly is an unfair labor practice to require workers to pay tribute to a private association (the union) as a condition of continued employment.

This argument has superficial appeal, but it is weakened by the fact that our economy is predominantly nonunion. In principle, so long as there are many employers and potential employers, they should be free to offer any terms they want to attract employees. Employers might require payments to a pension plan, a labor union, or the Communist party, or they might insist that workers sign a yellow-dog contract, and none of this would interfere with the freedom of individuals to contract for employment in the labor market. In fact, legally to prohibit employers from offering particular packages of compensation to individual employees does interfere with freedom. Most observers fail to understand that an exchange of labor services for money, voluntarily arrived at, constitutes an agreement by both individuals.

Why do employers require employees to pay dues to a labor union? They do not require payments to the Communist party. The primary answer is that many employers find it cheaper to grant this concession to union pressure than to accede to other union demands. The employer, in a sense, hands over to union headquarters dues from both willing and unwilling employees. In this sense, compulsory dues tend to be a symptom of union monopoly power rather than the cause of union power, although this assertion has all the difficulties of any chicken-and-egg argument.

To a large extent, the controversy over compulsory dues is misplaced. Compulsory dues and similar "abuses" of monopoly power in the labor market are not the main problem. Monopoly power is there to be abused; it has no other purpose. The real public-policy issue is the creation and support of private monopoly power. Some well-intentioned people believe that the fundamental answer to abuses of union power is state right-to-work laws or more detailed regulation of unions by the federal government. This may be the more politically practical approach, but it is not really a satisfactory answer. Taft-Hartley and Landrum-Griffin bear silent witness to this point. The most harmful thing that could happen to unions is deregulation of the labor market. Union monopoly power would shrivel without extensive labor laws and without government intervention that supports unions. Repeal of the Wagner Act, no matter how politically unrealistic, would be a stunning loss to unionists, because it is very difficult to exercise a monopoly power that has disappeared.

Political Stability

Economic analysis of unions is similar to the analysis of other monopoly problems. Although economists generally do not have much good to say about monopolies, most of them do not want to appear hostile to unions either, so the common solution has been to ignore unions and their actions. The few contemporary economists who venture into the area diplomatically balance their remarks. An important example is Albert Rees: "If the union is viewed solely in terms of its effects on the economy, it must in my opinion, be considered an obstacle to the optimum performance of our economic system." This distinguished labor economist further says that unions "help to protect the minimum consensus that keeps our society stable" and provide workers with "organized representation in public affairs." Rees concludes that "the economic losses imposed by unions are not too high a price to pay for successful performance of this [social and political] role."[49]

This rationale for unions and union methods is common in the academic community. I do not pretend to be an expert on "social stability," but it is difficult to see how unions promote stability. Henry Simons was far wiser when he observed in 1944 that

Organized economic warfare is like organized banditry and, if allowed to spread, must lead to total revolution, which will, on very hard terms, restore some order and enable us to maintain some real income instead of fighting interminably over its division among minorities. . . .a community which fails to preserve the discipline of competition exposes itself to the discipline of absolute authority.[50]

Unions must maintain a more-or-less constant war mentality among their memberships. Periodic disruptions in the flow of production of goods and services must be engineered to gain economic "victories," reinforce identity of the enemy among the rank and file, and engender the members' gratitude.

Granted, union officials provide organized workers with political representation, but what kind of representation? Most observers assume, without evidence, that union lobbying must reflect the views of organized workers and probably all lower-income and disadvantaged people as well. But a recent study of this belief found little evidence of a close correlation between members' preference and AFL-CIO lobbying in Congress.[51] Dan Heldman and Deborah Knight compared data in surveys published by leading pollsters with AFL-CIO political goals on a variety of issues. Even on narrow union issues there were major gaps between union members' views and the AFL-CIO views. On compulsory membership (union security) and common situs picketing the polls in the 1960s showed close splits or majorities supporting AFL-CIO views, but in the 1970s members' views changed. A Roper poll in 1977, for example, found that 58% of union members supported right-to-work laws, 63% endorsed Section 14b of the Taft-Hartley Act, and 64% favored picketing limited to a specific contractor. Union officials have spent many years "educating" their memberships on these issues and apparently have failed. The AFL-CIO ordinarily regards people with such views as reactionaries, but apparently the group includes a majority of union members.

Most legislation favored by union officials actually harms nonunion workers, so they are unlikely to favor union lobbying positions. Union wage rates and entry restrictions permanently push a large number of underprivileged workers into the low-wage corners of our economy, including illegal activity. Minimum-wage laws and the restriction of highly-paid craft and industrial workers reduce opportunities for entry-level employment of teenagers, blacks, southern workers, elderly workers, and female workers. Other union-promoted interventions harm people, including union members, in their capacity as consumers (for example, restrictions on competition from foreign goods and preventing closure of unprofitable plants) and in their capacity as taxpayers, because union officials favor all expansions of the public sector, more public employees, and bigger salaries for civil servants.

There is a hint of condescension in the claim that unions provide workers with political representation. We are left vaguely to believe that employees would go unrepresented in the political process without unions or that some unspecified doom would surely follow any reduction in the political power of big unions. This is no more sensible than the 1960s argument that the federal government should spend billions right now to prevent burning and rioting in our central cities. The Marxist view is that the upper classes occasionally appease the masses with welfare doles (bread and circuses) in order to avoid revolution and seizure of ill-gotten capitalist booty. This approach leaves little room for reasoned discussion of principles to guide individual behavior or to guide action by the state, nor does it suggest a promising positive model or explanation of human behavior. The ultimate argument for the special immunities of unionists is to allow us to keep the lid on, to suppress the strong susceptibility of working people to revolution and communism, to extend the life of capitalism for a few more years. Unions of working people must have special legal privileges or else labor will not tolerate the remnants of capitalism and free markets.

The most improbable aspect of the argument is the belief that hard hats are inherently revolutionary. No evidence is offered, nor do advocates carefully demonstrate that use of organized force (laws and regulations) on behalf of organized unionists forestalls incipient radicalism. Perhaps a relevant question is whether commentators on the left have ever worked for a living with their hands or have ever met any blue-collar workers. In the high spirits of the 1960s, some radicals went off campus into blue-collar work places in order to spread the good word. The campaign disappeared within a few weeks, presumably in the face of unpromising early returns.

11
Capitalism, Socialism, and Unionism

*There are a thousand hacking at the branches of
evil to one who is striking at the root.*
—Thoreau

*The history of mankind is a long record of
obstacles placed in the way of the more efficient
for the benefit of the less efficient.*
—Ludwig von Mises

U nionism stays enshrouded in mystery for most observers. Collective
bargaining, strikes, and settlements under duress remain practices in
search of an appealing theory. Many people of good will praise the existence of labor unions yet remain vaguely uncomfortable with the
idea. One of the popular naivetés of our times is to embrace unions as
an abstract ideal and then condemn them when they act like unions.
The fervent wish of most commentators—on the right, to the left, and
in between—is to embrace unionism and hope that it doesn't harm
their children. Yet real understanding depends on considering unions
and public policy toward them with an unflinching eye. If my analysis
of the real nature of unionism is false, my most fervent hope is that it
will be challenged and corrected in open public debate. Detachment
and reason, not compassionate rhetoric, will guide us to labor policies
that coincide with reality and facilitate the accomplishment of the aims
shared by most people in the West.

This chapter shows that unions fit into neither capitalism nor socialism, as generally conceived, and analyzes why this is so. Property in
jobs and industrial democracy are two specific modifications of either
capitalism or socialism that cannot withstand logical scrutiny.

Unionism is shown to be simply a subset of the man-made restrictions on human action. The chapter concludes with a discussion of the future of U.S. unionism, and I urge a restoration of equality before the law as the correct goal for our labor policies.

The Emotional Need for Unions

Although a few old-time industrialists denounced unions in no uncertain terms, most conservatives today publicly praise labor unions, presumably because conservatives mean it rather than because they seek respectability or just want to gain a hearing. Neo-conservatives like Irving Kristol, Daniel Bell, and Robert Nisbet provide an erudite defense of unions, though they acknowledge the grievous problems of unionism. The essence of their rationalization is that unions are a vital component in the web of institutions that stand between the state and the individual, just as the nuclear or extended family, churches, schools, the Red Cross, and social clubs do. What they describe as "free trade unions" fit well in a liberal order because such unions are an essentially conservative force, according to this view. Labor unions give "workers" (presumably the "little people") a sense of place, a sense of belonging in an otherwise rootless, changing industrial-technical society. As a source of traditional authority, unions are valuable for their reactionary, guildlike nature. Tribal organizations confer "dignity" and status on individuals and lift them out of a role as depersonalized cogs in an immense machine. On the negative side, however, neo-conservatives worry about the union impulse to power, the union ability to bring an economy (or at least sectors of an economy) to a grinding halt, and to extort higher wages in an increasingly interdependent society. So neo-conservatives mark time, viewing unions as a balance of good and evil, a potent political force, perhaps to be won over as a political ally for economic growth and a check on environmentalists. Unspecified ointments are supposed to clear up the acne of unionism.

The left has an even less comfortable relationship with unionism. The collectivist rhetoric and bellicose talk of unionists warms the hearts of those on the left, who have traditionally believed that unions are all too mild in their response to the exploitation of capitalists who expropriate too much of the social product. Unions at least raise the workers' consciousness, fight capitalists, and promote solidarity, by this view, but they never really gain worker control over decisions, and they never usher in a socialist revolution. Leftist intellectuals always loved unions for their revolutionary potential rather than for the conservative behavior that pleases observers in the center or on the right. Except for high points like the Industrial Workers of the World before World War I and the CIO unions in the 1930s and 1940s, the potential was never realized, and real leftists tend to denounce unionists for having accommodated reactionary capitalism and for their narrow vision, corruption, and loss of missionary zeal. "Bought off" sums up the left's contempt for unionism, especially for "business unionism."

Many people, including labor relations specialists, hold to the middle ground, comforted by the fact that unionists are criticized by both the right and left for completely different reasons. This middle view is a muddled notion that unions are a mixture of good and bad. Specific strikes, disruptions, and wage settlements can annoy, even anger these people but they retain a sentiment that unions are a good concept, even if imperfectly realized. Unions supposedly contribute to the working of a pluralist, polyglot society, a countervailing force in a political economy composed of large, powerful groups. As one labor expert wrote, "These [labor] policies grew from a pragmatic case-by-case search for workable answers to concrete questions."[1] Although this sounds terribly practical and in line with the allegedly nonideological temperament of America, the drawback is that such a sequence of policy rulings is "unprincipled," even if the rulings are rendered by "impartial" academics. This differs from the rule of law, which attempts a consistent application of normative principles of a legal or social kind. The middle ground resembles what passes as political theory in international affairs, where something called a balance of power is supposed to be good, although the questions about how the power is distributed, in whose hands it is held, for what purposes it is used, by what values it is guided, and with what laws of motion it is ruled are more important, though neglected and lacking answers.

Nothing in this mishmash of contemporary political views truly satisfies. There is an unspoken suspicion among many that unionism is an idea whose time has passed, that unionism's finery is nonexistent, playing out its string as an opaque ideology.

The only way to understand unionism is to return to economic truths. If we consider the two coherent patterns of social organization —capitalism and socialism—the striking fact is that unions fit into neither pattern. This provides the essential clue to their nature: Unions are restraints on trade in an interventionist economy—a portion of the confused and growing regulations, legislation, rulings, and prohibitions. Unions are throwbacks to a society of privilege, status, and accidents of birth; they are wayside stops in an erratic drift from a polity of pressure groups to (it seems) a totalitarian state.

Economic Systems and Unionism

Whether called competitive enterprise, free enterprise system, laissez-faire, free trade, economic freedom, or the unhampered market economy, capitalism's hallmarks are voluntary exchange, mutual consent as the primary mode of organization, the value of individual choice, and the preeminence of the private sector. Its essential features are private property rights, the rule of law, liberty of contract, and a government whose role is confined to that of an umpire and impartial protector of personal freedom from aggression and assault. The rights to pick up and move, to accept or reject offers, and to invest capital or labor time with anyone are secured by government in a capitalist nation. There is no balance of power to worry about, because each individual in a sense is sovereign, secure in his or her rights, not the subject of anyone else.

Is this democratic? Yes, in an important sense it is, in both economic and political terms. Elections are held daily in the marketplace, and all are free to enter, without man-made restraint, wherever individuals believe they can improve their personal circumstances, including the acceptance of wage offers. Consequences of individual decisions in such a world are "capitalized" on decision-makers. Individuals are held responsible for their actions. Those who please buyers best will prosper in the free market, and those who fail will lose control over resources and be left to find other employment. Such a system is not capitalist-controlled or worker-controlled. It is consumer-controlled. The end purpose of all economic activity is consumption, and capitalism puts the customer first. Interventions in a capitalist order usually serve producer interests, either in or out of government. Politically, capitalism is democratic, too, because it is a necessary, although not sufficient, condition for democracy.

Capitalism of course never existed in this pure form, although England and the United States came close in the nineteenth century, probably the greatest period of human advance in history. During the twentieth century we moved into what has been called the mixed economy, the welfare state, the transfer society, the redistributionist state, the middle way, or interventionism. Although widely described as "progressive," this lurching movement is actually regressive, with power over economic decisions gradually removed from individual citizens to those in central government. The on-budget and off-budget expansion of the public sector at the expense of the productive sector marks an uneven drift toward the totalitarian state, with everyone's income, not just that of Social Security recipients, being subject to political control, bureaucratic intervention, and central planning. It is a return to a form of feudal bondage by means of ad hoc interventions by interest groups with fleeting political clout. Economists often serve as rationalizing theoreticians, basing arguments for intervention on alleged, though not empirically demonstrated, failures of the invisible hand.

Where do unions fit in the interventionist state? As another self-interested producer group, their main purpose is to extract higher pay for their leaders and members and to preserve and expand their power and privilege by nearly any means possible. To believe otherwise is to engage in self-deception about how people can be trusted with market power created by intervention. Every economy has conflicts between producers and consumers. Producers want to preserve the existing mode of production, whether capitalist (investor) or worker (employee). Consumers are footloose, though, with no stake in the existing structure of investment. They want the cheapest prices and highest quality they can find, and they care little about how or where the goods were produced. The alleged harshness of capitalism is due to self-interested economizing by consumers, a group that includes all of us. In free markets, conflicts between producers and consumers are reconciled in a benign way because government confines its role to the prevention of force and fraud. Political activism, however, has produced an ongoing parade of protectionist favors for concentrated producer interests, the foremost being unionism, with its unmatched rights of private coercion.

Accumulating restrictions eventually must result in the thoroughgoing collectivist state, usually termed "socialist." Whether of the fascist, Nazi, communist, or democratic socialist variety, its essence is central political power over economic decisions. Although urged in the name of worker control or industrial democracy, common ownership of the means of production places awesome power over everyone's livelihood in the hands of political authorities. Under the restrictions and prohibitions of a socialist system, the only way to accomplish the daily chores of living on a remotely coordinated basis is by chain of command, by subordination. And where do strong, independent unions fit in a socialist state? They don't, if only because no economic planning can be done on a sustained basis if disruptive power is in the hands of noncentral authorities. Unions can only be branches of the bureaucracy under socialism.

The common classification of economic systems into two discrete types, capitalist and socialist, is useful to clarify thought, but it misrepresents reality. The economic system that offers the greatest degree of individual freedom is capitalism, whereas socialism, which is really feudalism or strong mercantilism, offers the least. In between are all the real-world systems, from individualist nations to collectivist states, from relatively few man-made restraints on personal freedom to the subjugation of one individual by another. Trade unions are simply a subset, though a sizable one, of the man-made restrictions that impede people's rights to trade with one another. Unions are one of the impediments of our times, barriers to profitable exchange in the interventionist state. The free trade union movement has little to do with "free" and even less to do with facilitating the trade. Unions are not difficult to understand, if we abandon the rhetoric of compassion and analyze their actual practices reasonably rather than emotionally.

No one ever coherently explained what a rigorously unionized society would be like. Perhaps this is the ultimate source of people's unease over unionism. No one ever has filled this theoretical void, despite numerous attempts. If the logic of unionism and collective bargaining (strike threat) is valid, it is only natural for us to ask why it should not be extended to physicians' unions, grocers' unions, automobile dealers' unions, landlords' unions, nurses' unions, oil industry unions, or lenders' unions. All should insist on decent prices for their products. Collective bargaining can be encouraged everywhere, with centralized negotiations. When it fails to reach agreement on prices, wages, and other terms, after hard negotiations, then muscle, violence, and endurance settle things. No one openly advocates this as an ideal unionized society, but no other portrait makes sense. Private force, piracy, and extortion would prevail, and victims would have no recourse for their losses.

Syndicalism, a turn-of-the-century doctrine that advocated control over production by organized bodies of workers, sounds somewhat more sensible. Thoroughgoing syndicalists, however, like anarchists, say the state must be abolished. The doctrine unfortunately never specified how prices or wages should be determined for various products and industries, or how workers could gain entry into production units controlled by unionists, or how savings would be allocated across enterprises, and so on. In other words, syndicalism is a kind of shallow romanticism, like other left-wing theories. Search the literature high and low, and you will find no theory of an ordered unionist society. Nor can there be such a society.

Something Old: Jobs as Property

To confirm the theory that unionism is just restrictionism of a special kind, consider the old issue of jobs as property. This notion goes back at least to the Middle Ages and, more recently, has formed a central tenet of the theories of John R. Commons and Selig Perlman. Can anybody legitimately "own" a job? Does it make any sense? Consider what we mean by a human right. The crucial philosophical feature of a right (a just or lawful claim) is that all human beings can simultaneously hold the right equally. So, for instance, rights to life, liberty, and the pursuit of happiness are true human rights that are retained by each person without jeopardizing the equal right of another. Any person's right of private property extends only to the point where it coexists harmoniously with the equal property rights of other members of society. Much the same may be said regarding the rights of free speech, assembly, worship, bearing arms, and so on.

A right to a "job" cannot meet this test because everyone cannot simultaneously hold that right. Someone is obliged to fulfill the other person's "right" by supplying the job. That makes one person the slave of the other, or at least subjugates one person's will to another's. The same objection holds for assertions that everyone has the "right" or owns an "entitlement" to a decent education, medical care, a guaranteed income, ad infinitum. Who is compelled to supply these commodities? If others are obligated to fulfill our wants, those others become our slaves rather than free citizens.

In a free society, an employment relationship is an exchange voluntarily undertaken between free individuals. The employer provides wages, benefits, and tools in return for labor services. Prior to the 1930s both parties were free to terminate their relationship at will. Either party could make a unilateral, private decision to continue or discontinue an employment relationship. The conventional expression is that employers fire employees, and employees quit their employers, but the act is the same. We can equally well say that an employee fires his or her employer, or sends the employer packing. Exchange relations are relations among sovereigns or equals, not superiors and subordinates.

The labor legislation of the 1930s, however, moved us away from employment relationship as mutual service between equals. The right to strike was central to this development because, correctly understood, it is a form of human bondage. What do strikers assert as their "rights," decreed by legislation? They claim the right to quit their jobs —but not *really* quit. Quitting means severing a business relation with owners of a business, while striking means quitting the job yet staying on the payroll. The striker retains the job he or she "owns," regardless of employer preference. Employers often are compelled to reinstate strikers, sometimes without regard for misconduct during a strike and independent of the mayhem and damage strikers may cause.[2] It is a formula for irresponsibility, even savagery. These incentives and immunities account for the common threats and violent behavior of organized workers—not "alienation" from their work or the economic system, as the academic and intellectual left typically claim. More important, the NLRB holds the employer in a form of involuntary servitude, in that the employer cannot terminate an employee's service. Although it is technically possible to replace strikers with "permanent" replacements, in many instances it is practically impossible because the NLRB finds the employer guilty of an unfair labor practice. Employers basically have little protection either from the NLRB or from the courts, nor do workers who want to enter work places to accept wages and working conditions scorned by strikers.

The current situation is a reversal of the relation between the "employer" and employee of a feudal society in which serfs were bound to landowners by a variety of restrictions. Employers now suffer a limited form of bondage to employees who strike, or damage the business, or do incompetent work. The courts reinstate employees for almost any reason, often with back pay. If the same principle were applied without regard to status, private citizens could no longer make unilateral decisions to terminate employment relationships. No employee could quit an employer without just cause, and employees could be found guilty of unfair labor practices to their employers and forced to return to their original employer, and provide the employer with "back output." Mediators, conciliators, arbitrators, government boards, commissions, and courts would have to rule on the fairness of each proposed dismissal by employer or employee in the economy, currently averaging over 4 million separations per month. The rationale, of course, for the current biased legal treatment is labor's alleged disadvantage, and the resulting duty of government to balance the gains from trade in labor markets.

Unions do not want symmetric treatment of equals before the law; they want special privilege over jobs. They already have it in a limited form. What are the economic consequences of treating jobs (employers) as the property of incumbent workers? This situation amounts to a tax on economic progress, with all concomitant side effects.[3] Suppose, for example, that incumbent workers compel employers to pay a severance tax if their jobs are made obsolete by new production techniques. The first question is, why single out this form of displacement (change)? Jobs are lost when firms disappear through competitive pressures or managerial incompetence or when assets become obsolete for any reason. Do the holders of such jobs also deserve compensation? Should slide rule manufacturers be compensated by electronic calculator firms because owners failed to foresee the decline in demand for their services or assets? If the answer is yes, foresight will be less accurate because penalties for error diminish, and resources will be less efficiently allocated in the future.

Suppose companies know that they will have to make severance payments in such situations. If firms and workers can predict future displacements, wages will be smaller and lifetime earnings, on average, will also be smaller, because termination payments will make up the expected difference. It amounts to a deferred wage-insurance plan, so it accomplishes no redistribution from investors to workers, but simply transfers income from workers to those who are laid off. If technical change is wholly uncertain, all workers share in wage reductions until dismissal rates are sorted out. The rate of displacement by technical change cannot be predicted perfectly, mistakes are made in either direction, and wages can be too low or too high after the fact, but market corrections continuously operate to bring wages to market-clearing rates. Unions disrupt this process by imposing ransom payments on the owners of assets who want to divest themselves of old production techniques. Assets are subject to the same uncertainties as labor, although unions propose no protections for owners in the form of rights to jobs for assets. Few are surprised to find that people put their interests before all else, but obstructions for well-paid incumbent workers in the name of social justice are sometimes hard to treat seriously. Property in jobs does not include jobs for the workers who would otherwise produce the new equipment, nor does it include guaranteed employment after machinery becomes obsolete.

Regarding jobs as property rights is not progressive. It is a return to the restrictions of two centuries ago when workers could not freely contract for mutually profitable employment. It is a mild form of slavery, with employers prosecuted as lawbreakers when they seek to terminate or revise an employee's service. Over the long run, it is just another complication in the bewildering maze of restrictions on productive activities, with losses spread over all income earners and consumers in the economy.

Something New: Industrial Democracy

A European import called "industrial democracy," "codetermination," or "participatory management" may emerge as a new variant of union power. Douglas Fraser, when he was UAW president, was one of eighteen directors of the Chrysler Corporation, a first for a major U.S. union. The virtually unanimous judgment in Washington was that federally guaranteed money would never have been forthcoming for Chrysler if the UAW had not mustered all of organized labor's lobbying power. More union representatives on U.S. company boards may follow. This idea has spread very far in Europe, and many Western governments require employee and/or union representation on corporate boards and the shop floor, with more drastic ownership legislation pending in Sweden and the Netherlands to hasten the transition to socialist, labor-managed firms. Presently, governments in the Netherlands, Norway, Sweden, Austria, Denmark, Luxembourg, West Germany, and France impose labor participation schemes, and it is an active issue in Great Britain as an alternative to further nationalization of industry. Japan thus far has avoided legislation requiring worker participation, though many major corporations have modest forms of on-the-job participation.

The methods of codetermination vary from country to country. In Holland, for example, a supervisory board, roughly equivalent to a board of directors, chooses new board members, but employees as well as shareholders have veto power over any appointment. In Denmark, Sweden, and Norway, workers have a quota of seats reserved on boards of large companies although labor representatives are always in a minority. The legislation has proceeded furthest in Germany and Sweden. At the shop-floor level, works councils, cooperation committees, or employee representation bodies called by some other name have extensive powers of codetermination. Management must gain their consent before taking various actions such as making changes in working hours or shop rules, closing a plant, hiring, laying off, firing, and transferring employees. Although works councils are forbidden by law to strike, they have the right to be informed and consulted on "matters or projects of essential importance to employees," and this amounts to having an opportunity to gain concessions on virtually anything, because they can always withhold their consent in order to realize unrelated objectives. The system is like a bomb waiting to explode. Shop stewards win about 80% of the seats in employee elections on union-supported slates, but there is tension between the works councils and regional and national union leaders because they represent separate centers of power. Shop-floor councils are even more powerful in Sweden than in Germany.[4]

At the board level, the legislation has gradually increased labor representation in Germany. In 1947 some iron and steel companies in the British-occupied zone of Germany "voluntarily" set aside one-half of their board seats for worker-elected representatives, a concession to the newly revived unions. In 1951 union pressure induced the Bundestag to make union representation on company boards mandatory for the iron and steel industries. It was extended to other industries in 1952, but conservatives successfully restricted labor directors to one-third of the board. In 1976, however, it was upped to one-half, although board chairmen retain a tie-breaking vote for the management side. Some labor directors are chosen by direct employee election, and others are appointed by trade unions.

The rationales for these compulsory-representation schemes range from the sincere to the insincere, and proponents range from those who see such schemes as a worthwhile modification of capitalist enterprise to those who cynically see them as another step toward personal power or as a means of hastening the demise of capitalism. The argument for labor representation goes like this: workers under a capitalist system lead fragmented, dreary lives; the quality of the work process is unsatisfying because it is always sacrificed to capitalist dominance and profits; workers never understand the whole production process, never identify with their fellow workers, never see the final product; in a word, workers are "alienated." Supposedly alienation is unavoidable because workers do not own or control the means of production, do not participate in choice of production techniques, do not choose the commodities to produce, and so on. Therefore, goes the story, they cannot have humane and meaningful lives without a "labor bench" to represent them in company decisions. They must offset the "capital bench" at the work place, which otherwise will run the show. The political appeal of these schemes is the promise to expand employee control over the firm's work environment and to redistribute income by reducing the share of income allegedly going to the bosses.

The probability that such schemes will be actively promoted in the United States seems high, though a less socialistic or European-sounding label than codetermination will probably be used. American unionists are experiencing diminishing economic and political clout, and the rhetoric of "democratic determination" by employees has a politically seductive appeal. It is, in fact, an almost logical extension of the language in the 1935 Wagner Act. Douglas Fraser, for example, rebuts all challenges to "democratization" at Chrysler and in the rest of the auto industry with a single question: "Why should corporations have a sole monopoly on decisions that affect so many workers, their families and their communities?"[5] Of course Fraser does not propose that consumers, auto shareholders, and the public sit on the UAW board, even though UAW leaders "affect so many people's lives." If the principle is good, it ought to be extended to other situations, but union arguments overlook any unpleasant implications. As with labor participation by means of profit-sharing schemes, unionists refuse to accept any financial risk or share any losses; they want access only to profits.

These schemes can be considered from two points of view: their effect on private-property rights and their economic consequences. The traditional right of private property granted American citizens the right to control the use of land, buildings, factories, and other assets to which they held title. As the proprietor, for instance, an employer had the right to place limits, as he wished, on the activities of workers on his property. Workers usually were admitted to the property to perform work for which they were hired. Other activities—say, company parties —might or might not be permitted, as the employer wished. Gradually, these rights have eroded. For instance, union organizers must be permitted to use the owner's property to distribute union pamphlets or speak to employees. Compelling the shareholders who supply the equity capital to appoint labor representatives as directors of the business certainly reduces their property rights over investment, but it is only a matter of degree compared with previous political restrictions imposed in the name of labor's welfare.

If Congress should adopt such legislation, the economic results are predictable. If the law is ineffective, firms may not be hampered in efficiently carrying out their productive activities, and labor representation will be window dressing for unionists. If the legislation is potent, however, a series of consequences could follow. Suppose unionists on company boards gain wages and working conditions that exceed what present union techniques can extract. The return to shareholders necessarily falls, and investors will not supply more capital to the "laboristic" sector. Production and employment will diminish unless more government intervention occurs. Employment and production will expand in small enterprises that have no mandatory labor representation, so unionists will press for compulsory codetermination for all firms and sectors of the economy. The ultimate result could be complete socialist control of the economy.[6]

Capitalism is open to all forms of enterprise: proprietorship, partnership, corporation, cooperatives, communes, nonprofit associations, and codetermined or labor-managed industry. If a codeterministic form of enterprise were a superior form of cooperation for labor, managers, and investors, it would flourish in open competition without government decree. The fact that codetermination and worker-managed enterprises on the Yugoslav model cannot survive except by government fiat implies that they are not an efficient mode of organization. In effect, compulsory codetermination protects codetermined enterprises from the competition of the more productive forms of enterprise that emerge in freer markets. Other forms of enterprise, like corporations, are simply outlawed. Workers who might want to trade in "democracy at the work place" for more income, by working in more efficient enterprises, are denied the choice. Worker participation is little more than old restrictions in new bottles.

The mind-set behind codetermination is that workers should be able to change their situation in the company right now, in a democratic way. This is naive. It ignores the cost of changing the production process, as well as the competitive feasibility of the change. It ignores mobility, the right of free movement of labor among jobs, industries, and enterprises, which permits individuals to find jobs to which they are better suited and in which they are happier. It ignores the main voting device to signal employers about what mixes of wages, benefits, and working conditions workers like best. Codetermination presumes that firms rather than individual employees must adjust. Nor is there any reason to believe that "democratic" decisions by incumbents at the work place will coincide with what is best for labor as a whole. Nepotism, entry restrictions on hiring, shortsightedness by workers having short remaining tenure with the firm, and large, persistent inequalities among comparable workers in different shops, plants, and industries cannot be cured when the free market is suppressed. Without transferable property rights in capital, there is little incentive to preserve or increase the capital stock. As with other laboristic schemes, the system cannot withstand logical scrutiny. It is unstable and simply accelerates the drift toward central control.

What has been the experience in Europe? Development continues, but preliminary signals confirm the theoretical analysis. Managers issue public statements praising the shop-floor councils, saying that they foster cooperation and worker understanding of the company's problems and prospects, but these statements appear to be placating gestures to unionists. Privately, these same managers complain about the costs due to delayed decision-making, declining morale and authority at the middle- and lower-management levels, and increasing instances of unions withholding consent in order to extract unrelated concessions.

Boardroom problems are worse. In Germany the social atmosphere has worsened as unions and management contest decisions on the boards.[7] Even when managers win decisions, they fear worker discontent in an increasingly politicized atmosphere. Unionists are angry at their minority status despite their nominal parity. Complete parity would mean more deadlocks in a decision-making process that already has slowed considerably. Union members have a conflict of interest on the board and have been passing secret information to their unions to use in negotiations. Companies now make more decisions outside board meetings. None of these effects favors capital formation, economic growth, or competitive efficiency, and, if allowed to proceed, they must inevitably reduce the level of real income in Europe. Union officials enjoy more economic and political power, though this effect probably will prove fleeting.

The Future

There is nothing certain or inevitable about the future. It will be determined by the choices of individuals and the prevailing ideas that influence government policy. There are always conflicting tendencies in the present. Which will seize the day cannot be confidently forecast in advance. Some main stirrings are easily identified, though. Labor unions are in serious difficulty, especially in the long run. What unions will be like in the twenty-first century is unclear, but the survivors will be less blue-collar, less industrial, less male, less white, and less manual labor. Automation is proceeding, and, although there are arguments on the opposite side, the net effect is likely to diminish the effectiveness of strikes because capital-intensive operations like, say, the telephone company or oil refining, can maintain production for long periods by using supervisory help and nonunion employees. Nor is the general public fond of strikes or the brazen grasping for "more" by public-employee unions. The air traffic controllers' illegal strike during the summer of 1981 was a potent example of the latent public support that exists for politicians who have the courage to defy union power.

The public is no more likely in the future to tolerate crippling strikes, the unplugging of society, than it has in the past. Unions continue to attract a smaller and smaller share of the labor force. Their image in the mind of the general public is poor and unlikely to improve. Proposition 13 and its offspring promise to restrain the expansion of the public sector, at least at the state and local level, and to restrict the amount of tax dollars that will go to public employees. The Reagan election and the conservative drift in the country diminish prospects for pro-union interventions.

No one proudly points to leading-edge examples like New York City or Great Britain and says, "Look at the glories of a unionized community." The resilience of the marketplace has checked many harmful effects of unions in the U.S. economy, and the distortions are likely to diminish over time. The bread-and-butter industries of American unionism—steel, autos, rubber, oil, food processing, mining, railroads, building trades—are decaying or stagnating, or else the unions' share of activity is falling. Reduction in transportation and communication costs is harming unions by expanding markets over time. Growth of international trade threatens the protections enjoyed by unionists. Some old-style regulation is being relaxed—in trucking, for instance—but new-style regulation is expanding—for example, safety and environmental intervention, which is not quite so directly helpful to union monopoly.

The shift of industry toward the Sunbelt is another adverse development. Young workers appear more individualistic than older workers and less fearful of a 1930s-style economic depression, so-called employer power, or loss of employment. They are not so receptive to the old-style drum-beating from union headquarters, and unions have not hit on a new recipe for selling their product. Friends in the academic community urge unions to tailor their message to the growing number of white-collar, technical, and professional employees, but prospects are poor. Between 1970 and 1980 the number of white-collar employees increased by 12.5 million, to 50.5 million, while blue-collar employees increased by only 2.7 million, to 30.5 million. The situation will grow worse for unions. Few white-collar workers seem to view themselves as "workers," and many identify with management. In 1981 unions won only 45% of representation elections, the smallest percentage in NLRB history, and the union victory percentage has been declining one percentage point each year. In 1980 employees represented by unions voted to toss their union out in 75% of 902 decertification elections, the second highest percentage in thirty years. Heavily unionized enterprises and industries stagnate or decline. Booming high-technology firms expand, produce, hustle, and stay nonunion. These firms offer engineers, programmers, office workers, and others as much personal growth as individuals can accomplish. Collectivist cries of solidarity, militance, and the company as "enemy" increasingly often fall on deaf ears.

Unions are trying to refine their image by soft-sell approaches, TV advertising, hiring young black women as organizers, and so on. Unions and historians raised $15 million in 1981–82 to produce a ten-part public TV series about American workers. But inflation can help union organizing considerably more than sweet talk. An inflationary malaise fosters a catch-up mentality, especially since cost-of-living adjustments in union contracts have widened the union-nonunion gap; people are frustrated by zero growth in real disposable income, and some are more receptive to unionism as the answer to employees' financial ills. An economic system with rapid inflation has increasing instability, which generally is a fertile ground for unionism. Another favorable development for unions is that many state and local governments have adopted laws that permit government managers to sign collective contracts compelling employees to pay union dues, an arrangement previously prohibited in most governmental units. Some police departments have been organized by the Teamsters' Union, whose officials remain unsurpassed in felony convictions among union leaders. More Teamster control of police departments opens up new vistas for Teamster revenues and expanded union lawlessness due to nonenforcement, a particularly unfavorable development for the unorganized workers who might risk crossing picket lines in order to support their families.

On balance, if government has the courage to stop inflation and allows economic growth to revive, the prospects for expanding unionism are negligible. Despite brave talk about a "new era of cooperation" between unions and management and revitalization of American industry, time is running against unionism. Although many people are impressed by the sheer magnitude of union membership, the numbers are very misleading, and not just because of inflated union claims.[8] Movements have adherents, individuals who freely choose allegiance. Big unionism, though, never was based on choice by employees, despite some hardworking and dedicated unionists, because the bulk of unionism in this country has always rested on various forms of coercion.

Organizing voluntary adherents to the ideals of unionism will play no significant role in the evolution or demise of big-time unionism. Organizing campaigns are basically a diversion, like welfare fraud, which distracts us from the main problem of coercive redistribution of income. Although organizing campaigns gain some members, they essentially are public relations events, orchestrated to convince an inattentive public that this is the main method of gaining membership. Despite massive governmental intervention on behalf of unionism, organizing campaigns remain extremely expensive in time, effort, and money, yield little in new dues and members, and are not the primary means of maintaining unionism. American employees remain skeptical of unionism, so unions basically avoid laborious persuasion of individual employees in favor of pressure on employers and government. A secondary union intent is to secure concessions from managements by threats of organizing campaigns rather than by the actual rigors of organization.

The 1980s are critical because it is not so much where you are that counts as where you are going. The union movement really cannot tolerate a sustained period of membership decline because it produces the wrong psychological aura. A minority group growing smaller looks more and more like a labor elite, and its claims, demands, and stridency begin to look more and more like shallow posturing to the public. As Bennett and Johnson have written, "every time a representation election is lost by a union, or a union is decertified, or membership overall drops, the union's promise of economic betterment loses some degree of credibility."[9] Even the recent moves toward union cooperation in autos and steel look like ad hoc expediency by unionists whose dues income has declined rather than a new direction for unionism. In the political arena, where influence is even more intensely psychological, reduced funding and a growing perception of a weakening union movement reduce political candidates' beliefs that unions can turn out the vote for or against. Unions are on the edge of a precipice, a slippery slope, a situation akin to their floundering in the late 1920s and early 1930s. Since the Republican resurgence in 1980, there is no doubt that unionists are struggling to find new cosmetics, a new angle. The uncertain calls for industrial democracy, worker-management cooperation, the Japanese model, "anything," nervously find partisans.

The most immediate effect of the emerging decline in union organization is to rely on "pushbutton unionism"—union reliance on pressure directed at employers and government to keep members. Techniques are diverse, but they all depend on bypassing employees. Criminal threats and violence toward employers to force them to recognize a union as the bargaining agent are techniques polished to a fine art by some unions. Pension fund and related financial pressure, as demonstrated in the J. P. Stevens case, are major weapons. Pledges of strict or "benign" neutrality extracted by unionists from employers have been pioneered by unions in the auto and rubber industries. "Packing" new plants temporarily with union workers during a union-representation election is another tactic. Accretion agreements force an employer to unionize all new divisions automatically, thereby "saving" election expenses.

Government supplies a wide range of measures to maintain union membership, as I have documented in previous chapters. Bennett and Johnson, however, correctly highlight the subtle web of government contract provisions that impose unionism in various ways.[10] For instance, HUD's housing assistance requires local governments to demonstrate that they have collective bargaining agreements with construction unions in the area. Under the Urban Mass Transit Act of 1964, the city of Albuquerque, New Mexico, was refused federal funds because national officials of the United Transportation Union (UTU) disapproved of a collective contract its local had signed with the city government: one "benefit" the union contract lacked was a compulsory-membership clause. The Health and Human Services Department has informed all health care providers that it will reimburse expenses for collective bargaining but not for funds spent to encourage or discourage unionization—say, hiring consultants to avoid unionization. Since few enterprises spend money to encourage their employees to unionize, the purpose is obvious. The "mild" Labor Law Reform bill of 1977, although defeated, would have debarred any firm found guilty of "unfair labor practices" by the NLRB from all federal contracts for three years. And so it goes. What cannot be won among employees can be won indirectly in Washington, and the success of unions in

Washington is difficult for an economist to foresee, though it is the crucial ingredient in the survival of big unionism.

The Way Out: Restore Equality before the Law

Irving Kristol has observed that unions do not sponsor the *Harvard Trade Union Review* as a counterpart to the *Harvard Business Review,* nor do they sponsor conferences on trade unions, nor do they subsidize research on unionism: "It's almost as if they don't want to explain themselves to the world, or have anyone else do the explaining for them. And this condition is not peculiarly American. It prevails in all countries where free trade unions exist."[11] The reason is clear: unionists do not spend a great deal of time explaining themselves because no one, including unionists, can construct a clear, yet pleasing version of what they are and what they do. Unions are antisocial outfits, selfish sectional groups that try to benefit their members, by use of force and threat, at the expense of everyone else. Ultimately, even union members count for little because only power for the decisive coalition of union leaders counts. Stripped of the deceptive language of compassion for the poor, unionism is labor monopoly, pure and simple. The inarticulateness of the union vision is not surprising. Why encourage exposure and open discussion of unionism's methods and purposes? A movement based on appeal to prejudice and emotion, it is power without responsibility, shrill demands without accountability.

To proclaim these truths is not antilabor, nor even antiunion. It is protruth. Proemployee. Propeople. Most people, including me, have little objection to free associations of workingmen, so long as they do not seek to impose their will by force. A few economists like W. H. Hutt, for whom I have the highest regard, argue that even this concession is unsatisfactory because the mere threat of strike disruptions by organized workers diminishes and distorts investment and thereby the real flow of wages. True, but from a legal or political point of view, this economic truism does not imply that prohibiting labor unions as combinations or collusions in restraint of trade would be a desirable policy. Desirable policies are not only consonant with the Western values of individual freedom, material prosperity, and peace, but also are effective in principle and practice. Little good can come of repressive measures directed against labor unions; in fact, they might strengthen unions in their continual political campaign to be treated as underdogs in an oppressive capitalist society.

Unionism is a rejection of free markets, open competition, and individual freedom in favor of their opposites: monopoly power, private coercion, and aggrandizement of personal rule. In a perverse way unions fit our age, so intent are they on forcibly designing pleasing outcomes, constructing restrictions, harassing successful businesses, impeding the accumulation of productive capital, and subverting the pricing mechanism in its task of coordinating human activity. Despite the brilliant success of free markets on both logical and empirical grounds, there is a widespread bias against them that is hard to explain. George Gilder has puzzled over it: "Evidently, there is something in the human mind, even when honed at Oxford or the Sorbonne, that hesitates to believe in capitalism: in the enriching mysteries of inequality, the inexhaustible mines of the division of labor, the multiplying miracles of market economics, the compounding gains from trade and prosperity."[12]

Fortunately, we need not solve this mystery to understand what sorts of public policies will restore individual freedom in the labor market and drastically diminish the union problem. Outlawing unions or strikes or repressing unions in any special way would be the wrong thing to do. Taft-Hartley and Landrum-Griffin offer rich testimony about the likelihood of further federal intervention to tame these organizations.

Instead, the right thing to do is to deregulate. Try freedom for a change. Repeal, abolish, rescind, revoke, and do away with the Railway Labor Act, the Norris–La Guardia Act, and the National Labor Relations Act. Also abolish the commissions, executive orders, state laws, rulings, administrative orders, and regulations derived from the three major statutes. Restore the rule of law in labor relations by treating unions in a manner consistent with the way everyone else is treated under contract and tort law. Treat workers and worker organizations as responsible adults, not as children who are exempt from the rules of peaceable conduct.

If we dispense with the privileges and immunities of unions, labor disputes will be resolved just as other disputes are, by peaceful and private means and ultimately in the courts. Would the courts be overwhelmed? This is a supply-and-demand problem that has solutions, but there are two good reasons to believe that this is not a troublesome problem. First, the volume of disputes, labor brawls, and labor violence will decline precipitously because legislative repeal removes the props that advanced unionism to its current size and influence. Strong unionism in the United States will virtually disappear without its special-interest legislation. Second, direct access to the courts will further decrease the problem because more vigorous private and public prosecution of organized aggression will reduce the profit from strong-arm tactics. People will learn that labor brawls result from legal exemptions, not from workers' revulsion toward capitalism.

What the state has granted, it can take away. The current privileges are extensive, and it may be well to summarize them as Senator Barry Goldwater did before the American Bar Association in 1962. What the list loses in complexity and subtlety, it gains in basic truth:

1. Almost total immunity under antitrust laws.
2. Immunity from taxation.
3. Ability to use union funds for purposes not directly related to collective bargaining, even if union dues are compulsory (a less clear "truth" today than in 1962).
4. Immunity from injunction by federal courts.
5. Power to compel employees to pay union dues as a condition of keeping their jobs.
6. Power to represent all employees in a bargaining unit, no matter how small the majority of those voting, including those compelled to join and those denied membership.
7. Power to compel employers to bargain "in good faith" with "certified" union officials.
8. Power to deny membership to employees in a bargaining unit.
9. Power to compel enterprises to make their private property available for use by union officials.
10. Comparative immunity from payment of damages for personal and property injury inflicted on anyone by union members engaged in strikes, picketing, and other tactics in disputes.
11. Power to strike for objectives not related to a collective-bargaining dispute.
12. Power to examine an enterprise's books and records, including confidential data on costs, earnings, and prices.
13. Relative immunity from state labor law under the doctrine of federal preemption.[13]

With this list of privileges, the wonder is not that corruption exists in unions, but that honesty exists. No one is to be trusted with much power, a rule our legislation on labor unions has repeatedly violated. Our economy and society can easily tolerate the weak and dispersed unions that may survive in an open economy, but not the giant centers of coercive power created by compliant politicians. As John Davenport wrote, "Precisely because government is by nature coercive, its powers must be *limited* and *jealously guarded*. Our difficulties today stem largely from the fact that we have broken both rules."[14]

Some may declare this list of repeals unrealistic. Perhaps, but it is nice to know what labor policies can best promote prosperity and human freedom. Furthermore, political realities are constantly changing, and what is politically impossible one moment is possible the next. Where will the opposition come from? From the net beneficiaries of the labor-conflict system, namely, union officials and the arbitrators, mediators, conciliators, fact finders, and consultants in the academic and legal communities. They will complain vigorously, but open discussion, public debate, and reasoned argument could easily lead to abolition of union privilege and a system of justice that administers "blindly" instead of peeking at status. The opposition is thinly based and so dependent on prejudice and emotion that ideas and evidence may be more potent than usual.

The logical and empirical case for free trade, domestic and foreign, rather than "free trade" unions, must continue to be made. Inflation, unemployment, and union tyranny will plague us until people learn the true nature of unionism. Maybe it will take more impoverishment, more industrial warfare, and more suffering to teach people what so-called collective bargaining is all about. They are very close to that state in Britain, where even a Labour member of Parliament recently admitted that trade unions are destroying the living standards of workingmen in the country. I hope that we do not sink to the British standard of living, or impose "industrial democracy," or look to other false idols to alleviate our union and industrial problems. We took a wrong turn in 1947 by trying to patch a bad law, and we have been patching it ever since. Repeal is the answer.

Although a great deal has been written about human rights, the most fundamental right is the right to life—that is, the right to work in order to earn a living. Human freedom and dignity are impossible without that right. We should immediately restore the right of every American to raise his or her income by accepting any remuneration a prospective employer may offer, free from union threat and intimidation, no matter how much these trades supposedly harm the interest of those with higher incomes. The time for dissembling is over.

Table A-1

Labor Union and Employee Association Membership, 1950–78

Item	Unit	1950	1955	1960	1965	1970	1972	1974	1976	1978
Number of unions, total........	Number .	209[1]	199	184	191[2]	185	177	175	175	174
Unions affiliated with AFL-CIO.......	Number .	137	139	134	129	120	113	111	112	108
Union membership	1,000 ...	15,000	17,749	18,117	18,519	20,752	20,893	21,643	21,171	21,784
AFL-CIO	1,000 ...	12,400	16,062	15,072	15,604	15,978	6,507[1]	16,938	16,699	17,024
Independent or unaffiliated unions	1,000 ...	2,600	1,688	3,045	2,915	4,773	4,386	4,705	4,472	4,760
Male[3]......................	1,000 ...	(NA)	(NA)	14,733	(NA)	16,408	16,315	16,985	16,481	16,636
Female[3]	1,000 ...	(NA)	(NA)	3,304	(NA)	4,282	4,524	4,600	4,648	5,106
White-collar membership[3]	1,000 ...	(NA)	2,463[4]	2,192	(NA)	3,353	3,434	3,762	4,068	4,067
Percent of total membership	Percent..	(NA)	13.6[4]	12.2	(NA)	16.2	16.5	17.4	19.2	18.7
U.S. members[5]................	1,000 ...	14,267	16,802	17,049	17,299	19,381	19,435	20,199	19,634	20,246
Percent of total labor force	Percent..	22.0	24.4	23.6	22.4	22.6	21.8	21.7	20.3	19.7
Percent of nonagric. employment	Percent..	31.5	33.2	31.4	28.4	27.5	26.4	25.8	24.5	23.6
Canadian members of U.S. unions	1,000 ...	733	947	1,068	1,220	1,371	1,458	1,444	1,537	1,538
Association membership[6]	1,000 ...	(NA)	(NA)	(NA)	(NA)	1,868	2,221	2,610	3,028	2,561
Female membership	1,000 ...	(NA)	(NA)	(NA)	(NA)	1,116	1,212	1,438	1,790	1,559
White-collar membership	1,000 ...	(NA)	(NA)	(NA)	(NA)	1,564	1,768	2,119	2,605	2,185

NA - not available. Estimates based on average number of dues-paying members of unions with headquarters in the U.S. Certain unions did not report as members persons not required to pay dues, such as apprentices and workers retired, unemployed, in armed forces, or involved in work stoppages. Excludes single-firm and local unaffiliated unions; includes local unions directly affiliated with the AFL-CIO, except as noted. Employee associations are similar to unions. See also *Historical Statistics, Colonial Times to 1970*, series D 933–934 and D 946–951.

1. 1949 data.
2. 1966 data.
3. Excludes local unions directly affiliated with AFL-CIO.
4. 1956 data.
5. Excluding Canadians.
6. Covers professional and state employee associations engaged in collective bargaining in more than one state in two or more cities.

Source: U.S. Bureau of Labor Statistics, *Handbook of Labor Statistics*, annual; *Directory of National Unions and Employee Associations, 1979*.

Table A-2

Membership in Large Unions, 1968–80

Union	1968	1972	1976	1980
Teamsters (Ind.)	1,755	1,855	1,889	1,891
Automobile workers (Ind.)	1,473	1,394	1,358	1,357
Food and commercial[1]	1,052	1,162	1,209	1,300
Steelworkers[2][3]	1,352	1,400	1,300	1,238
State, county (AFSCME)	364	529	750	1,098
Electrical (IBEW)	897	957	924	1,041
Carpenters	793	820	820	832
Machinists	903	758	917	745
Service employees (SEIU)	389	484	575	650
Laborers (LIUNA)	553	600	627	608
Communications workers	357	443	483	551
Teachers (AFT)	165	249	446	502
Clothing and textile workers[3][4]	569	539	502	455
Engineers, operating	350	402	420	423
Hotel and restaurant	459	458	432	400
Plumbers	297	[5]228	[5]228	352
Garment, ladies (ILGWU)	455	428	365	323
Musicians	283	315	330	299
Government (AFGE)	295	293	260	255
Postal workers[6]	[7]166	239	252	251
Electrical (IUE)	324	290	238	233
Letter carriers	210	220	227	230
Paperworkers[3][8]	328	389	300	219
Retail, wholesale	175	198	200	215
Government (NAGE) (Ind.)	(NA)	100	150	200
United transportation[9]	(NA)	248	265	190
Mine workers (Ind.)[10]	(NA)	213	277	185
Iron workers	168	176	179	184
Railway, steamship clerks[11]	280	238	211	180
Firefighters	133	160	174	178
Painters	200	208	195	164
Electrical (UE) (Ind.)	167	165	165	162
Transit union	134	130	150	162
Bakery, confectionery[12]	(NA)	146	135	160
Oil, chemical workers	173	172	177	154
Sheetmetal workers	140	153	153	154
Rubber	204	183	211	151
Boilermakers	140	132	145	145
Bricklayers	160	149	135	135
Transport workers	98	150	150	130
Postal employees[12] (Ind.)	(NA)	(NA)	(NA)	125
Printing and graphic (IPGCU)	(NA)	(NA)	109	122

Table A-2 (Continued)
Membership in Large Unions, 1968–80

Union	1968	1972	1976	1980
Woodworkers	96	106	109	112
Office employees (OPEIU)	76	83	99	107
Maintenance of way	125	142	119	101

NA Not available.

In thousands. AFL-CIO (except as noted) unions reporting 100,000 members or more in 1980 with headquarters in U.S.

"Ind." - independent or unaffiliated unions.

1. In 1979, Retail clerks merged with Meat Cutters to form Food and Commercial Workers.

2. Intl. Union of Mine, Mill, and Smelter Workers, and Intl. Union of District 50 merged with United Steelworkers of America in 1967 and 1972, respectively.

3. Figures for all years represent the union as constituted after merger.

4. In 1976, Amalgamated Clothing Workers of America merged with Textile Workers Union of America to form Amalgamated Clothing and Textile Workers Union.

5. AFL-CIO per capita reports.

6. American Postal Workers Union formed in 1971 by merger of the postal clerks union and 4 other unions.

7. Postal clerks only.

8. United Papermakers and Paperworkers merged with Intl. Brotherhood of Pulp, Sulphite, and Paper Mill Workers in 1972 to form United Paperworkers International Union.

9. Merged with Brotherhood of Railroad Trainmen and three other railroad unions in 1969. 1980 excludes retired members.

10. 1980 excludes retired workers.

11. Includes Transportation-Communication Employees Union.

12. American Bakery and Confectionery Workers Intl. Union and Bakery and Confectionery Workers' Intl. Union of America merged in 1969.

13. Includes associate members.

Source: U.S. Bureau of Labor Statistics, *Directory of National Unions and Employee Associations, 1975, News,* Sept. 18, 1981; unpublished data.

Table A-3

National Unions—Number and Members, by Industry, 1970 and 1978

(Excluding employee associations and local unions directly affiliated with the AFL-CIO)

Industry Group	Number, All Unions[1]		Number, AFL-CIO Unions[1]		Members, All Unions[2] (1,000)		Members, AFL-CIO[2] Unions (1,000)		Percent Members, 1978	
	1970	1978	1970	1978	1970	1978	1970	1978	All	AFL-CIO
All unions	185	174	120	108	20,689	21,742	15,916	16,982	100.0	100.0
Manufacturing[3]	100	94	73	64	9,173	8,119	6,666	6,119	37.3	36.0
Food and kindred products[4]	25	24	17	16	905	595	588	575	2.7	3.4
Tobacco manufactures	8	4	5	3	38	37	37	37	.2	.2
Textile mill products	10	11	4	7	191	156	177	149	.7	.9
Apparel and related products	16	15	11	11	852	683	936	667	3.1	3.9
Lumber and wood products[5]	13	18	8	14	215	262	208	260	1.2	1.5
Furniture and fixtures	17	10	13	8	214	174	187	160	.8	.9
Paper and allied products	20	21	12	17	453	389	391	364	1.8	2.1
Printing, publishing, allied industries	18	18	15	13	370	281	357	270	1.3	1.6
Chemicals and allied products	26	25	19	15	362	219	151	201	1.0	1.2
Petroleum refining and related industries..............	12	13	7	10	79	77	69	73	.4	.4
Rubber and misc. plastics products .	19	24	13	19	271	269	248	253	1.2	1.5
Leather and leather products	13	15	10	13	140	119	134	118	.5	.7
Stone, clay, glass, concrete products	22	22	17	19	284	293	234	277	1.3	1.6
Primary metals industries	16	13	11	12	787	774	667	688	3.6	4.1
Fabricated metal products.........	33	29	21	19	917	613	719	438	2.8	2.6
Machinery, except electrical	23	18	16	13	550	670	278	411	3.1	2.4
Electrical machinery equipment, supplies	19	15	11	9	1,033	715	793	492	3.3	2.9

Transportation equipment	21	13	15	10	1,109	1,110	291	306	5.1	1.8
Nonmanufacturing[3]	104	96	73	70	9,198	9,998	7,390	7,811	46.0	46.0
Mining and quarrying[6]	15	14	8	10	368	428	154	149	2.0	.9
Contract construction[7]	28	29	21	23	2,576	2,884	2,476	2,711	13.3	16.0
Transportation	44	31	34	26	2,441	1,748	1,425	1,254	8.0	7.4
Telephone and telegraph	10	7	7	6	533	547	483	547	2.5	3.2
Electric, gas, sanitary services	17	15	12	14	312	356	268	353	1.6	2.1
Wholesale and retail trade	24	21	15	13	1,549	1,713	1,315	1,059	7.9	6.2
Service industries	48	47	31	29	1,286	1,824	1,166	1,548	8.4	9.1
Government	60	62	34	39	2,318	3,625	1,860	3,052	16.7	18.0
Federal	56	51	31	30	1,370	1,384	927	967	6.4	5.7
State and local	19	45	16	41	948	2,242	933	2,085	10.3	12.3

1. Nonadditive: many unions have membership in more than one industry group.
2. Membership computed by applying reported percentages to total membership, including that outside the U.S.
3. Includes industries not shown separately.
4. Includes beverages.
5. Except furniture.
6. Includes crude petroleum and natural gas production.
7. Building and special trade.

Source: U.S. Bureau of Labor Statistics, *Directory of National Unions and Employee Associations, 1971* and *1979*.

Table A-4
Labor Union Membership—Total and Percentage of Nonagricultural Employment, by States, 1964–78

State	Total (1,000)				Percent of Employment	
	1964	1970	1976	1978	1970	1978
U.S................	17,188	19,757	19,874	20,459	28.0	23.6
Ala.[1]	151	204	229	257	20.2	19.2
Alaska..............	21	25	50	43	26.9	26.2
Ariz.[1]	81	96	117	122	17.5	13.8
Ark.[1]...............	112	95	102	109	17.8	15.0
Calif................	1,888	2,137	2,148	2,184	30.8	23.7
Colo	124	152	175	172	20.5	15.2
Conn	244	290	309	296	24.2	21.9
Del. ...	36	48	49	52	22.5	21.7
Fla.[1]	201	299	365	367	13.9	11.7
Ga.[1]...	150	251	261	271	16.1	13.6
Hawaii	50	82	129	120	27.9	32.1
Idaho	32	38	41	47	18.3	14.3
Ill.	1,394	1,548	1,451	1,497	35.8	31.5
Ind.	522	657	621	643	35.5	29.3
Iowa[1]...............	150	186	192	212	21.1	19.2
Kans.[1]	109	112	125	117	16.5	12.8
Ky.	187	250	275	274	27.5	22.4
La	147	193	'213	'227	18.5	16.0
Maine	57	61	67	74	18.4	18.3
Md.[2]	352	463	440	458	23.4	21.0
Mass	572	573	570	611	25.1	24.4
Mich	962	1,195	1,165	1,223	39.8	34.6
Minn	339	378	385	411	28.7	24.4
Miss.[1]	53	76	87	103	13.2	12.4
Mo.................	546	594	572	578	35.7	30.0
Mont	63	60	60	67	29.8	24.1
Nebr.[1]	78	86	87	92	17.8	15.3
Nev.[1]...............	49	66	69	80	32.5	22.9
N.H.	44	45	43	48	17.3	13.3
N.J.................	814	768	697	683	29.4	23.0
N. Mex	34	43	50	54	14.7	12.1
N.Y.	2,507	2,555	2,358	2,753	35.7	39.2
N.C.[1]...............	89	137	141	147	7.7	6.5
N. Dak.[1]	21	28	26	34	17.2	14.7
Ohio	1,148	1,413	1,289	1,294	36.4	29.5
Okla	86	124	126	138	16.1	13.5
Oreg	198	218	221	232	30.7	23.1

Table A-4 (Continued)
Labor Union Membership—Total and Percentage of Nonagricultural Employment, by States, 1964–78

State	Total (1,000)				Percent of Employment	
	1964	1970	1976	1978	1970	1978
Pa	1,450	1,617	1,642	1,595	37.2	34.2
R.I.	89	89	114	108	25.9	27.1
S.C.¹	52	81	68	76	9.6	6.7
S. Dak.¹	14	21	21	24	11.9	10.3
Tenn.¹...............	184	274	288	303	20.6	17.7
Tex.¹	370	523	563	575	14.4	11.0
Utah¹...	58	75	62	68	20.9	13.0
Vt	22	24	30	33	16.2	17.5
Va.¹.................	179	245	252	258	16.7	12.7
Wash...............	367	434	453	496	40.2	33.1
W. Va	192	221	232	226	42.8	36.8
Wis	400	482	506	522	31.5	27.8
Wyo.¹	19	19	25	28	17.4	14.9
Unallocated	181	108	133	60	NA	NA

NA - Not Applicable.
1. State has a right-to-work law.
2. Includes District of Columbia.

Source: U.S. Bureau of Labor Statistics, *Directory of National and International Labor Unions in the United States, 1965; Directory of National Unions and Employee Associations, 1971, 1977,* and *1979.*

Table A-5
Work Stoppages by State, 1978 and 1979

State	Work Stoppages[1]		Workers Involved[2] (1,000)		Days Idle During Year (1,000)	
	1978	1979	1978	1979	1978	1979
U.S..............	4,230	4,827	1,623	1,727	36,922	34,754
N. Eng.:						
Maine	24	15	7	3	214	65
N.H.	15	13	3	3	61	47
Vt	11	11	1	2	12	26
Mass	117	138	25	29	331	531
R.I.	36	44	7	17	75	150
Conn	55	61	8	25	239	1,114
Mid. Atl.:						
N.Y.	328	394	111	130	2,084	2,027
N.J..............	219	273	51	55	556	1,032
Pa	480	612	155	167	4,064	2,762
E. No. Cent.:						
Ohio	441	508	141	170	3,757	3,573
Ind..............	211	193	62	59	1,497	1,547
Ill...............	341	394	136	222	3,037	4,233
Mich	300	349	94	91	1,757	1,593
Wis	110	84	28	26	573	977
W. No. Cent.:						
Minn	91	112	35	28	775	573
Iowa	47	60	13	46	186	747
Mo..............	92	123	39	37	701	988
N. Dak	5	3	3	1	17	8
S. Dak..........	3	11	1	2	7	53
Nebr	14	14	14	13	79	79
Kans	21	23	15	11	120	107
So. Atl.:						
Del..............	23	20	9	7	139	54
Md..............	46	41	14	15	231	402
D.C.	26	8	6	8	64	183
So. Atl.:						
Va	69	56	35	24	1,291	525
W. Va	142	183	36	36	3,393	526
N.C.	31	31	12	14	125	277
S.C..............	21	11	10	3	69	64

Table A-5 (Continued)
Work Stoppages by State, 1978 and 1979

State	Work Stoppages[1]		Workers Involved[2] (1,000)		Days Idle During Year (1,000)	
	1978	1979	1978	1979	1978	1979
Ga	40	76	24	30	203	470
Fla	50	42	20	21	228	435
E. So. Cent.:						
Ky	102	157	63	52	2,093	729
Tenn	91	106	40	37	749	914
Ala	69	92	22	27	1,069	667
Miss	29	27	12	7	202	252
W. So. Cent.:						
Ark	28	22	9	6	121	151
La	38	36	21	18	236	484
Okla	23	31	10	7	262	195
Tex	91	82	52	37	636	816
Mt.:						
Mont	19	21	8	2	56	46
Idaho	15	11	5	5	41	14
Wyo	5	9	9	5	125	68
Colo	37	24	17	8	186	232
N. Mex	21	16	9	6	224	46
Ariz	31	15	20	10	318	165
Utah	11	16	5	9	205	60
Nev	11	19	3	4	44	68
Pac.:						
Wash	94	75	41	17	1,471	780
Oreg	44	33	20	15	570	251
Calif	296	403	124	145	2,295	3,352
Alaska	12	8	2	2	58	23
Hawaii	18	12	12	12	100	275

1. Work stoppages affecting more than 1 State are counted as separate stoppages in each State affected, and workers involved and days idle are allocated among the appropriate States.

2. Workers counted more than once if involved in more than 1 stoppage during year.

Source: U.S. Bureau of Labor Statistics, *Analysis of Work Stoppages,* annual.

Notes

Chapter 1, THE ENDURING CONTROVERSY OVER LABOR UNIONS

1. H. Gregg Lewis, *Unionism and Relative Wages in the United States* (Chicago: University of Chicago Press, 1963), p. 6.

2. Basic sources of membership statistics are the U.S. Bureau of the Census, *Historical Statistics of the United States, Colonial Times to 1970;* U.S. Bureau of Labor Statistics, *Handbook of Labor Statistics,* annual; and *Directory of National Unions and Employees' Associations, 1979,* Bulletin 2079, September 1980. (See Appendices A-1 to A-4 of this book for more membership statistics.)

3. Adam Smith, *The Wealth of Nations,* ed. by Edwin Cannan (New York: Modern Library, 1937), Book I, Chapter VIII.

4. Quoted by W. H. Hutt, *The Theory of Collective Bargaining* (London: King, 1930), p. 25; reprinted by The Institute of Economic Affairs, London, 1975. Original in R. G. Hawtrey, *The Economic Problem* (London: Longmans, Green, 1926), p. 29.

5. Smith, *Wealth of Nations* (n. 3, above).

6. Quoted by Hutt, *Theory* (n. 4, above).

7. Alfred Marshall, *Principles of Economics,* 8th ed. (London: Macmillan, 1920), pp. 471–72.

8. Quoted by Hutt, *Theory* (n. 4, above), p. 44.

9. Sidney Webb and Beatrice Webb, *Industrial Democracy* (London: Longmans, Green, 1920), pp. 840–41.

10. Irving Kristol, "Understanding Trade Unionism," *The Wall Street Journal,* 23 October 1978, p. 24.

11. Nicholas von Hoffman, "The Last Days of the Labor Movement," *Harper's,* December 1978, p. 28.

12. Clark Kerr, "Industrial Relations Research: A Personal Retrospective," *Industrial Relations,* May 1978, p. 142.

13. George Strauss and Peter Feuille, "Industrial Relations Research: A Critical Analysis," *Industrial Relations,* October 1978, pp. 259–77.

14. Richard B. Freeman and James L. Medoff, "The Two Faces of Unionism," *The Public Interest,* Fall 1979, pp. 69–93.

15. Hutt, *Theory* (n. 4, above); Henry C. Simons, "Some Reflections on Syndicalism," *Journal of Political Economy*, 52 (March 1944), pp. 1-25; H. Gregg Lewis, "The Labor Monopoly Problem: A Positive Program," *Journal of Political Economy*, 59 (August 1951), pp. 277-87; Fritz Machlup, *Political Economy of Monopoly* (Baltimore: Johns Hopkins University Press, 1952); Ludwig von Mises, *Human Action* (New Haven, Conn.: Yale University Press, 1949); Milton Friedman, "Some Comments on the Significance of Labor Unions for Economic Policy," in David McCord Wright, ed., *The Impact of the Union* (New York: Harcourt Brace, 1951).

Chapter 2, THE ECONOMIC NATURE OF UNIONISM

1. John Hutchinson, *The Imperfect Union: A History of Corruption in American Trade Unions* (New York: Dutton, 1970), p. 9.

2. Finis Welch, "The Rising Impact of Minimum Wages," *Regulation*, November-December 1978, pp. 28-37.

3. Leon Appelbaum found that 40% of the union leaders in 94 locals in Milwaukee who were in office in 1960 were not in office by 1962, in "Officer Turnover and Salary Structures in Local Unions," *Industrial and Labor Relations Review*, 19 (January 1966), pp. 224-30; see also Leon Appelbaum, "A Comparison of Officer Turnover and Salary Structures in Local Unions," *Labor Law Journal*, December 1969, pp. 795-802; Leon Appelbaum and Harry R. Blaine, "Compensation and Turnover of Union Officers," *Industrial Relations*, 14 (May 1975), pp. 156-57.

4. Ernest van den Haag, "Labor Unions in a Free Market," *Imprimis*, Hillsdale College, March 1979.

5. L. F. Dunn, "Quantifying Nonpecuniary Returns," *Journal of Human Resources*, 12 (Summer 1977), pp. 347-59.

6. George J. Borjas, "Job Satisfaction, Wages, and Unions," *Journal of Human Resources*, 14 (Winter 1979), pp. 21-40.

7. Richard B. Freeman, "The Effect of Unionism on Worker Attachment to Firms," *Journal of Labor Research*, 1 (Spring 1980), pp. 29-61.

8. Thomas Kochan, "How American Workers View Labor Unions," *Monthly Labor Review*, April 1979, pp. 23-31.

9. Douglass V. Brown and Charles A. Meyers, in Benjamin Aaron, Clyde W. Summers, and Joseph Shister, eds., *Public Policy and Collective Bargaining* (New York: Harper & Row, 1962).

10. A formal model is presented in Morgan O. Reynolds, "Whatever Happened to the Monopoly Theory of Labor Unions?" *Journal of Labor Research*, 2 (Spring 1981), pp. 163-73.

11. Edward H. Chamberlin, *The Economic Analysis of Labor Union Power* (Washington, D.C.: American Enterprise Institute, 1963), p. 31.

12. Arthur J. Goldberg, "Labor and Antitrust," in William G. Bowen and Orley Ashenfelter, eds., *Labor and the National Economy* (New York: Norton, 1975).

13. *Economic Report of the President,* January 1982, pp. 256–57, 327. Without inventory valuation and capital consumption adjustments, post-corporate-tax profits were $154 billion in 1981.

14. The employee share of income is slightly inflated by the fact that public-sector employees' compensation adds to labor income but not to corporate income. The *1980 Economic Report of the President,* p. 41, shows that labor's share in nonfinancial corporate business was seven-eighths in data excluding capital consumption adjustment and all petroleum and coal companies. Probably the most accurate statement to make is that labor receives just under 90% and investors just over 10% of the income (value added) from corporate activity.

15. Quotation reprinted in *Pathfinder,* Texas A&M University, May–June 1979, p. 6.

16. Henry C. Simons, "Some Reflections on Syndicalism," *Journal of Political Economy,* 52 (March 1944), p. 22.

17. This section is based on Sylvester Petro, *The Labor Policy of the Free Society* (New York: Ronald, 1957), p. 114.

18. *Sacramento Bee,* 30 December 1980.

19. Milton Friedman and Rose Friedman, *Free to Choose* (New York: Harcourt Brace Jovanovich, 1980), p. 242; formal models are in Earl A. Thompson, "On Labor's Right to Strike," *Economic Inquiry,* 18 (October 1980), pp. 640–53, and Michael T. Maloney, Robert E. McCormick, and Robert D. Tollison, "Achieving Cartel Profits through Unionization," *Southern Economic Journal,* 45 (October 1979), pp. 628–35.

20. Simons, "Some Reflections" (n. 16, above).

21. Milton Friedman, *Capitalism and Freedom* (Chicago: University of Chicago Press, 1962), p. 22.

22. Sylvester Petro, *Power Unlimited* (New York: Ronald, 1959), p. 213.

Chapter 3, THE MYTHOLOGY OF UNIONISM

1. Felix Frankfurter and Nathan Greene, *The Labor Injunction* (New York: Macmillan, 1930), p. 25.

2. Archibald Cox and Derek C. Bok, *Cases and Materials on Labor Law,* 7th ed. (New York: Foundation Press, 1969), p. 71.

3. W. H. Hutt, *The Theory of Collective Bargaining* (London: King, 1930); reprinted by Institute of Economic Affairs, London, 1975.

4. Benjamin Klein, Robert G. Crawford, Armen A. Alchian, "Vertical Integration, Appropriable Rents, and the Competitive Contracting Process," *Journal of Law and Economics,* 21 (October 1978), pp. 297–326.

5. Ludwig von Mises, *Human Action,* 3rd ed. (Chicago: Regnery, 1963), p. 492.

6. Herbert R. Northrup, "The Case for Boulwarism," *Harvard Business Review,* 41 (September–October, 1963), pp. 86–87.

7. W. H. Hutt, *The Strike-Threat System* (New Rochelle, N.Y.: Arlington House, 1973), p. 47.

8. Quoted in William Leiserson, *American Trade Union Democracy* (New York: Columbia University Press, 1959), p. 88.

9. Quoted in C. Wright Mills, *The New Men of Power: America's Labor Leaders* (New York: Harcourt, Brace, 1948), p. 60.

10. Reprinted in Neil W. Chamberlain, ed., *Sourcebook on Labor* (New York: McGraw-Hill, 1958), pp. 94–169; see also Leo Bromwich, *Union Constitutions* (New York: Fund for the Republic, 1959).

11. U.S. Bureau of Labor Statistics, *Directory of National Unions and Employee Associations, 1975* (Washington: U.S. Government Printing Office, 1977), Bulletin 1937, p. 3.

12. Mills, *New Men* (n. 9, above), p. 130.

13. House Education and Labor Committee, U.S. House of Representatives, *Hearings on Labor-Management Relations,* pursuant to H. Res. 115, 83d Congress, 1st session, 9–13 March 1953, Washington, D.C., pp. 1026–29.

Chapter 4, THE NEW RATIONALE FOR UNIONISM

1. Kenneth E. Boulding, "Collective Bargaining and Fiscal Policy," *Industrial Relations Research Association,* proceedings, December 1949, p. 52.

2. Richard B. Freeman and James L. Medoff, "The Two Faces of Unionism," *The Public Interest,* 57 (Fall 1979), pp. 69–93. Critical analysis includes Morgan O. Reynolds, "The New Rationale for Unionism," *Journal of Social and Political Studies,* 5 (Fall 1980), pp. 259–69; Leo Troy, C. Timothy Koeller, and Neil Sheflin, "The Three Faces of Unionism," *Policy Review,* 14 (Fall 1980), pp. 95–109; John T. Addison, "Are Unions Good for Productivity?" *Journal of Labor Research,* 3 (Spring 1982), pp. 125–38; John T. Addison and A. H. Barnett, "The Impact of Unions on Productivity," *British Journal of Industrial Relations,* 20 (July 1982), pp. 145–62; W. H. Hutt, "The Face and Mask of Unionism," *Journal of Labor Research,* 4 (Summer 1983), pp. 197–211; Lionel Robbins, et al., *Trade Unions: Public Goods or Public Bads?* (London: Institute of Economic Affairs, 1978).

In what is rapidly becoming a minor industry, see also Charles Brown and James L. Medoff, "Trade Unions in the Production Process," *Journal of Political Economy,* 86 (June 1978), pp. 355–78; Richard B. Freeman, "The Exit-Voice Tradeoff in the Labor Market: Unionism, Job Tenure, Quits, and Separations," *Quarterly Journal of Economics,* 94 (1980), pp. 643–74; Richard B. Freeman, "Individual Mobility and Collective Voice in the Labor Market," *American Economic Review,* 66 (May 1976), pp. 361–68; Kim Clark, "Unions and Productivity in the Cement Industry," unpublished Ph.D. diss., Harvard University, 1978; Oliver E. Williamson, Jeffrey E. Harris, and Michael L. Wachter, "Understanding the Employment Relation: The Analysis of Idiosyncratic Exchange," *Bell Journal of Economics,* 6 (Spring 1975), pp. 250–78; and Richard B. Freeman and James L. Medoff, *What Do Unions Do?* (New York: Basic Books, 1984).

3. Freeman and Medoff, "The Two Faces" (n. 2, above), p. 93.

4. The authors fail to specify exactly who desires new social conditions. If everyone does, nothing except the laws of nature would impede the change.

5. Unless otherwise specified, all quotations and page citations for Freeman and Medoff in this chapter refer to "The Two Faces" (n. 2, above).

6. Richard B. Freeman, "The Effect of Unionism on Worker Attachment to Firms," *Journal of Labor Research,* 1 (Spring 1980), pp. 29–61; Richard B. Freeman, "The Exit-Voice Tradeoff" (n. 2, above), pp. 643–74.

7. Freeman and Medoff, The Two Faces" (n. 2, above); J. Frantz, Senior Honors thesis, Harvard University, March 1976, cited by Freeman and Medoff; Kim Clark, "Unionization and Productivity: Microeconometric Evidence," *Quarterly Journal of Economics,* 94 (December 1980), pp. 613–39; Steven Allen, "Unionized Construction Workers Are More Productive," mimeo (Washington, D.C.: Center to Project Workers' Rights, November 1979); Freeman, Medoff, and Connerton, work in progress, cited by Freeman and Medoff.

8. Richard B. Freeman, "Unionism and the Dispersion of Wages," *Industrial and Labor Relations Review,* 34 (October 1980), pp. 3–23.

9. Ibid., p. 23.

10. Thomas Hyclak, "Unions and Income Inequality: Some Cross-State Evidence," *Industrial Relations,* 19 (Spring 1980), pp. 212–15.

11. Norman Hill, "The Double Speak of Right-to-Work," *American Federationist,* 87 (October 1980), p. 16. See also Bill Cunningham, "Bringing Productivity into Focus," *American Federationist,* 86 (April 1979), pp. 1–8, which reprints an excerpt from Brown and Medoff, "Two Faces" (n. 2, above); and "Are the Unions Dead, or Just Sleeping?" *Fortune,* 20 September 1982, pp. 98ff.

12. See, for instance, F. A. Hayek, *Capitalism and Historians* (Chicago: University of Chicago Press, 1954).

13. William Leiserson, "The National Union: Basic Governmental Unit," in Richard L. Rowan, ed., *Readings in Labor Economics and Labor Relations* (Homewood, Ill: Irwin, 1976).

14. Albert Rees, "The Effects of Unions on Resource Allocation," *Journal of Law and Economics,* 6 (October 1963), p. 75.

15. Gilbert Burck, "A Time of Reckoning for the Building Unions," *Fortune,* 4 June 1979, pp. 82–96.

16. *Pathfinder,* Texas A&M University, September-October 1980, pp. 1–2. See also Roderick Martin, *New Technology and Industrial Relations in Fleet Street* (Oxford: Clarendon Press, 1981); Paul A. Weinstein, *Featherbedding and Technological Change* (Boston: Heath, 1965); Clarence B. Carson, *Throttling the Railroads* (Indianapolis: Liberty Fund and Foundation for Economic Education, 1971); Frank Knox and Jossleyn Hennessy, *Restrictive Practices in the Building Industry* (London: Institute of Economic Affairs, 1966); David Graham Hutton, *Source-book on Restrictive Practices in Britain* (London: Institute of Economic Affairs, 1966).

17. Paul T. Hartman, *Collective Bargaining and Productivity: The Longshore Mechanization Agreement* (Berkeley: University of California Press, 1969).

18. Rees, "Effects of Unions" (n. 14, above), pp. 75–76.

19. Although there are instances of unions cooperating with management to

improve productivity—in the needle trades, for example—such cooperation occurs only when unionized firms are under severe competitive pressures, endangering the industry and hence the existence of the union. This behavior reinforces the view that with "business as usual," unions restrict productivity.

20. Thomas Beecroft, "A Study of Union Elections and Their Influence on Relative Stock Prices," mimeo (College Station: Texas A&M University, August 1979).

21. An example is Charles R. Greer, Stanley A. Martin, and Ted A. Reusser, who in "The Effect of Strikes on Shareholder Returns," *Journal of Labor Research,* 1 (Fall 1980), pp. 217-29, found that returns for firms varied with the duration of strikes, generally increasing with strike length. Also, Richard S. Ruback and Martin Zimmerman found that unionization lowered the equity value of a firm by 3.8% in "Unionization and Profitability: Evidence from the Capital Market," mimeo (Cambridge, Mass.: Massachusetts Institute of Technology and National Bureau of Economic Research, Inc., presented at the Conference on the Economics of Trade Unions, 6-7 May 1983).

22. W. H. Hutt, *The Strike-Threat System* (New Rochelle, N.Y.: Arlington House, 1973), p. 158; see also Troy et al., "Three Faces" (n. 2, above); and ch. 7 in this book. The hypothesis that positive inducements or reinforcements induce greater responsiveness than negative punishments is well accepted in psychology and animal research, too.

23. Martin Anderson, *The Federal Bulldozer* (Cambridge, Mass.: MIT Press, 1964); Jerome Rothenberg, *Economic Evaluation of Urban Renewal* (Washington, D.C.: Brookings Institution, 1967).

24. *The Wall Street Journal,* 11 December 1980, p. 29. Original "Survey of Business Opinion" conducted October 1980 by Dow Jones & Company.

25. Troy et al., "Three Faces" (n. 2, above).

26. Albert Rees, *The Economics of Trade Unions* (Chicago: University of Chicago Press, 1977), pp. 91-93; George Johnson, "Economic Analysis of Trade Unionism," *American Economic Review Proceedings,* 65 (May 1975), pp. 23-28; David Metcalf, "Unions and the Distribution of Earnings," *British Journal of Industrial Relations,* 20 (July 1982), pp. 163-69.

27. Peter Wiles, "Are Trade Unions Necessary?" *Encounter,* September 1956, p. 7.

28. Stephen Early, "Union Democracy in Mineworkers, Steelworkers, and Teamsters Unions," *San Fernando Valley Law Review,* 1978, p. 43.

29. *Monthly Labor Review,* December 1980, p. 69.

30. Arthur Shenfield, "Trade Union Power and the Law," *Modern Age,* Summer 1980, pp. 262-63.

Chapter 5, OLD UNIONISM AND GOVERNMENTAL SUPPORT

1. See, for instance, James A. Gross, *The Reshaping of the National Labor Relations Board* (Albany, N.Y.: State University of New York Press, 1981), and the book review by Morgan O. Reynolds in the *Journal of Economic History,* 42 (December 1982), pp. 950-51.

2. W. H. Hutt, *The Strike-Threat System* (New Rochelle, N.Y.: Arlington House, 1973), p. 23.

3. William E. Leuchtenburg, "The New Deal and the Analogue of War," in John Braeman, Robert H. Bremmer, and Everett Walters, eds., *Change and Continuity in Twentieth Century America* (Columbus: Ohio State University Press, 1964), p. 87.

4. The friendship formed between Roosevelt and Frankfurter produced an extraordinary correspondence. See Max Freedman, ed., *Roosevelt and Frankfurter: Their Correspondence, 1928-45* (Boston: Little, Brown, 1967). Frankfurter's memo to FDR on 8 June 1941 states his version of the common view of labor writers about labor markets: "The day of industrial absolutism is done. All our experience since the industrial revolution demonstrates that employers as a class cannot be relied upon, voluntarily and out of the goodness of their hearts, to give a square deal to unorganized labor; this has been precluded by the pressure of immediate self-interest and the inexorable workings of the competitive system" (p. 604).

5. Leuchtenburg, "New Deal" (n. 3, above), pp. 87-90.

6. Ibid., p. 88.

7. See Morgan O. Reynolds, "Understanding Political Pricing of Labor Services: The Davis-Bacon Act," *Journal of Labor Research,* 3 (Summer 1982), pp. 295-309.

8. Section 7a was originally interpreted as meaning "proportional" collective bargaining; that is, if a particular union received 55% of the votes, it represented only that 55%, and so forth, rather than the compulsory majority rule of today. Edwin Witte noted that the essential provisions of 7(a) were "but restatements of principles first recognized by the National War Labor Board" in "The Background of the Labor Provisions of the N.I.R.A.," *University of Chicago Law Review,* 1 (1934), p. 573. For a portrayal of the transition to majority rule, see Kim McQuaid, *Big Business and Presidential Power* (New York: Morrow, 1982), ch. 1, pp. 39-47. Thanks to Murray Rothbard for this point.

9. Many scholars also argue that the NLRA was a prerequisite to the growth of Big Labor and, ultimately, to the development of the alliance between organized labor and the Democratic party; Daniel A. Sipe, "A Moment of the State: The Enactment of the National Labor Relations Act, 1935," unpublished Ph.D. diss., University of Pennsylvania, 1981.

10. Section 2 of the Norris–La Guardia Anti-Injunction Act is noteworthy for its colorful declaration of public policy, borrowed from two sources: Chief Justice Taft's opinion in the *American Steel Foundries* case and the language of the Railway Labor Act. The public policy statement of Norris–La Guardia also served as the forerunner of the policy statement in the Wagner Act. By the turn of the century it was commonplace to write about "the individual unorganized worker who is commonly helpless to exercise actual liberty of contract and to protect his freedom of labor" (Norris–La Guardia Act, Section 2); and to speak of the worker as defenseless: "A single employee was helpless in dealing with an employer. . . unable to leave the employ and to resist arbitrary and unfair treatment. . . . Union was essential to give laborers opportunity to deal on equality with their employer." (*American Steel Foundries* v. *Tri-City Cent. Trades Council,* 257 U.S. 184 [1921]).

11. Benjamin Aaron, "The Labor Injunction Reappraised," *UCLA Law Review,* 10: 292 (1963), p. 295.

12. For examples, see ibid.; Charles O. Gregory and Harold A. Katz, *Labor and the Law,* 3d ed. (New York: Norton, 1979), pp. 174–84; Edwin F. Beal, Edward D. Wickersham, and Philip K. Kienast, *The Practice of Collective Bargaining,* 5th ed. (Homewood, Ill.: Irwin, 1976), pp. 137–38; Juanita M. Kreps, Philip L. Martin, Richard Perlman, and Gerald G. Somers, *Contemporary Labor Economics and Labor Relations,* 2d ed. (Belmont, Calif.: Wadsworth, 1980), p. 149; Lloyd G. Reynolds, *Labor Economics and Labor Relations,* 8th ed. (Englewood Cliffs, N.J.: Prentice-Hall, 1982), pp. 506–7.

13. For evidence of similarity in union-nonunion pay, see Albert F. Hinrichs, *The United Mineworkers of America and the Non-Union Coal Fields* (New York: Columbia University Press, 1923). See also the evidence from multiple sources that annual wages were 20% higher, or more, for unorganized miners than for unionized miners, in *Hitchman Coal & Coke Co.* v. *Mitchell et al.,* 202 F. 512 (1912), pp. 540–42. For evidence of higher nonunion wages in coal mining today, see "Maverick Mine," *The Wall Street Journal,* 23 October 1978, p. 1, and "Digging for Dollars," *The Wall Street Journal,* 10 November 1978, p. 1.

14. The Federal District Court described the events that had angered the Hitchman employees: "The men did not want to quit work, and tried to get permission from their union officials to continue loading engine coal, for the reason that, if they were not allowed to do so, the Baltimore & Ohio Railroad Company would haul in nonunion coal, and have it loaded into their engines from plaintiff's tipple and bins under the terms of plaintiff's contract with the railroad company.... The strike was called, coal was hauled from an Ohio union mine with which settlement had been made by the union by the railroad, and loaded on its engines over plaintiff's tipple..... This national strike was finally settled in July, 1906, by the adoption of the 1903 [pay] scale, which plaintiff from the start had offered to pay. But in the meantime the Hitchman miners had been promised benefits by the union which were not paid, and they were incensed because the Ohio coal had been allowed to be hauled and loaded on its engines by the railroad over plaintiff's tipple, and because plaintiff *Hitchman's* original proposition to pay the 1903 scale had not been accepted" (202 Federal Reporter 553 [1913]). For an extensive treatment of a similar incident, see Sylvester Petro, *The Kingsport Strike* (New Rochelle, N.Y.: Arlington House, 1967).

15. Alvin F. Goldman, *The Supreme Court and Labor-Management Relations Law* (Lexington, Mass.: Lexington Books, 1976), pp. 18–19; Felix Frankfurter and Nathan Greene, *The Labor Injunction* (New York: Macmillan, 1930), pp. 148–49.

16. "Unionizing Employees under Contract Declared Illegal by United States Supreme Court," *Monthly Labor Review,* 6 (January 1918), pp. 146–47.

17. Ibid., p. 149.

18. A number of writers classify today's union security provisions compelling union membership and/or dues payments as a condition of continuing employment in the same category as nonunion oaths. For example, in *The Constitution of Liberty* (Chicago: University of Chicago Press, 1960), Friedrich Hayek says that "unions should not be permitted to keep non-members out of any employ-

ment. This means that closed- and union-shop contracts (including such varieties as the 'maintenance of membership' and 'preferential hiring' clauses) must be treated as contracts in restraint of trade and denied the protection of the law. They differ in no respect from the 'yellow-dog contract' which prohibits the individual worker from joining a union and which is commonly prohibited by law'' (p. 278). Strictly speaking, a yellow-dog contract demands nonunion status only as a condition of continuing in the *same* employment relationship. If nonunion oaths generally were considered a disadvantage in working conditions *and* if labor markets were competitive, employers would have to pay higher wages in order to compensate workers for insisting on such a disadvantage.

Right-to-work laws are directly related to this issue because they prohibit collective agreements requiring union membership or payment of union dues as a condition of employment. Milton Friedman appears to differ from Hayek in his policy recommendation because Friedman opposes right-to-work laws on the grounds that such laws restrict liberty of contract, that is, the freedom of private parties to agree to union security clauses if they wish. See Milton Friedman, *Capitalism and Freedom* (Chicago: University of Chicago Press, 1962), pp. 115-17. Legal versions of the argument are *Adair* v. *U.S.* (208 U.S. 161 [1908]) and *Coppage* v. *Kansas* (236 U.S. 1 [1915]), in which the Supreme Court invalidated federal and state legislation prohibiting nonunion oaths because the legislation denied freedom of contract.

Thomas Haggard makes a libertarian argument for right-to-work laws on somewhat different grounds than Hayek does, namely, by arguing that collective bargaining agreements are not true contracts in which enforceable promises of something of value are voluntarily exchanged between parties. See *Reason,* May 1979, pp. 34-37. According to this view, laws properly prevent the state from enforcing unilateral employer promises obtained by coercive methods for which nothing is exchanged in return. Of course, this approach raises the more general question of what provisions, if any, in collective contracts would be enforceable by law. See also Haggard, *Compulsory Unionism, the NLRB, and the Courts* (Philadelphia: University of Pennsylvania Press, The Wharton School, 1977).

My view is that so long as there is a reasonably competitive open market with many employers and potential entrants, employees should be free to offer any terms of employment they wish. Similarly, employees should be free to offer, or demand, any terms they wish. Employers might require donations to a pension plan, a labor union, the Communist party, or the signing of a nonunion oath, and none would interfere with or restrain the freedom of individuals to trade in the labor market. Legally to constrain employers from offering particular packages of compensation to employees interferes with freedom. See Morgan O. Reynolds, "The Free Rider Argument for Compulsory Union Dues," *Journal of Labor Research,* 1 (Fall 1980), pp. 295-313.

19. Roscoe Pound, "Legal Immunities of Labor Unions," *Labor Unions and Public Policy* (Washington, D.C.: American Enterprise Association, 1958); Reprint No. 1, *Journal of Labor Research,* Fall 1979.

20. Sylvester Petro, "Injunctions and Labor Disputes: 1880-1932," *Wake Forest Law Review,* 14 (June 1978), pp. 341-576; reprint, Baylor Institute for Labor Policy Research, Reprint No. 1.

21. Archibald Cox and Derek C. Bok, *Cases and Materials on Labor Law,* 7th ed. (New York: Foundation Press, 1969), p. 71.

22. Goldman, *Supreme Court* (n. 15, above), p. 7.

23. On 29 June 1886, Congress enacted a law to legalize the incorporation of national trade unions, and they could incorporate with "the right to sue and be sued, to implead and be impleaded." The act was passed with the support of organized labor, which believed that it would enhance respectability and end the doctrine of criminal conspiracy that still surrounded unionism. A statement at the AFL convention in 1886 declared, "The law is not what was desired...but it recognizes the principle of the lawful character of trades unions, a principle we have been contending for years." No union made an effort to secure a charter under the law, and by 1901 Samuel Gompers said at the AFL convention, "Some years ago the Federal Congress passed a law for the incorporation of our trade unions. Beyond question the advocates of that bill really believed they were doing the organized workers a real service; but at the time, and since, we have repeatedly warned our fellow-unionists to refrain from seeking the so-called protection of that law."

This was the opening round of a concerted effort against incorporation, prompted by the Taff-Vale case in England. In this case, a railroad had sued unionists for damages of $150,000, which it claimed to have suffered during a strike. The House of Lords held that a *registered* trade union was subject to civil suits for damages, that it was collectively responsible for the acts of its officers as individuals, and that its funds could be attached to satisfy claims. The decision was instrumental in producing the 1906 Trades Disputes Act, which provided complete immunity from torts and ordinary contract law for unionists. It was a vote-catching expediency by men in the Liberal party, who nevertheless failed to forestall the formation of the Labour party and the gradual demise of their own party.

In America a political movement sprang up to make incorporation of trade unions mandatory. In April 1903, for instance, a member of this group, the National Civic Federation, said, "When the suggestion is made to the average labor leader that such incorporation ought to be enforced, we at once meet with the answer that it would be fatal to their methods, which is an open confession that their methods are illegal and wrong." The episode ended when Senator Sheppard of Texas submitted a bill, which later became Public Act 306, to repeal the incorporation act of 1886, and it passed both houses without discussion on 22 July 1932. "Historical Review of Trade-Union Incorporation," *Monthly Labor Review,* January 1935, pp. 38–43, is the source of all quotations used in this note.

24. Edwin E. Witte, *The Government in Labor Disputes* (New York: McGraw-Hill, 1932), p. 84; reprint, New York: Arno, 1969; Frankfurter and Greene, *The Labor Injunction* (n. 15, above), report the earliest injunction in the early 1880s, p. 21; James M. Landis and M. Manoff, *Cases on Labor Law,* 2d ed. (Chicago: Foundation Press, 1942), pp. 39–40, say that American labor injunctions "date back to the Railway strike of 1877," when Judge Drummond, circuit judge for the Seventh Circuit, found strikers guilty of contempt for interfering with the general orders of the court directing the receivers of the railroads to operate their trains (citations omitted).

25. Irving Bernstein, *The Lean Years: A History of the American Workers, 1920-1933* (Boston: Houghton Mifflin, 1960), p. 400.

26. Sylvester Petro, "Injunctions" (n. 20, above).

27. *Union Pac. Ry.* v. *Reuf,* 120 F. 102, 120-21 (C.C.C. Neb., 1902), cited by Petro, ibid., p. 373. Literature on union violence includes Graham Adams, *Age of Industrial Violence, 1910-1915* (New York: Columbia University Press, 1966); Hugh D. Graham and Ted R. Gurr, *Violence in America,* rev. ed. (Beverly Hills, Calif.: Sage Publications, 1979); Charles Stevenson, "The Tyranny of Terrorism in the Building Trades," *Reader's Digest,* June 1973, pp. 89-94, "The Construction Unions Declare War," *Reader's Digest,* July 1973, pp. 79-83, "Labor Violence—A National Scandal," *Reader's Digest,* August 1973, pp. 153-58, "Yes, Construction Terrorism is Real," *Reader's Digest,* December 1973, pp. 85-89. Periodicals frequently report incidents of violence and vandalism in labor disputes; for instance, an AP wirephoto in the *Houston Chronicle,* 22 July 1982, p. 1, shows strikers pelting a car with bricks and rocks at the Iowa Beef Processing Plant at Dakota City, Nebraska; *Time,* 28 September 1981, p. 16, shows union miners demolishing a fence at Kerr-McGee's nonunion mine in Galatia, Illinois; and a government informant alleged that the Hotel Employees' and Restaurant Employees' Union paid him to bomb two Tahoe, Nevada, casinos during labor disputes (*Wall Street Journal,* 29 September 1982, p. 50). See also Randolph H. Boehm, *Organized Crime and Organized Labor* (Washington, D.C.: Foundation for the Advancement of the Public Trust, 1975) and Armand J. Thieblot, Jr., and Thomas R. Haggard, *Union Violence: The Record and the Response by Courts, Legislatures, and the NLRB* (Philadelphia: The Wharton School, University of Pennsylvania, 1983) for more on this neglected topic.

28. Of 524 reported cases of labor injunction in federal and state courts from 1880 to 1932, unions sought to enjoin employers' actions in 33 cases and gained a partial injunction in only one case. By comparison, unions sought to enjoin tactics by other *unionists* in nearly as many reported cases, 26, as they sought to enjoin employers. See Petro, "Injunctions" (n. 20, above), p. 388 and Appendix I.

29. Henry George, "The Condition of Labor: An Open Letter to Pope Leo XIII," *The Land Question* (New York: Robert Schalkenbach Foundation, 1982 [1891]), p. 77.

30. U.S. Bureau of the Census, *Historical Statistics of the United States, Colonial Times to 1970* (Washington, D.C.: U.S. Government Printing Office, 1975), Part 1, p. 1710.

31. Witte, *Government in Labor Disputes* (n. 24, above), p. 84.

32. *Monthly Labor Review,* 102 (September 1979), p. 59.

33. John E. Abodeely, *The NLRB and the Appropriate Bargaining Unit* (Philadelphia: University of Pennsylvania Press, 1971); Robert E. Williams, Peter A. Janus, and Kenneth C. Huhn, *NLRB Regulation of Election Conduct* (Philadelphia: University of Pennsylvania Press, 1974); A. R. McFarland and W. S. Bishop, *Union Authorization Cards and the NLRB* (Philadelphia: University of Pennsylvania Press, 1969); W. N. Coke and F. H. Gantschi III, "Political Bias in NLRB Unfair Labor Practice Decisions," *Industrial and Labor Relations Review,* 35 (July 1982), pp. 539-49.

34. To head the new Agricultural Adjustment Administration in 1933, Presi-

dent Roosevelt named George N. Peek, "a hard bitten farm-belt agitator who had served as 'a sort of generalissimo of industry' under the War Industries Board." See Leuchtenburg, "New Deal" (n. 3, above), pp. 112–13.

35. John E. Kwoka, "Pricing under Federal Milk Market Regulation," *Economic Inquiry,* 15 (July 1977), pp. 357–84.

36. *Monthly Labor Review,* 102 (September 1979), p. 58.

37. A few exceptions occur in sports, entertainment, and higher education, in which some collective contracts specify only wage floors, above which individuals can negotiate (the so-called star system). Thanks to Dan C. Heldman for making this point.

38. National Labor Relations Board, *Legislative History of the Labor-Management Relations Act, 1947* (Washington, D.C.: U.S. Government Printing Office, 1948), Vol. 1, pp. 1493–96; Vol. 2, p. 2680; National Labor Relations Board, *Legislative History of the National Labor Relations Act* (Washington, D.C.: U.S. Government Printing Office, 1936), Vol. 1, pp. 1531, 1570–91, 1574–76.

39. The cases are *Senn* v. *Tile Layers' Protective Union,* 301 U.S. 468 (1937); *Lauf* v. *E.G. Shinner & Co.,* 303 U.S. 323 (1938); *New Negro Alliance* v. *Sanitary Grocery Co., Inc.,* 303 U.S. 552 (1938); *Milk Wagon Drivers' Union* v. *Lake Valley Farm Products,* 311 U.S. 91 (1940).

40. Litigation continues to test the outer limits of the exemption. Some labor organizations fail to qualify for the labor union exemption because members do not have an "employment relationship" with an enterprise—say, truckers, painters, or fishermen who attempt to fix product prices rather than hourly wage rates. In *Connell Construction Co.* v. *Plumbers Local 100,* 421 U.S. 616 (1975), the Supreme Court by a 5–4 vote found the union in violation of the Sherman Act after its picket forced Connell, a general contractor, to subcontract mechanical work to firms with bargaining agreements with the union.

41. An important exception is the Supreme Court's opinion in *Boys Markets, Inc.* v. *Retail Clerks Local 770,* 398 U.S. 235 (1970), that federal district courts can enjoin strikes that violate the no-strike clause in a union contract when the contract provides for binding arbitration of the dispute over which the strike was called.

42. Benjamin Aaron, "Labor Injunctions in the State Courts," *Virginia Law Review,* 50 (November 1964), pp. 1147–64; John R. Commons and John B. Andrews, *Principles of Labor Legislation,* 4th rev. ed., 1936 (reprinted by Augustus M. Kelly, New York, 1967), pp. 415–17.

43. The similarity between labor and agricultural cartels is highlighted by Wisconsin, which enacted a union anti-injunction act in 1929. Bernstein, *Lean Years* (n. 25, above), p. 395, says the act was maneuvered through the legislature by adding a provision that contracts obligating farmers not to join cooperative associations would be unenforceable, another kind of yellow-dog contract. For more on state labor law, see Charles C. Killingsworth, *State Labor Relations Acts* (Chicago: University of Chicago Press, 1952); Sanford Cohen, *State Labor Legislation, 1937–1947* (Columbus: Ohio State University Press, 1948).

44. See, for instance, John E. Abodeely, "Injunctive Powers under the National Labor Relations Act," in Richard L. Rowan, ed., *Collective Bargaining:*

Survival in the 70's? (Philadelphia: Wharton School, University of Pennsylvania Press, 1972), pp. 106–26.

45. The executive council of the AFL in its report at the 1937 convention declared that as a consequence of the "impetus to growth, which followed directly upon the decision of the United States Supreme Court upholding the constitutionality of the Wagner Labor Relations Act, the A.F. of L. and its constituent national and international unions had gained nearly a million members." *Monthly Labor Review,* December 1937, p. 1427.

46. Bernstein, *Lean Years* (n. 25, above), pp. 15–17; Philip D. Bradley, "Involuntary Participation in Unionism," Reprint No. 1, *Journal of Labor Research* (Fall 1979), pp. 28–32.

47. Charles W. Hickman, "Labor Organizations' Fees and Dues," *Monthly Labor Review,* 100 (May 1977), pp. 19–24; Florence Peterson, *Handbook of Labor Unions* (Washington, D.C.: American Council on Public Affairs, 1944); Florence Peterson, *American Labor Unions* (New York: Harper, 1945 and 1952).

48. Florence Peterson, then director of industrial relations in the Bureau of Labor Statistics, wrote in 1945 that "the total amount of money which passes in and out of all union treasuries currently amounts to several hundred million dollars a year" (Peterson, *American Labor Unions,* p. 113). This is probably a substantial underestimate. J. B. S. Hardman calculated total income for unions at $400 million per year during the late 1940s. He also cited a $400-million figure published in *Life* magazine in 1948 and official estimates of $390 million in 1943 and $478 million in 1946 published by the Bureau of Internal Revenue. See J. B. S. Hardman, "'Dollar Worth' of the Unions," in J. B. S. Hardman and Maurice F. Neufeld, eds., *The House of Labor* (New York: Prentice-Hall, 1951), p. 411. See also Philip Taft, "Dues and Initiation Fees in Labor Unions," *Quarterly Journal of Economics,* 60 (February 1946), pp. 219–41.

49. Peterson, *Handbook* (n. 47, above), p. 104.

50. Florence Peterson, "Industrial Relations in 1938," *Monthly Labor Review,* March 1939, p. 493.

51. Steven Brill, *The Teamsters* (New York: Harper & Row, 1978), p. 13.

52. National unions and employee associations numbered 210 in 1976 and their collective bargaining coverage was estimated at 26.8 million members and nonmembers. See U.S. Bureau of Labor Statistics, *Directory of National Unions and Employee Associations,* 1977, Bulletin 2044, December 1979, pp. 58, 78.

53. *Guidebook to Labor Relations, 1980,* 19th ed. (Chicago: Commerce Clearing House, 1979), p. 9.

54. *Labor Relations Reference Manual* (Washington, D.C.: Bureau of National Affairs, 1938), Volume 1-A, pp. 818–38.

55. Ibid., p. 780.

56. Ibid., pp. 780–81.

57. U.S. Bureau of Labor Statistics, *Directory of National Unions and Employee Associations, 1977,* Bulletin 2044, December 1979.

58. Charles C. Killingsworth, "Arbitration Then and Now," *Labor Arbitra-*

tion at the Quarter-Century Mark (Washington, D.C.: Bureau of National Affairs, 1973), pp. 21-22.

59. Orley Ashenfelter and John H. Pencavel, "American Trade Union Growth: 1900-1960," *Quarterly Journal of Economics,* 83 (August 1969), pp. 434-48.

60. Rex Cottle, Hugh Macaulay, and Bruce Yandle, *Labor and Property Rights in California Agriculture* (College Station: Texas A&M University Press, 1982); Patty Newman, "Who's Bankrolling the UFW?" *Reason,* November 1979; Erik Larson, "Internal Strains Split UFW," *The Wall Street Journal,* 17 May 1982, p. 33.

61. J. Carl Cabe, *Foreman's Unions: A New Development in Industrial Relations* (Urbana: University of Illinois Press, 1947); Charles P. Larrowe, "A Meteor on the Industrial Relations Horizon: The Foreman's Association of America," *Labor History,* 2 (Fall 1961), pp. 259-94.

62. Gary M. Fink, ed., *Labor Unions* (Westport, Conn.: Greenwood, 1977), pp. 283-85.

63. Witte, *Government in Labor Disputes* (n. 24, above), pp. 66, 265-84; Bernstein, *Lean Years* (n. 25, above), ch. 11; Paul F. Brissenden, "Campaign Against the Labor Injunction," *American Economic Review,* 23 (March 1933), pp. 42-54; Robert F. Koretz, ed., *Statutory History of the United States, Labor Organizations* (New York: Chelsea House, 1970), Chapters 23-25; Arthur M. Schlesinger, Jr., *The Coming of the New Deal* (Boston: Houghton Mifflin, 1958), Chapters 23-25; James A. Gross, *The Making of the National Labor Relations Board* (Albany, N.Y.: State University of New York Press, 1974); Richard C. Cortner, *The Wagner Act Cases* (Knoxville: University of Tennessee Press, 1964); Philip Ross, *The Government as a Source of Union Power* (Providence, R.I.: Brown University Press, 1963); Irving Bernstein, *The New Deal Collective Bargaining Policy* (Berkeley: University of California Press, 1950); and Gross, *Reshaping* (n. 1, above), p. 268 (references).

64. George Stigler, "The Economic Theory of Regulation," *Bell Journal of Economics and Management Science,* 2 (Spring 1971), pp. 3-21, and Sam Peltzman, "Toward a Theory of Government Regulation," *Journal of Law and Economics,* 19 (August 1976), pp. 211-40, develop the interest-group explanation of politics; Joseph Reid, "Understanding Political Events in the New Economic History," *Journal of Economic History,* 37 (June 1977), pp. 302-28, supports the argument that politicians can and do pursue their own ideology; and James B. Kau and Paul H. Rubin, "The Impact of Labor Unions on the Passage of Economic Legislation," *Journal of Labor Research,* 2 (Spring 1981), pp. 133-45, and "Self Interest, Ideology, and Logrolling in Congressional Voting," *Journal of Law and Economics,* 22 (October 1979), pp. 365-84, provide empirical analysis of the politics of labor unions.

65. Witte, *Government in Labor Disputes* (n. 24, above), p. 266.

66. Koretz, *Statutory History* (n. 63, above), pp. 240-41.

67. William Manners, *Patience and Fortitude: A Biography of Fiorello La Guardia* (New York: Harcourt, Brace, Jovanovich, 1976); Fiorello H. La Guardia, *The Making of an Insurgent: An Autobiography* (Philadelphia: Lip-

pincott, 1948, reprinted by Capricorn Books, New York, 1961); Arthur Mann, *La Guardia: A Fighter Against His Times, 1882-1933* (Chicago: University of Chicago Press, 1969); Howard Zinn, *La Guardia in Congress* (Ithaca, N.Y.: Cornell University Press, 1959); *Guide to U.S. Elections* (Washington, D.C.: Congressional Quarterly, 1975).

68. Bernstein, *Lean Years* (n. 25, above), p. 262.

69. Norman L. Zucker, *George W. Norris: Gentle Knight of American Democracy* (Urbana: University of Illinois Press, 1966); Richard L. Neuberger and Stephen B. Kahn, *Integrity: The Life of George W. Norris* (New York: Vanguard Press, 1937); Richard Lowitt, *George W. Norris: The Making of a Progressive* (Syracuse, N.Y.: Syracuse University Press, 1963), *The Persistence of a Progressive, 1913-1933* (Urbana: University of Illinois Press, 1971), *The Triumph of a Progressive* (Urbana: University of Illinois Press, 1978); George W. Norris, *Fighting Liberal* (New York: Macmillan, 1945).

70. *Monthly Labor Review,* November 1933, p. 1121.

71. *Monthly Labor Review,* October 1937, p. 875.

72. For example, see the twenty-page bibliography assembled in "Injunctions in Labor Disputes: Select List of Recent References," *Monthly Labor Review,* September 1928, pp. 631-50; and articles in the *American Labor Legislation Review* from Vol. 12 (1922) to Vol. 20 (1930).

73. See G. William Domhoff, *The Higher Circles* (New York: Random House, 1970), ch. 6.

74. Edwin E. Witte, "IRRA Presidential Address," *Industrial Relations Research Association, Proceedings of First Annual Meeting,* 29-30 December 1948, pp. 6-20. Witte also noted the burgeoning literature in industrial relations and remarked, "But I protest against the use made of some of the recent studies by people who have an axe to grind."

75. *Industrial Relations Research Association, Proceedings of the Second Annual Meeting,* 30 December 1949.

76. Edwin E. Witte, *Historical Survey of Labor Arbitration* (Philadelphia: Wharton School, University of Pennsylvania Press, 1952), p. 51.

77. Katherine Seide, ed., *A Dictionary of Arbitration and Its Terms* (Dobbs Ferry, N.Y.: Oceana, 1970), p. 154.

78. R. W. Fleming, *The Labor Arbitration Process* (Urbana: University of Illinois Press, 1965), p. 13: Walter E. Baer, *The Labor Arbitration Guide* (Homewood, Ill.: Dow-Jones-Irwin, 1974), p. 12. The U.S. Bureau of Labor Statistics reports that 98.8% of contracts have grievance clauses and 96.1% have arbitration clauses; see BLS, *Characteristics of Major Collective Bargaining Agreements,* Bulletin 1957, 1977, p. 94.

79. *Labor Relations Yearbook* (Chicago: Commerce Clearing House, 1980), p. 347.

80. Paul R. Hays, *Labor Arbitration: A Dissenting View* (New Haven, Conn.: Yale University Press, 1966), pp. 53-54.

81. U.S. Federal Mediation and Conciliation Service, *31st Annual Report,* FY1978, p. 43.

82. Paul M. Herzog and Morris Stone, "Voluntary Labor Arbitration in the United States," *International Labor Review,* 82 (October 1960), pp. 301-26.

83. *The Wall Street Journal,* 29 July 1980, p. 1.

84. Killingsworth, "Arbitration" (n. 58, above). Killingsworth tells a revealing anecdote about the original meeting of the National Academy of Arbitrators in 1947: "There was a photographer on hand to take pictures of a group of the leading lights, and when the photographer said, 'smile, say "cheese,"' a wag in the group said 'No, you must realize you are dealing with arbitrators. You should say "Fees."'" (p. 29)

85. J. A. Raffaele, "Needed: A Fourth Party in Industrial Relations," *Labor Law Journal,* 13 (March 1962), pp. 230–44.

86. Milton Friedman and Rose Friedman, *Free to Choose* (New York: Harcourt, Brace, Jovanovich, 1979), p. xix.

87. Domhoff, *Higher Circles* (n. 73, above), p. 219.

88. George Stigler, "Is American Capitalism at High Noon?" *Competition,* 3 (November-December 1982), pp. 3–4.

89. Benjamin J. Taylor and Fred Witney, *Labor Relations Law,* 2nd ed. (Englewood Cliffs, N.J.: Prentice-Hall, 1975), pp. 157, 580.

90. Morgan O. Reynolds, "Free Rider" (n. 18, above), p. 306; see also Dan C. Heldman, *American Labor Unions: Political Values and Financial Structure* (Washington, D.C.: Council on American Affairs, 1977); Dan C. Heldman, James T. Bennett; and Manuel H. Johnson, *Deregulating Labor Relations* (Dallas: Fisher Institute, 1981).

Chapter 6, FEDERAL REGULATION OF WAGES

1. U.S. Comptroller General, *The Davis-Bacon Act Should Be Repealed* [HRD 79-18] (Washington, D.C.: General Accounting Office, 27 April 1979).

2. George Fowler, "Davis-Bacon Needs a Decent Burial," *Nation's Business,* March 1979, pp. 57–60.

3. *The Wall Street Journal,* 10 March 1981, p. 1.

4. Robert W. Merry, "This Year's Hot Labor Issue," *The Wall Street Journal,* 24 May 1979, p. 20.

5. Eugene J. McAllister, "Davis-Bacon: A Costly Contradiction," *A Heritage Foundation Backgrounder,* 14 June 1979; see also John P. Gould and George Bittlingmayer, *Davis-Bacon Act: The Economics of Prevailing Wage Laws* (Washington, D.C.: American Enterprise Institute, 1980); Armand J. Thieblot, Jr., *The Davis-Bacon Act,* Labor Relations and Public Policy Series, Report No. 10 (Philadelphia: University of Pennsylvania Press, 1975); Robert S. Goldfarb and John F. Morrall III, "The Davis-Bacon Act: An Appraisal of Recent Studies," *Industrial and Labor Relations Review,* 34 (January 1981), pp. 191–206; and Morgan O. Reynolds, "Understanding Political Pricing of Labor Services: The Davis-Bacon Act," *Journal of Labor Research,* 3 (Summer 1982), pp. 295–309.

6. Fowler, "Davis-Bacon" (n. 2, above).

7. "Adobe Is Adorable, But Today's Pueblos Can't Build With It," *The Wall Street Journal,* 4 February 1980, p. 1.

8. Herbert C. Morton, *Public Contracts and Private Wages: Experience Under the Walsh-Healey Act* (Washington, D.C.: Brookings Institution, 1965).

9. U.S. Department of Labor, *Annual Report, Fiscal Year 1966* (Washington, D.C.: U.S. Government Printing Office, 1966), p. 177.

10. Morton, *Public Contracts* (n. 8, above), pp. 51–53.

11. Jacob Mincer, "On-the-Job Training: Costs, Returns, and Some Implications," *Journal of Political Economy,* 70 (Part 2, Supplement, October 1962), pp. 50–73.

12. Finis Welch, "The Rising Impact of Minimum Wages," *Regulation,* November–December 1978, pp. 28–37.

13. See also Walter E. Williams, "Government Sanctioned Restraints that Reduce Economic Opportunities for Minorities," *Policy Review,* Fall 1977, pp. 7–30; George E. Tauchen, "Some Evidence on Cross-Section Effects of the Minimum Wage," *Journal of Political Economy,* 89 (June 1981), pp. 529–47.

14. John Cogan, "The Decline in Black Teenage Employment: 1950–1970," *American Economic Review,* 72 (September 1982), pp. 621–38.

15. Jude Wanniski, *The Way the World Works* (New York: Simon and Schuster, 1978), p. 282. See also Simon Rottenberg, "Minimum Wages in Puerto Rico," in Simon Rottenberg, ed., *The Economics of Legal Minimum Wages* (Washington, D.C.: American Enterprise Institute, 1981), pp. 327–39.

Chapter 7, ECONOMIC EFFECTS OF UNIONISM

1. H. Gregg Lewis, *Unionism and Relative Wages in the United States* (Chicago: University of Chicago Press, 1963).

2. C. J. Parsley, "Labor Unions and Wages: A Survey," *Journal of Economic Literature,* 18 (March 1980), pp. 1–31; Leonard W. Weiss, "Concentration and Labor Earnings," *American Economic Review,* 56 (March 1966), pp. 96–117; Frank P. Stafford, "Concentration and Labor Earnings: A Comment," *American Economic Review,* 58 (March 1968), pp. 174–81; Paul M. Ryscavage, "Measuring Union-nonunion Earnings Differences," *Monthly Labor Review,* 97 (December 1974), pp. 3–9; Orley Ashenfelter, "Union Relative Wage Effects: New Evidence and a Survey of Their Implications for Wage Inflation," mimeographed, Princeton University, Princeton, N.J., 1976.

3. Bibliography in Parsley, "Labor Unions" (n. 2 above). See also H. Gregg Lewis, "Union Relative Wage Effects: A Survey of Macro Estimates," *Journal of Labor Economics,* 1 (January 1983), pp. 1–18.

4. Randall J. Olsen, "Comment on 'The Effect of Unions on Earnings and Earnings on Unions: A Mixed Logit Approach,' " *International Economic Review,* 19 (February 1978), pp. 259–61; Peter Schmidt and Robert P. Strauss, "The Effect of Unions on Earnings and Earnings on Unions: A Mixed Logit Approach," *International Economic Review,* 17 (February 1976), pp. 204–12.

5. Albert Rees, *The Economics of Trade Unions,* 2d ed. (Chicago: University of Chicago Press, 1977), p. 74.

6. Peter F. Drucker, "The Danger of Excessive Labor Income," *The Wall Street Journal,* 6 January 1981, p. 30.

7. Yale Brozen, *Revitalizing the American Economy* (Kansas City: University of Missouri, Kansas City, 1981); see also Yale Brozen, "Government and the Rich," *National Review,* 34 (9 July 1981), especially pp. 822-23.

8. *The Wall Street Journal,* 12 January 1981, p. 19.

9. *The Wall Street Journal,* 6 January 1981, p. 1.

10. A rare exception is Richard B. Freeman, "The Effect of Unionism on Fringe Benefits," *Industrial and Labor Relations Review,* 34 (July 1981), pp. 489-509, who found that unionism raised the proportion of wages paid in the form of fringes, especially in the categories of life-accident-health, pensions, vacations, and holiday pay. See also Louis F. Rossiter and Amy K. Taylor, "Union Effects on Health Insurance," *Industrial Relations,* 21 (Spring 1982), pp. 167-77.

11. Harry G. Johnson and Peter Mieszkowski, "The Effects of Unionization on the Distribution of Income: A General Equilibrium Approach," *Quarterly Journal of Economics,* 84 (November 1970), pp. 539-71; Albert Rees, "The Effects of Unions on Resource Allocation," *Journal of Law and Economics,* 6 (October 1963), pp. 69-78.

12. Richard Posner, "The Social Costs of Monopoly and Regulation," *Journal of Political Economy,* 83 (August 1975), pp. 807-28.

13. James T. Bennett, Dan C. Heldman, and Manuel H. Johnson, *Deregulating Labor Relations* (Dallas: Fisher Institute, 1981). The authors estimate the total social cost of all regulations and restrictions in the labor sector at some $170 billion annually, or $3,000 for a family of four.

14. See, for instance, Simon Kuznets, *Modern Economic Growth* (New Haven, Conn.: Yale University Press, 1966), pp. 402-09, 420-26.

15. Irving Kravis, "Income Distributions: Functional Share," in David L. Sills, ed., *Encyclopedia of the Social Sciences* (New York: Crowell Collier and Macmillan, 1960), vol. 7, pp. 132-35.

16. Rees, *Economics* (n. 5, above), p. 89.

17. The issue has been so dormant and the conclusion so widely confirmed by scholars that only pre-1965 studies exist. See Martin Bronfenbrenner, *Income Distribution Theory* (Chicago: Aldine, 1971), especially pp. 83-87; Norman J. Simler, *The Impact of Unionism on Wage-Income Ratios in the Manufacturing Sector of the Economy* (Minneapolis: University of Minnesota Press, 1961).

18. Drucker, "Danger" (n. 6, above).

19. *The Wall Street Journal,* 20 October 1977, p. 1.

20. *The Wall Street Journal,* 26 August 1981, p. 15.

21. See Lewis, *Unionism* (n. 1, above); Rees, *Economics* (n. 5, above); Johnson and Mieszkowski, "Effects" (n. 11, above).

22. Martin Feldstein, "Temporary Layoffs in the Theory of Unemployment," *Journal of Political Economy,* 84 (October 1976), pp. 937-58.

23. Quoted from John Maynard Keynes, *Essays in Persuasion,* 1931, in Alan Reynolds, "What Do We Know about the Great Crash?," *National Review,* 9 November 1979, p. 1418. Also see F. A. Hayek, *1980s Unemployment and the Unions,* Hobart Paper No. 87 (London: Institute of Economic Affairs, 1980).

24. Daniel K. Benjamin and Levis A. Kochin, "Searching for an Explana-

tion of Unemployment in Interwar Britain," *Journal of Political Economy,* 87 (June 1979), pp. 441–78.

25. Harry G. Grubel and Michael A. Walker, eds., *Unemployment Insurance* (Vancouver, B.C.: Fraser Institute, 1978).

26. Leonard P. Adams, *Public Attitudes Toward Unemployment Insurance* (Kalamazoo, Mich.: Upjohn Institute, 1971), ch. 2.

27. Joseph M. Becker, *Experience Rating in Unemployment Insurance* (Baltimore: Johns Hopkins University Press, 1972), p. 231.

28. Armand J. Thieblot and Ronald M. Cowin, *Welfare and Strikes: The Use of Public Funds to Support Strikes* (Philadelphia: Wharton School, University of Pennsylvania Press, 1972), p. 263.

29. Ibid., p. 216.

30. Quoted in Emerson P. Schmidt, *Union Power and the Public Interest* (Los Angeles: Noah Publishing, 1973), p. 133.

31. Ibid., p. 139.

32. Ed Baines and Bob Windrem, "Six Ways to Take Over a Union," *Mother Jones,* August 1980, p. 36.

33. James D. Compton, "Victory at GE: How It Was Done," *American Federationist,* July 1970.

34. John Gennard, *Financing Strikers* (New York: Halsted, 1977).

35. Armand J. Thieblot, "Review of Financing Strikers," *Industrial and Labor Relations Review,* 32 (July 1979), pp. 554–55.

Chapter 8, NEW UNIONISM IN THE PUBLIC SECTOR

1. These figures are approximate because various sources differ according to year, definitions of full-time versus part-time employment, inclusion of special government districts, etc. See Nicolaus Henry, *Governing at the Grass Roots: State and Local Politics* (Englewood Cliffs, N.J.: Prentice-Hall, 1980), pp. 274–82; John Burton, "The Extent of Collective Bargaining in the Public Sector," in Benjamin Aaron et al., eds., *Public-Sector Bargaining* (Washington, D.C.: Bureau of National Affairs, 1979), pp. 1–43; and David Lewin and Shirley B. Goldenberg, "Public Sector Unionism in the U.S. and Canada," *Industrial Relations,* 19 (Fall 1980), pp. 239–56. When the expressions "unionized," "organized," or "proportion in unions" are used, I intend them to mean dues-paying members reported by unions rather than numbers represented by unions, numbers under collective contracts, or some other variant of what unionization might mean.

2. Lawrence M. Spizman, "Public Employee Unions: A Study in the Economics of Power," *Journal of Labor Research,* 1 (Fall 1980), p. 265.

3. *Nation's Business,* February 1979, p. 40.

4. Ralph J. Flynn, *Public Works, Public Workers* (Washington, D.C.: New Republic, 1975), p. 1.

5. This section draws on Charles A. Baird, *Unionism and the Public Sector,* Original Paper 15 (Los Angeles: International Institute for Economic Research, August 1978). For the views of a former advocate of public-sector

bargaining now turned staunch critic, see Myron Lieberman, *Public-Sector Bargaining: A Policy Reappraisal* (Lexington, Mass.: Lexington Books, 1980).

6. Donald M. Fisk, Herbert Kiesling, and Thomas Muller, *Private Provision of Public Services* (Washington, D.C.: Urban Institute Press, 1978), p. 99; see also James T. Bennett and Manuel H. Johnson, *Better Government at Half the Price* (Ottawa, Ill.: Caroline House, 1981); John M. Greiner, et al., *Productivity and Motivation: A Review of State and Local Government Initiatives* (Washington D.C.: Urban Institute Press, 1981); Peter M. Mieszkowski and George E. Peterson, eds. *Public Sector Labor Markets* (Washington, D.C.: Urban Institute Press, 1981).

7. Thomas R. Haggard, "Legal Sources of Union Political Privileges," in *Union Coercive Power,* Symposium Proceedings, Chicago, Ill., 7 April 1978, National Right to Work Committee, p. 23.

8. Robert J. Thornton, "The Elasticity of Demand for Public School Teachers," *Industrial Relations,* 18 (Winter 1979), pp. 86–91; see also Orley Ashenfelter and Ronald G. Ehrenberg, "The Demand for Labor in the Public Sector," in Daniel Hamermesh, ed., *Labor in the Public and Nonprofit Sectors* (Princeton, N.J.: Princeton University Press, 1975), pp. 55–78.

9. Morgan O. Reynolds, "Whatever Happened to the Monopoly Theory of Labor Unions?" *Journal of Labor Research,* 2 (Spring 1981), pp. 61–72.

10. Winston Bush and Arthur Denzau, "The Voting Behavior of Bureaucrats and the Public Sector Growth," in Thomas E. Borcherding, ed., *Budgets and Bureaucrats: The Sources of Governmental Growth* (Durham, N.C.: Duke University Press, 1977); Bruno S. Frey and Werner W. Pommerehne, "How Powerful Are Public Bureaucrats as Voters?," *Public Choice,* 38, 3 (1982), pp. 253–62.

11. George J. Borjas, *Wage Policy in the Federal Bureaucracy* (Washington, D.C.: American Enterprise Institute, 1980).

12. James T. Bennett and Manuel H. Johnson, *The Political Economy of Federal Government Growth, 1959–1978* (College Station: Center for Education and Research in Free Enterprise, Texas A&M University, 1980).

13. Douglas K. Adie, *An Evaluation of Postal Service Wage Rates* (Washington, D.C.: American Enterprise Institute, 1977).

14. *Business Week,* 3 August 1981, p. 26.

15. Sharon Smith, "Are Postal Workers Over- or Underpaid?" *Industrial Relations,* 15 (May 1976), pp. 175–76.

16. Joseph F. Quinn, "Postal Sector Wages," *Industrial Relations,* 18 (Winter 1979), pp. 92–96.

17. Reported in *Houston Post,* 25 July 1981, p. 14a.

18. Sharon Smith, "Pay Differences between Federal Government and Private Sector Workers," *Industrial and Labor Relations Review,* 29 (January 1976), pp. 179–97.

19. Sharon Smith, "Public/Private Wage Differentials in Metropolitan Areas," mimeo, Federal Reserve Bank of New York, n.d.

20. Joseph F. Quinn, "Wage Differentials among Older Workers in the Public and Private Sectors," *Journal of Human Resources,* 14 (Winter 1979), pp. 41–62.

21. U.S. Congressional Budget Office, *Alternative Approaches to Adjusting Compensation for Federal Blue-Collar Employees* (Washington, D.C.: U.S. Government Printing Office, November 1980).

22. James L. Freund, "Market and Union Influences on Municipal Employee Wages," *Industrial and Labor Relations Review,* 27 (April 1974), pp. 391–404.

23. David Shapiro, "Relative Wage Effects of Unions in the Public and Private Sectors," *Industrial and Labor Relations Review,* 31 (January 1978), pp. 193–204.

24. David Lipsky and John Drotning, "The Influence of Collective Bargaining on Teachers' Salaries in New York State," *Industrial and Labor Relations Review,* 27 (October 1973), pp. 18–35.

25. Richard B. Victor, "The Effects of Unionism on the Wage and Employment Levels of Police and Firefighters," *Rand Paper P-5924* (August 1977).

26. Alan G. Balfour, "More Evidence that Unions Do Not Achieve Higher Salaries for Teachers," *Journal of Collective Negotiations,* 3 (Fall 1974), pp. 289–303.

27. *Public Sector Bargaining and Strikes,* 3rd ed. (Vienna, Va.: Public Service Research Council, 1978).

28. William H. Baugh and Joe A. Stone, "Teachers, Unions, and Wages in the 1970s: Unionism Now Pays," *Industrial and Labor Relations Review,* 35 (April 1982), pp. 368–76.

29. William W. Brown and Courtenay C. Stone, "Academic Unions in Higher Education: Impacts on Faculty Salary, Compensation and Promotions," *Economic Inquiry,* 15 (July 1977), pp. 385–96.

30. See James T. Bennett and Manuel H. Johnson, *Demographic Trends in Higher Education: Collective Bargaining and Forced Unionism?* Original Paper 20, (Los Angeles: International Institute for Economic Research, May 1979), pp. 18–21.

31. James P. Begin, "Grievance Mechanisms and Faculty Collegiality: The Rutgers Case," *Industrial and Labor Relations Review,* 31 (April 1978), p. 308. See also Joseph Garbarino, "Faculty Unionization: The Pre-Yeshiva Years, 1966–1979," *Industrial Relations,* 19 (Spring 1980), pp. 221–30.

32. Bennett and Johnson, *Demographic Trends* (n. 30, above), p. 25.

33. Roger W. Schmenner, "The Determination of Municipal Employee Wages," *Review of Economics and Statistics,* 55 (February 1973), pp. 83–90; Orley Ashenfelter, "The Effect of Unionization on Wages in the Public Sector: The Case of Firefighters," *Industrial and Labor Relations Review,* 24 (January 1971), pp. 191–202; Ronald G. Ehrenberg, "Municipal Government Structures, Unionization, and the Wages of Firefighters," *Industrial and Labor Relations Review,* 27 (October 1973), pp. 36–48; Casey Ichniowski, "Economic Effects of Firefighters' Unions," *Industrial and Labor Relations Review,* 33 (January 1980), pp. 198–211; Ronald G. Ehrenberg and Gerald Goldstein, "A Model of Public Sector Wage Determination," *Journal of Urban Economics,* 2 (July 1975), pp. 223–45; Ann P. Bartel and David Lewin, "Wages and Unionism in the Public Sector: The Case of Police," *Review of Economics and Statistics,* 63 (February 1981), pp. 53–59; and *The Wall Street Journal,* 1 May 1979, p. 1.

34. U.S. Bureau of Labor Statistics, *State Government Employee Compensation, 1972* (Washington: U.S. Government Printing Office, 1976), Bulletin 1899.

35. Anthony H. Pascal, "The Organization of Local Public Employees: Implications for the Cost and Quality of Services," paper presented at the Annual Meeting of the Western Economic Association, Las Vegas, Nevada, 21 June 1979.

36. Bartel and Lewin, "Wages and Unionism" (n. 33, above).

37. Quinn, "Wage Differentials" (n. 20, above).

38. Robert Tilove, *Public Employee Pension Funds,* A Twentieth Century Fund Report (New York: Columbia University Press, 1976), pp. 338–40.

39. *Sacramento Bee,* 25 January 1981, p. B7.

40. Morley Gunderson, "Public Sector Compensation in Canada and the U.S.," *Industrial Relations,* 19 (Fall 1980), p. 268. See also David Shapiro, "Relative Wage Effects of Unions in the Public and Private Sectors," *Industrial and Labor Relations Review,* 31 (January 1978), pp. 193–204.

41. Public Service Research Council, *Public Sector Bargaining* (n. 27, above).

42. Harry C. Katz, "Municipal Pay Determination: The Case of San Francisco," *Industrial Relations,* 18 (Winter 1979), pp. 44–58. See also Randolph H. Boehm and Dan C. Heldman, *Public Employees, Unions and the Erosion of Civic Trust: A Study of San Francisco in the 1970s* (Frederick, Md.: University Publications of America, 1982).

43. David Y. Denholm, "Standing Up to Union Bosses," *Conservative Digest,* 5 (October 1979), p. 37.

Chapter 9, INFLATION AND UNIONISM

1. See *Public Opinion,* December 1979–January 1980.

2. Milton Friedman, "Using Escalators to Help Fight Inflation," *Fortune,* July 1974, p. 94.

3. James M. Buchanan and Richard W. Wagner, *Democracy in Deficit* (New York: Academic Press, 1977).

4. Frank H. Knight, "Lippmann's *The Good Society,*" *Journal of Political Economy,* 46 (December 1938), p. 869.

5. Robert L. Schuettinger and Eamonn F. Butler, *Forty Centuries of Wage and Price Controls* (Washington, D.C.: Heritage Foundation, 1979). See also J. L. Fallick and R. F. Elliot, eds., *Incomes Policies, Inflation and Relative Pay* (Boston: Allen & Unwin, 1981); D. J. B. Mitchell, *Unions, Wages, and Inflations* (Washington D.C.: Brookings Institution, 1980).

6. Albert Rees, *The Economics of Work and Pay* (New York: Harper & Row, 1979), p. 223.

7. "Carter's Final Budget," *The Wall Street Journal,* 16 January 1981, p. 7.

8. Henry Hazlitt, *The Inflation Crisis, and How to Resolve It* (New Rochelle, N.Y.: Arlington House, 1978), p. 98.

9. Tom Bethell, *Treating Poverty: Wherein the Cure Gives Rise to the Disease* (Los Angeles: International Institute for Economic Research, 1980), p. 6.

10. Ibid., pp. 6-8. See also Edgar K. Browning and Jacquelene M. Browning, *Public Finance and the Price System,* (New York: Macmillan, 1979), ch. 8; Philip K. Robins, et al., *A Guaranteed Annual Income: Evidence from a Social Experiment* (New York: Academic Press, 1980).

11. Dwight Lee, *The Inflationary Impact of Labor Unions* (College Station, Texas: Center for Education and Research for Free Enterprise, Texas A&M University, 1980); Dan C. Heldman and Deborah L. Knight, *Unions and Lobbying: The Representation Function* (Arlington, Va.: Foundation for Advancement of the Public Trust, 1980). See also Graham K. Wilson, *Unions in National Politics* (London: Macmillan, 1979).

12. *Policy Review,* Winter 1981, p. 173.

13. Lee, *Inflationary Impact* (n. 11, above), p. 16. Original in *AFL-CIO News,* 3 December 1978, p. 2.

14. Ibid., p. 18. Original in *AFL-CIO Legislative Alert,* 11 February 1980, p. 3.

15. Ibid., p. 18.

16. A. W. J. Thomson, "Trade Unions and the Corporate State in Britain," *Industrial and Labor Relations Review,* 33 (October 1979), p. 52.

17. Arthur Shenfield, "The Rise of Trade Union Power in Britain," *Journal of Social and Political Studies,* 2 (1977), pp. 88-89.

Chapter 10, CONTRADICTIONS OF UNIONISM

1. *The Militant,* 20 October 1978.

2. "Labor Comes to a Crossroads," *Time,* 4 September 1978, p. 40.

3. Herbert Stein, "Let's Hold a 'No Business Day,'" *The Wall Street Journal,* 7 January 1980, p. 13; "Big Business Day = Anti-Consumer Day," *Pathfinder,* Texas A&M University, March–April 1980, p. 1.

4. Lane Kirkland, *AFL-CIO American Federationist,* September 1979, p. 4.

5. William B. Gould, *Black Workers in White Unions* (Ithaca, N.Y.: Cornell University Press, 1977); Herbert Hill, *Black Labor and the American Legal System* (Washington, D.C.: Bureau of National Affairs, 1977); Julius Jacobson, ed., *The Negro and the American Labor Movement* (Garden City, N.Y.: Anchor Books, 1968); F. Ray Marshall, *The Negro and Organized* Labor (New York: Wiley, 1965); H. W. Risher, Jr., *The Negro in the Railroad Industry* (Philadelphia: University of Pennsylvania Press, 1971); Sterling D. Spero and Abram L. Harris, *The Black Worker* (New York: Kennikat Press, 1931); Booker T. Washington, "The Negro and the Labor Unions," *Atlantic Monthly,* July 1913, pp. 756–67; Benjamin W. Wolkinson, *Blacks, Unions, and the EEOC* (Lexington, Mass.: Heath, 1973).

6. Quoted in W. Elliot Brownlee and Mary M. Brownlee, *Women in the American Economy* (New Haven, Conn.: Yale University Press, 1976), pp.

213–15, originally published in *American Federationist,* October 1897, pp. 186–87.

7. Fiona McNally, *Women for Hire: A Study of the Female Office Worker* (New York: St. Martin's Press, 1979), p. 119.

8. Ibid., p. 120.

9. Ronnie Steinberg Ratner, ed., *Equal Employment Opportunity for Women* (Philadelphia: Temple University Press, 1980), pp. 227–28.

10. Walter E. Williams, et al., *Black America and Organized Labor: a Fair Deal?* (Washington, D.C.: Lincoln Institute, 1980), pp. 31–32. See also Walter E. Williams, *The State Against Blacks* (New York: McGraw-Hill, 1982).

11. U.S. Congress, *National Employment Priorities Act of 1979* (H.R. 5040 and S. 2400).

12. Barry Bluestone and Bennett Harrison, *Capital and Communities: The Causes and Consequences of Private Disinvestment* (Washington, D.C.: Progressive Alliance, 1980), p. 7.

13. Richard B. McKenzie, "The Case for Plant Closures," *Policy Review,* Winter 1981, p. 130. See also Richard B. McKenzie, ed., *Plant Closings: Public or Private Choices?* (Washington: Cato Institute, 1982).

14. *The Wall Street Journal,* 13 January 1981, p. 4.

15. Jeremy Rifkin and Randy Barber, *The North Will Rise Again* (Boston: Beacon Press, 1978). See also "Symposium on Union Use of Employee Pension Funds," *Journal of Labor Research,* 2 (Fall 1981).

16. *The Wall Street Journal,* 6 June 1980, p. 8.

17. *Houston Chronicle,* 9 March 1980, p. B7.

18. *U.S. News & World Report,* 8 September 1980, p. 33.

19. Clark Kerr, "Unions and Union Leaders of Their Own Choosing," in Richard L. Rowan, ed., *Readings in Labor Economics and Labor Relations,* 3d ed. (Homewood, Ill.: Irwin, 1976), p. 205.

20. Derek C. Bok and John T. Dunlop, *Labor and the American Community* (New York: Simon and Schuster, 1970), p. 69.

21. Robert F. Kennedy, *The Enemy Within* (New York: Harper, 1960), pp. 211–12 and 277–78.

22. Ibid., p. 211.

23. Murray I. Gurfein, "Racketeering," *Encyclopedia of the Social Sciences* (New York: Macmillan, 1934), Vol. 13, p. 45.

24. Ibid.

25. U.S. Department of the Treasury, Bureau of Alcohol, Tobacco, and Firearms, "Explosive Incidents," *1978 Annual Report* (Washington: U.S. Government Printing Office, 1979).

26. C. Wright Mills, *The New Men of Power: America's Labor Leaders* (New York: Harcourt, Brace, 1948), p. 186.

27. Karl O. Mann, *Readings in Labor Relations* (from *The Wall Street Journal*) (Princeton, N.J.: Dow Jones, 1974), p. 51.

28. "How Washington Winks at Corruption in Unions," *U.S. News & World Report,* 23 January 1978, p. 64.

29. Walter Gellhorn, "Address on Receiving the Hillman Award," in Neil W. Chamberlain, ed., *Sourcebook on Labor* (New York: McGraw-Hill, 1959), pp. 210–15.

30. *The Wall Street Journal,* 7 January 1980, p. 13.

31. *Business Week,* 12 May 1980, pp. 86–89.

32. "The Six-Figure Set—City's Labor Leader Elite," *Chicago Tribune,* 23 October 1977. Also consider this excerpt from Steven Brill, *The Teamsters* (New York: Simon and Schuster, 1978), p. 338: "He [Jackie] may be good," explained PROD's research director, Robert Windem, referring to Presser, a Teamster officer. "But is he $200,000 good, with no real education and with even people he negotiates against not getting paid that much? Also, he's the king of severance and pension plans from the Teamsters covering him. This is just a rip-off that avoids the embezzlement statutes."

33. "How Washington Winks" (n. 28, above).

34. Ibid. See also *The Wall Street Journal,* 15 November 1979, p. 48.

35. Sara Gramm, "The Election Base of National Union Executive Boards," *Industrial and Labor Relations Review,* 32 (April 1979), pp. 295–311.

36. J. David Edelstein and Malcolm Warner, *Comparative Union Democracy* (New York: Wiley, 1976).

37. Ed Baines and Bob Windrem, "Six Ways to Take Over a Union," *Mother Jones,* August 1980, pp. 34–47.

38. "Union Corruption, Worse than Ever," *U.S. News & World Report,* 8 September 1980, pp. 33–36. See also Jonathan Kwitny, *Vicious Circles: The Mafia in the Marketplace* (New York: Norton, 1979).

39. For example, Mancur Olson, *The Logic of Collective Action* (Cambridge, Mass.: Harvard University Press, 1971); Allan G. Pulsipher, "The Union Shop: A Legitimate Form of Coercion in a Free-Market Economy," *Industrial and Labor Relations Review,* 19 (July 1966); Paul Sultan, "The Union Security Issue," in Joseph Shister, Benjamin Aaron, and Clyde W. Summers, eds., *Public Policy and Collective Bargaining* (New York: Harper & Row, 1962).

40. Morgan O. Reynolds, "The Free Rider Argument for Compulsory Union Dues," *Journal of Labor Research,* 1 (Fall 1980), pp. 295–313.

41. Ralph Elliott, "The Impact of Right-to-Work Laws on Union Activity," *Journal of Social and Political Studies,* 5 (Winter 1980), pp. 81–93; David Gilbert, "A Statistical Analysis of the Right-to-Work Controversy," *Industrial and Labor Relations Review,* 19 (July 1966), pp. 533–38; James W. Kuhn, "Right-to-Work Laws—Symbols or Substance?" *Industrial and Labor Relations Review,* 14 (July 1961), pp. 587–94; Keith Lumsden and Craig Petersen, "The Effect of Right-to-Work Laws on Unionization in the United States," *Journal of Political Economy,* 83 (December 1975), pp. 1237–48; William J. Moore and Robert J. Newman, "On the Prospects for American Trade Union Growth: A Cross-Section Analysis," *Review of Economics and Statistics,* 57 (November 1975), pp. 435–45; William J. Moore, "Membership and Wage Impact of Right-to-Work Laws," *Journal of Labor Research,* 1 (Fall 1980), pp. 349–68; Robert Swidinsky, "Bargaining Power under Compulsory Unionism," *Industrial Relations,* 21 (Winter 1982), pp. 62–72.

42. Reynolds, "Free Rider" (n. 40, above).

43. *Independence Examiner,* 8 December 1978, and *The Wall Street Journal,* 26 December 1978, p. 1

44. Daniel Pollit, "Union Security in America," *The American Federa-*

tionist, AFL-CIO, 80 (October 1973), pp. 16–22; reprinted in Richard L. Rowan, ed., *Readings in Labor Economics and Labor Relations*, 3d ed. (Homewood, Ill.: Irwin, 1976).

45. Lloyd G. Reynolds, *Labor Economics and Labor Relations,* 6th ed. (Englewood Cliffs, N.J.: Prentice-Hall, 1974), pp. 506–7.

46. Milton Friedman, *Capitalism and Freedom* (Chicago: University of Chicago Press, 1962), pp. 115–17.

47. Thomas R. Haggard, "Right to Work," *Reason,* May 1979, pp. 34–37.

48. E. Clyde Robbins, *Selected Articles on the Open versus Closed Shop* (Minneapolis: Wilson, 1912), p. 81.

49. Albert Rees, *The Economics of Trade Unions,* 2d ed. (Chicago: University of Chicago Press, 1977), p. 187.

50. Henry C. Simons, "Some Reflections on Syndicalism," *Journal of Political Economy,* 52 (March 1944), pp. 4–5.

51. Dan C. Heldman and Deborah L. Knight, *Unions and Lobbying: The Representation Function* (Arlington, Va.: Foundation for Advancement of the Public Trust, 1980).

Chapter 11, CAPITALISM, SOCIALISM, AND UNIONISM

1. Irving Bernstein, *The New Deal Collective Bargaining Policy* (Berkeley: University of California Press, 1950), p. 130.

2. John R. Erickson, "Forfeiture of Reinstatement Rights Through Strike Misconduct," *Labor Law Journal,* October 1980, pp. 602–16.

3. See Simon Rottenberg, "Property in Work," *Industrial and Labor Relations Review,* 15 (April 1962), pp. 402–5.

4. Irving Geiger, "The Movement for Industrial Democracy in Western Europe," *Challenge,* May-June 1979, pp. 14–21.

5. *The New York Times,* 27 April 1980, Sect. 3, p. 15.

6. For a more extensive analysis, see Eirik G. Furubotn, *The Economics of Industrial Democracy: An Analysis of Labor Participation in the Management of Business Firms* (College Station, Texas: Center for Education and Research in Free Enterprise, Texas A&M University, 1979) and the bibliography therein.

7. *The Wall Street Journal,* 10 December 1979, p. 1.

8. Dan C. Heldman, "Making Policy in a Vacuum: The Case of Labor Relations," *Policy Review,* 10 (Fall 1979), pp. 75–88.

9. James T. Bennett and Manuel H. Johnson, *Pushbutton Unionism* (Fairfax, Va.: George Mason University, 1980), p. 7.

10. Ibid.

11. Irving Kristol, "Understanding Trade Unionism," *The Wall Street Journal,* 23 October 1978, p. 24.

12. George Gilder, "The War against Wealth," *American Spectator,* October 1979, p. 11.

13. Based on Maurice Finks, *What's Wrong with our Unions* (Indianapolis: Bobbs-Merrill, 1963), pp. 49–50.

14. John Davenport, "Unions, Unemployment, and Public Order," *Journal of Social and Political Studies,* 4 (Summer 1979), pp. 175–91.

Index

Only authors cited by name in the text are
included. For others, please see Notes.

LIBRARY
ST. LOUIS COMMUNITY COLLEGE
AT FLORISSANT VALLEY